720/2

The French Renaissance
and its Heritage

Pour Prof. Boase Marc Chagall.

THE
FRENCH RENAISSANCE
AND ITS HERITAGE

✳✳✳✳✳✳✳✳✳✳✳

essays presented to

Alan M. Boase

M.A., PH.D., *Officier de la Légion d'Honneur*
Professor Emeritus of French in
the University of Glasgow

by Colleagues, Pupils
and Friends

✳✳✳✳✳✳

Editorial Committee

D. R. Haggis   S. Jones   F. W. Leakey
E. G. Taylor   G. M. Sutherland

✳✳

Methuen & Co Ltd
LONDON

First published in Great Britain, 1968
by Methuen & Co Ltd
11 New Fetter Lane, London EC4
© Methuen 1968
Printed in Great Britain
by W & J Mackay & Co Ltd, Chatham

SBN 416 11500 4

Erratum
p. xi The first line on this page should be read as
the first line on p. xii

Distributed in USA
by Barnes & Noble Inc

Contents

Contents

Contents

Illustrations

Alan Martin Boase

A SCHOLAR'S LIFE cannot be resumed in the few dates, titles and places which indicate his various offices and publications; but certain deductions may be made from them.

In the case of ALAN BOASE, the retiring Marshall Professor of French in the University of Glasgow, who held that Chair from 1937 to 1965, it is not unimportant to note that his family, while originating in part from Cornwall, was long associated with Scotland. His father, Norman Boase, C.B.E., was a distinguished citizen, being President of the universally famous golf club at St Andrews, and his son is no mean golfer, as well as inheriting something of his father's capacity for affairs. It will also be noted that ALAN BOASE, being born in 1902, was one of that remarkable generation which had to consolidate and further the achievements of those predecessors who had founded the first schools of modern languages in our universities. As such modern subjects then had little status or tradition behind them, only men of unusual capacities could carry out this task.

ALAN BOASE had the good fortune of enjoying all the benefits of such venerable institutions as Eton, the Universities of Oxford and Cambridge, and the Sorbonne. Yet it is fitting that a scholar whose mind and temperament inclined him from the start to become a devotee of Montaigne, should have refused to take these or any other advantages for granted. While appreciating what Eton could provide, he kept his mind open to other conceptions of education, and to more experimental types of school. Although his career at New College, Oxford, was outstanding, he remained sceptical of the emphasis laid there on conventional philological studies, and he was right in reducing or modifying that element of French teaching in Glasgow, while always discovering the best-qualified staff to do it. Proceeding to Trinity College, Cambridge, for his postgraduate work under the late H. F. Stewart, he was fortunate in coming into direct contact with such original thinkers of his own generation as I. A. Richards and F. R. Leavis, and this inspired him to give a new impulse and direction to the teaching of French, comparable with that which has revolutionized English Studies in the universities in our time. Finally, at both Oxford and Cambridge he learnt to respect the tutorial and seminar systems, and their tradition of giving the undergraduate the utmost personal contact with his supervisor.

After these profitable years of study, instead of retreating to some comfortable academic haven, he ventured into the provinces, teaching first at Sheffield (1929–36), where he met his gifted wife, Grizelle Forster, the daughter of the late Professor E. S. Forster of that University. He did not come to Glasgow without professorial experience, having first occupied the Chair of French in the University College of Southampton.

ALAN BOASE thus assumed the Marshall Chair, not only with an academic and professional background of the highest order, but with matured views on the nature and orientation of French Studies. His lively and keenly pursued interests, not only in his own special field of the Renaissance, but also in education, the drama, the fine arts, history, politics, contemporary writing, enabled him to survey and dominate the entire range of his subject as few professors were then, or are now, capable of doing. While he could, and did, build upon the scholarly basis laid down by his predecessor, Professor Martin, for whose work he had every respect, he had also to take into account the type of recruitment and the degree-structures that already existed. His pupils ought to be eternally grateful for the way in which he insisted that as much attention must be given to the 'Ordinary' student as to any other. He had a most difficult task in extending and maintaining achievement ought to give pause to those who are in any way such teaching in small groups, in a rapidly expanding department. At the same time, by introducing a wide variety of optional subjects, he was able to provide some of those advantages which, as they demand great personal initiative as much as close personal supervision, had hitherto been the privilege of Oxford and Cambridge. Recognition was not slow to come to him for such efforts, in the award he received of the decoration of the Légion d'Honneur; or his election as Dean of his Faculty; or his part as a founder and President of the now indispensable Association of Professors of French; or the visiting professorships that he has held abroad.

It is evident that long before his regretted retirement ALAN BOASE had fully achieved most of the things he had set out to do, through the shaping of a Department of French Studies which can set an example to the universities in Britain and to those in many other countries, in its coherence, originality and modernity. At the same time he brought great honour to the University of Glasgow through the variety and quality of his numerous publications. While having proved himself, at an early age, to be a high authority on Montaigne, his most original contribution was thought, in France, to be his discovery of a most important and hitherto unknown poet, Jean de Sponde, whose poems and meditations he edited and expounded as no other French or British scholar could have done. Equally at home in contemporary French literature, his contribution to *France: A Companion to French Studies* was a model of what such scholarly essays ought to be. Quick to realize that a judicious choice of poems might be an act of criticism of the first order, he produced his comprehensive anthologies of French poetry, to which he gave many years of careful thought, and which have reformed and redirected taste in this domain throughout the country, both in the schools and in the universities.

The little that has been said here is enough to show that ALAN BOASE's academic adventure was as complete and as successful as any scholar's life can hope to be. His modesty over such a real ambitious. Glasgow has every reason to be proud of the devoted service of an unusually thoughtful, unusually sensitive, and unusually imaginative scholar and educator, who so profoundly respected and so honestly employed the gifts with which he found himself endowed. It is now our turn to respect those gifts. It is fitting, now, that some of those who are qualified to appreciate his qualities should join together in paying a tribute which he has so well deserved from the community of scholars. This we can only do in that humble form which is traditional in the academic world, but which is never perfunctorily offered. Those who have contributed to or supported this collection, and those who were his colleagues or pupils, or both, wish him, not retirement – a vain hope for one who will wither age, rather than yield to it – but the leisure and health which will enable him to give further evidence of his acute, spontaneous, and always generous mind. Of what has gone before, we can only say, in Samuel Johnson's words,

Nihil quod tetigit non ornavit.

F.H.S.

List of Major Publications
by Alan M. Boase

➤➤➤ ➤➤➤ ➤➤➤ ➤➤➤ ➤➤➤ ➤➤➤ ➤➤➤ ➤➤➤ ➤➤➤ ➤➤➤ ➤➤➤ ⬅⬅⬅ ⬅⬅⬅ ⬅⬅⬅ ⬅⬅⬅ ⬅⬅⬅ ⬅⬅⬅ ⬅⬅⬅ ⬅⬅⬅ ⬅⬅⬅ ⬅⬅⬅ ⬅⬅⬅

THE FORTUNES OF MONTAIGNE. A History of the Essays in France,
1580–1669, London, Methuen, 1935.

EDITIONS

Montaigne, *Selected Essays*, edited by Arthur Tilley and A. M.
Boase, Manchester University Press, 1934. (Revised edition
1954, with additional Essays, and new Preface by Alan M.
Boase.)

Jean Cocteau, *La Machine infernale* (with a Preface by Alan M.
Boase), London, Nelson, 1944.

Sponde, *Sonnets et Stances de la Mort*, introduction de Alan Boase,
Paris, Corti, 1948.

Sponde, *Poésies*. Texte établi par Alan Boase et François Ruchon.
Avec une 'Etude sur les poésies de Jean de Sponde' par Alan
Boase, Geneva, Cailler, 1949.

Sponde, *Méditations, avec un Essai de Poèmes chrétiens*. Introduction
de Alan Boase, Paris, Corti, 1954. (This long introduction
includes a section, pp. xiii–xcix, on 'La Vie de Sponde'.)

ANTHOLOGIES

The Poetry of France. From André Chénier to Pierre Emmanuel. An
Anthology with Introduction and Notes by Alan M. Boase,
London, Methuen, 1952.

The Poetry of France. Vol. I: *1400–1600.* An Anthology with Introduction and Notes by Alan M. Boase, London, Methuen, 1964.

The Poetry of France. Vol. III: *1800–1900.* An Anthology with Introduction and Notes by Alan M. Boase, London, Methuen, 1967.

ARTICLES

'Montaigne annoté par Florimond de Raemond', *Revue du XVe siècle*, XV (1928), pp. 237–78.

'Then Malherbe came', *The Criterion*, X (1930–1), pp. 287–306.

'Un lecteur hollandais de Montaigne: Pieter van Veen', in: *Mélanges offerts à M Abel Lefranc*, Paris, Droz, 1936, pp. 408–17.

'Montaigne et la sorcellerie', *Humanisme et Renaissance*, II (1935), pp. 402–21.

'French Literature: the Twentieth Century', in: *France: A Companion to French Studies*, ed. R. L. Graeme Ritchie, London, Methuen, 1937, pp. 352–401. (Fifth edition, revised, 1951, includes additional section on 'The Last Ten Years'.)

'Jean de Sponde, un poète inconnu', *Mesures*, V, no. 4 (15 October 1939), pp. 127–51.

'Poètes anglais et français de l'époque baroque', *Revue des sciences humaines*, XIV (1949), N.S. fasc. 55–6, pp. 155–84.

'Mr Turnell's Criticism', *Scrutiny*, XVI (1949), pp. 250–9.

'Du nouveau sur Jean de Sponde', *Mercure de France*, CCCXII, no. 1056 (1 August 1951), pp. 641–7.

'The Interpretation of *Les Lettres persanes*', in: *The French Mind. Studies in honour of Gustave Rudler*, ed. Will Moore, Rhoda Sutherland and Enid Starkie, Oxford, Clarendon Press, 1952, pp. 152–69.

'Tradition and Revaluation in the French Anthology, 1692–1960', in: *Essays presented to C. M. Girdlestone*, University of Durham, 1960, pp. 51–63.

'The Definition of Mannerism', in: *Proceedings of the Third Congress of the International Comparative Literature Association, 21–26 August 1961, Utrecht*, 's Gravenhage, Monton, 1962, pp. 143–55.

'Tradition et révision de valeurs dans l'anthologie française (1692–1960)', *Annales de la Faculté des Lettres et Sciences Humaines d'Aix*, xxxvi (1962), pp. 31–47.

'Critiques français, critiques anglais, ce qui les divise. Réponse à Yves Bonnefoy. Communication de Alan Boase (Glasgow) XVᵉ Congrès de l'Association, le 26 juillet 1963', *Cahiers de l'Association internationale des Études françaises*, no. 16 (March 1964), pp. 157–65.

'Le grand madrigalier', in: *De Ronsard à Breton, recueil d'essais. Hommages à Marcel Raymond*, Paris, Corti, 1967, pp. 85–89.

'The Early History of the *Essai* Title in France and Britain', in: *Studies in French Literature presented to H. W. Lawton by colleagues, pupils and friends*, Manchester University Press, 1968, pp. 67–73.

Gide's *Essai sur Montaigne*: an assessment

❯❯❯ ❯❯❯ ❯❯❯ ❯❯❯ ❯❯❯ ❯❯❯ ❯❯❯ ❯❯❯ ❯❯❯ ❯❯❯ ❯❯❯ ❮❮❮ ❮❮❮ ❮❮❮ ❮❮❮ ❮❮❮ ❮❮❮ ❮❮❮ ❮❮❮ ❮❮❮ ❮❮❮ ❮❮❮ ❮❮❮

IF THERE IS one fact about Gide's *Essai sur Montaigne* which is not in dispute, it is that it was intended to figure in a history of literature being prepared by André Malraux. Gide twice notes the fact in his diary at the time when he is working on the project. Albert Thibaudet corroborates it in an article written in advance of the date of publication of the *Essai*.[1] Louis Martin-Chauffier confers upon it the authority of a painstaking and knowledgeable editor.[2] Günter Krebber works it, with scholarly diligence, into a worthy study of Gide's criticism.[3] It is as though the parable of the widow's mites had run away with its audience. For the other fact which is just as certain is that, when the *Tableau de la Littérature française* at last appeared,[4] it did not include Gide's *Essai*.[5]

[1] *Nouvelles littéraires*, samedi, 30 mars 1929, 'Montaigne et André Gide'.

[2] *Œuvres complètes d'André Gide*, t. XV, p. ix.

[3] *Untersuchungen zur Ästhetik und Kritik André Gides* (Geneva, 1959), p. 109.

[4] *Tableau de la Littérature française. XVIIe – XVIIIe siecles. De Corneille à Chénier* (Paris, 1939).

[5] The reader may wish to be reminded that Gide's criticism of Montaigne comprises the following texts:

    (*a*) the *Essai sur Montaigne*, which we take to be the centre-piece;

    (*b*) *Suivant Montaigne*, published shortly before the *Essai*, in the June number of the *Nouvelle Revue Française*, 1929. The two were then incorporated in a single volume (J. Schiffrin, Ed. de la Pléiade, Paris, 1929);

    (*c*) the preface to a Montaigne anthology which Gide prepared at the request of an American publisher in 1939. Several firms shared the copyright: we quote from *Les Pages immortelles de Montaigne* (Ed. Corrêa, Paris, 1939).

The measure of agreement among the various texts is such that, except in our references, we do not distinguish between them.

1

There is an obvious explanation in the period of literary history – *De Corneille à Chénier* – which the 1939 *Tableau* sets out to cover. But it would be interesting to know when and for what reasons the decision was taken to limit the volume in this way. Did Gide precipitate the decision by publishing his contribution independently? Or was the decision to publish independently consequent on a change in the original plan? Neither is likely. Gide speaks about 'l'étude sur Montaigne que j'ai promise à Malraux' on the 14th of September 1928;[1] he is correcting the proofs on the 29th of January 1929;[2] Thibaudet's article appears on the 30th of March; the Pléiade edition of the *Essai sur Montaigne* carries an *achevé d'imprimer* of the 10th of June. There is no room here for a change of plan. The implication is rather that by publishing the *Essai* in advance of the corporate effort, and Thibaudet's article in advance of the *Essai*, it was intended to awaken interest in a forthcoming literary event.

But if such was the intention, then the *Essai* would have had to make a very deep impression or the public to be possessed of a very long memory, for the effect to have been achieved. For it was only in 1939 that something like the original project came to fruition. Here again, a piece of literary history is missing. M. André Vandegans, discussing the schemes initiated by Malraux when he became a close associate of the *N.R.F.*, writes:

> Enfin, dès 1928, il s'occupa de dresser le fameux *Tableau de la littérature française*, qui ne sera achevé que onze ans plus tard: on avait sans doute eu du mal à réunir toutes les collaborations que réclamait cette oeuvre collective.[3]

The suggestion makes up in plausibility what it lacks in precision. Whatever the reason, it seems likely that, as the delay grew longer, less importance would be attached to the connection between the *Essai* and the proposed history, until it was felt that there was no point in distorting any shape which the other contributions

---

[1] *Journal* (Bibliothèque de la Pléiade, 1948), p. 887.
[2] ibid., p. 911.
[3] *La jeunesse littéraire d'André Malraux* (J.-J. Pauvert, *sans lieu*, 1964), p. 271.

could assume – *De Corneille à Chénier*, for example – in order to accommodate it.[1]

Behind the *Essai*, an initiative of Malraux; behind its separate publication, a publicity motive: the study which emerged in these circumstances might be expected to stand in a loose relationship to its author, but such is not the case. Gide began by being oppressed by the obligation to write on Montaigne:

> Mon horizon est tout obstrué par ce roman que j'ai promis à l'Amérique (*L'École des Femmes*) . . . puis par ce portrait de Montaigne pour l'*Histoire de la Littérature* de Malraux. Il me tarde de n'avoir plus devant moi que . . . moi-même.[2]

On further reflection, however, it seemed to him that he might write about Montaigne without losing sight of current preoccupations:

> A dire vrai, ce livre (*L'École des Femmes*) ne m'intéresse guère . . . Il ne se relie pas étroitement à mes préoccupations actuelles, auxquelles je pourrais plus facilement donner vent dans l'étude sur Montaigne . . . où sans doute je trouverai prétexte légitime à exprimer quelques-unes des considérations qui me tiennent le plus à cœur.[3]

The speed with which he was able to complete the task – still talking about it in the future in mid-September, correcting the proofs in January – leads one to suppose that he was right, and that the subject lent itself to his mood of self-absorption. Thus the obligation became an opportunity, and Gide, if he did not propose, must have welcomed the idea that the *Essai* might be published without delay. For besides being a work of criticism, it was a manifesto, as a remark in the diary makes clear:

---

[1] The volume published by Gallimard in 1962 – *Tableau de la Littérature française. De Rutebeuf à Descartes* – must be supposed to stand in fairly tenuous relationship to anything that was planned for the earlier period some thirty years beforehand. The text of the *Essai sur Montaigne* is, however, reproduced there in something like the context for which it was intended.

[2] *Journal*, p. 886.

[3] ibid., p. 887.

Corrigé les épreuves de mon *Montaigne*. A le relire il me paraît que je m'y suis montré soucieux de ne rien forcer; que ma propre position, devant la philosophie que je dégage des *Essais*, va paraître bien incertaine. Pourtant, la période des hésitations est passée; mais combien ce que je voudrais à présent me paraît difficile à dire.[1]

What Gide aimed at, via his *Montaigne*, was some statement of ultimate wisdom, or at any rate, of *his* ultimate wisdom, such as he found in Book III of the *Essais*, by which time Montaigne,

parfaitement maître, non de lui-même (il ne le sera jamais et ne peut l'être), mais de son sujet, ne tâtonne plus; il sait ce qu'il veut dire . . . et il le dit excellemment . . .[2]

Although we believe that Gide, for all his grumbling, was peculiarly ready to write about Montaigne at the time when he did, this is not to suggest that his interest in Montaigne, relative to the date of publication of the *Essai*, was a recent or sudden development. Any such notion can be dismissed on the strength of the Indexes to the two Pléiade volumes of the *Journal*, together with the *Index détaillé des 'Œuvres complètes d'André Gide.'*[3] Frieda S. Brown has found enough encouragement in the mentions which Gide makes in his diary, between 1904 and 1906, of reading the *Essais*, to devote an article to 'Montaigne and Gide's *La Porte étroite*'.[4] She dwells longer on the component parts of the title considered separately than she does on their relationship to one another, but the conclusion, that Alissa's spiritual quest and end provide 'strong testimony for the truth of Montaigne's observation that men cannot transcend their limitations',[5] would seem to be valid.[6] Moreover, beside the probability that the moral line of *La Porte étroite* tends toward a Montaigne-type conclusion, there is the fact that several of the ideas expressed, in the *Essai, Suivant*

[1] *Journal*, p. 911.
[2] *O.C.*, t. XV, p. 6.
[3] Justin O'Brien; Asnières-sur-Seine, 1954.
[4] *PMLA*, vol. LXXXII, no. 1, March 1967, pp. 136–41.
[5] ibid., p. 140.
[6] Gide would, of course, also be familiar with Pascal's version of Montaigne's thoughts on the subject: 'le malheur veut que qui fait l'ange fait la bête'.

Montaigne, or the preface to the 1939 anthology, had been formulated at an earlier date, sometimes much earlier. Gide's objection to the *Apologie*, for example: that the vivacity of Montaigne's style is lost in the effort of systematic composition, is noted among the *Feuillets* or groups of undated fragments which he inserts at intervals in the *Journal*.[1] Also in the *Feuillets* is the quotation from Saint-Évremond, comparing Plutarch unfavourably with Sallust or Montaigne in the matter of their understanding of human complexity.[2] And in a diary entry, the notion of a martyred Gide-Montaigne after the manner of Dostoevsky's parable of the Grand Inquisitor.[3] So that, while there is reason to think that Gide attached particular importance to the effort to situate himself relative to Montaigne in the winter of 1928–9, there is no doubt but what the *Essai* represents the fruit of long acquaintance.

The frame of mind in which Gide, in 1928, approaches the task of writing about Montaigne – 'je trouverai prétexte légitime à exprimer quelques-unes des considérations qui me tiennent le plus à cœur'[4] – is such that no one would be very much surprised if his conclusions were suspect. We are all agreed that the critic's first duty is to extract himself from his inner maze and to focus on the product of another mind. When is there ever a legitimate pretext for doing otherwise? While we savour these general truths, we ought however to consider Gide's terms of reference. Thibaudet, in his article in the *Nouvelles littéraires*, explains the theory behind the forthcoming volume thus:

> L'idéal eût été de faire écrire le chapitre sur chaque auteur par son successeur ou son Epigone actuel . . .

And when the *Tableau* at last appears, the same guiding principle is enunciated in the preface – a preface written, not, as one might

---

[1] *Journal*, pp. 353–4. Although printed in the *Journal* between the consecutive entries for 1911 and 1912, this particular *Feuillet* might date from 1906, when – diary entry of *21 mars* – we find him 'patiently advancing' in the *Apologie*.

[2] ibid., p. 662.

[3] ibid., *30 novembre* (1924), p. 796.

[4] ibid., p. 887.

expect, by Malraux, but by Gide. (The reversal of roles is complete: Malraux figures as a contributor, with an essay on Laclos, while Gide provides the introductory comment which would normally be furnished by the editor. Why the latter? Would such a volume without the voice of Gide have been like a Metro-Goldwyn-Mayer film without the lion?) Gide explains the rationale of the volume in such a way as to make his subjective approach to the study of Montaigne seem unexceptionable:

> Chaque historien de la littérature a plus ou moins grand souci de considérer chaque auteur dans ses rapports avec son temps; de dénoncer des filiations, des influences; d'établir telles corrélations subtiles, telles motivations qui nous livrent enfin cet auteur, toutes pensées liées, beaucoup moins indépendant et original qu'il n'avait pu d'abord nous paraître et se croire lui-même . . .
>
> Notre propos est tout différent. Le seul rattachement que nous ayons cherché, dans la galerie de portraits que voici, c'est celui du peintre au modèle: l'effet d'une prédilection.[1]

We are bound to say that the description of a possible effect of literary history seems fair, though no more than Gide do we imagine that literary history can be dispensed with. More important, however, is the alternative which he proposes. In the situation he describes, the need for the critic to strive for understanding through objectivity does not arise. The understanding is intuitive, exists prior to the critical effort, guarantees its success. On the one hand, we may judge that this kind of argument is fraught with the difficulties which bother Icarus:

> Je n'extrais du plus beau syllogisme que ce que j'y avais mis d'abord. Si j'y mets Dieu, je l'y retrouve.[2]

On the other hand, in support of the view that critics of Montaigne are born, not made, Gide might refer us to the case of Pierre Hamp, in whose company he travels, together with Paul Desjardins, to Morocco, in 1923:

[1] op. cit., p. 7.
[2] *Romans* (Bibliothèque de la Pléiade, 1958), p. 1435, *Thésée*.

Ce qui fait que Hamp ne m'exaspère pas d'avantage, c'est qu'il exaspère encore bien plus Desjardins. C'est son assurance qui choque; il n'est point sot, mais il ne laisse habiter son esprit par rien que d'indubitable . . . On voudrait lui faire lire Montaigne, et l'on désespère de lui lorsqu'on apprend qu'il a pour livre de chevet les *Essais*.[1]

The *Essai sur Montaigne* and the *Tableau* set out from the assumption that certain insights may be granted to men of a certain cast of mind which are not the necessary perquisites of other men practising a particular discipline. He would be a presumptuous scholar who was not willing at least to entertain the notion.

In reality, of course, Gide exaggerates the difference between a subjective and a scholarly approach. At the beginning of the *Essai* he tenders a disclaimer the sense of which is broadly that of his remarks in the preface to the *Tableau* quoted above. He will leave it to scholars, he says, to determine the historical importance of Montaigne, and to say whether,

peut-être, avant lui, Erasme n'avait point posé les premières bases d'une humaine sagesse dont les peuples encléricalisés de l'Europe avaient en ce temps grand besoin. *Tel que je suis, je le prends tel qu'il est.*[2]

The *naïveté* of Gide's approach, which we are to infer from his 'Tel que je suis . . .', is altogether relative. Immensely well read, he was perfectly capable of situating Montaigne in a historical perspective. He was familiar with Pascal's reactions to Montaigne, with those of Sainte-Beuve and Emerson. His own appreciation of Montaigne the man and the stylist shows unmistakably that he had assimilated, whether consciously or not, the lessons of the Romantic reappraisal of the essayist. He was familiar also with the work of Pierre Villey, and had adopted Villey's central thesis of a development in Montaigne's thought: Stoic, Pyrrhonist, Epicurean. If he paid less attention to the Bordeaux text, it was from choice and not from ignorance. It would be a mistake therefore to

---

[1] *Journal*, p. 756.
[2] *O.C.*, t. XV, pp. 3–4; my italics.

suppose that Gide, in disclaiming any special competence, denies the need for information.

There is no reason why we should not accept the *Essai* on the terms on which it is offered to us. Thibaudet indeed, to whose scholarly concern with Montaigne the Pléiade edition and posthumously published study amply testify, positively welcomes the sort of criticism – 'partial et partiel' – which the *Essai* represents. His argument deserves to be reproduced:

> L'essai de Gide pourrait s'appeler *Montaigne et les problèmes gidiens*. Et voilà un dessein que j'approuve pleinement. Nous ne manquons pas d'excellents livres où Montaigne est étudié pour lui-même de manière historique et critique. Au besoin le grand travail de M. Pierre Villey dispenserait des autres. Mais une autre critique montaniste a été fondé par l'auteur ou les auteurs, quels qu'ils soient, de l'*Entretien avec M. de Saci*. Pascal ne s'intéresse dans Montaigne que dans la partie où il peut profiter et pascaliser, laissant le reste de côté. L'*Entretien avec M. de Saci* c'est un *Montaigne et les problèmes pascaliens* . . . Si nous possédions douze ou quinze *Montaigne et moi*, à la manière de Pascal et de Gide, quel trésor et quels recoupements![1]

A part of the interest of such studies would be proportional to the affection and esteem in which we held the figure of the commentator: there would still be 'celui qu'on gobe', as they used to say in the novels of Gyp, and 'celui qu'on ne gobe pas', but objections of principle would fall away. Not all of Thibaudet's readers have been convinced, however, for it is precisely an objection of principle which is brought by the only other scholar who has made a systematic attempt to evaluate Gide's criticism of Montaigne.

Günter Krebber, in his concluding chapter, represents Gide's sympathy for Montaigne as being on a par with his sympathy for Dostoevsky and for Goethe. These authors were for years his spiritual companions and advisers. In consequence, when he wrote about them what he had to say was inseparably bound up with some of the most personal elements of his thought. This is

[1] *Nouvelles littéraires*, samedi, 30 mars 1929.

borne out by a diary entry of 1922, at the time when he was lecturing on Dostoevsky:

> tout ce que je trouve le moyen de dire à travers Dostoïevsky et à l'occasion de lui, me tient à cœur et j'y attache une grande importance. Ce sera, tout autant qu'un livre de critique, un livre de confessions, pour qui sait lire; ou plutôt: une profession de foi.[1]

Quoting this remark, Herr Krebber comments:

> Die Gefahr einer solcher Kritik ist, dass sie zum Selbstporträt wird. Gide ist, wie früher gezeigt wurde, in seinen Montaigne-Essays dieser Gefahr erlegen, nicht aber in den Dostojewsky-Vorträgen und den Aufsätzen über Goethe.[2]

That the weakness of the Montaigne criticism had earlier been demonstrated is perhaps to claim too much. Three arguments had been advanced: (*a*) factors tending to limit the extent of Gide's sympathy with other authors were absent in the case of Montaigne; here, sympathy extended 'bis zur beinahe problemlosen Identifizierung';[3] (*b*) a summary of the contents of the *Essai sur Montaigne* enables us to recognize 'Angelpunkte den Moralkritik Gides';[4] (*c*) Gide preferred to read the *Essais* not in the Bordeaux version of the text but in the version of 1588; his account of Montaigne is based overwhelmingly on Book Three as it appeared in the 1588 edition. If we accept that (*a*) and (*b*) are accurate, it is still not clear why they constitute objections: there is no obvious reason why the state of affairs described in (*a*) should give rise to inferior criticism in the case of Montaigne, while the state of affairs described in (*b*) merely confirms the initial assumption – that there exists a family resemblance between Gide and Montaigne. The third argument looks to be more serious, but is unsupported by any discussion of what Gide might have neglected in Montaigne, so that we wonder whether Herr Krebber has spotted a major fault or a minor inconsistency: a selective approach to the

---

[1] *Journal*, p. 733.
[2] G. Krebber, op. cit., p. 153.
[3] ibid., p. 110.
[4] ibid., p. 111.

Essais on the part of Gide, combined with a professed admiration for their lack of system, caprice in the interest of sincerity, accommodation of opposites, etc. What we have in the earlier chapter, then, is not a demonstration of the way in which Gide has distorted Montaigne; at most, it is a demonstration of the fact that Gide, in writing about Montaigne, has produced 'ein indirektes Selbstporträt'.[1] But to say this is to say nothing. A portrait of Montaigne which resembles Gide will also resemble Montaigne where Gide is like Montaigne. And the idea that Gide is like Montaigne, as we have tried to show, is the *donnée* on which the whole enterprise – *Essai* and *Tableau* – is based. 'Il y a des chances,' says Thibaudet, 'que Racine ne se retrouve qu'assez changé en Giraudoux, Montesquieu en Valéry . . .',[2] but with Gide and Montaigne, where the affinity was real, the insight would be correspondingly profound. Was Thibaudet entitled to his view? The question as to whether the image which Gide projected of himself in the *Essai* resembles Montaigne, remains unanswered. As indeed does the question whether the image which Gide projected of himself resembled Gide.

There is no short cut to a verdict on the *Essai*. In order to judge, we are obliged to form our own picture of Montaigne, and then, contrasting it with that of Gide, to show in what respects it is more faithful. This is not an easy task, for as Gide has said, making an obvious point:

> Il n'est point d'auteur qu'il soit plus facile de tirer à soi, sans que précisément on puisse être accusé de le trahir, car il vous donne l'exemple et sans cesse se contredit et se trahit lui-même.[3]

Gide does not, of course, belong to the era before scholarly editing enabled students of Montaigne to see progression where formerly there had seemed to be contradiction. But he recognized, as one is bound to do, that passages of the *Essais* which stand in close proximity, whether by reason of subsequent

[1] G. Krebber, op. cit., p. 111.
[2] *Nouvelles littéraires*, samedi, 30 mars 1929.
[3] *Les Pages immortelles de Montaigne*, pp. 37–38.

addition or not, either must be read as cancelling one another (a futile option), or involve the reader in a process of explanation, assessment, preference. And he further recognized that by whichever of his 'mille visages' we are pleased to take Montaigne, the challenge of the others will remain. This can best be seen in the Notes to the *Essai* and its companion piece. Note 19, for example, intended to correct a bias in Gide's account of Montaigne's views on virtue:

> Montaigne, alors même qu'il affirme, reste si ondoyant, si divers . . . l'on pourrait nuancer à l'infini tout ce que je viens de dire . . . etc.[1]

Or the following Note, correcting a possibly false impression of Montaigne's ultimate scale of values:

> Montaigne crut devoir apporter à ces déclarations dernières quelques retouches, sur le fameux exemplaire de Bordeaux. Il serait aussi indécent de n'en point tenir compte, que de les trop mettre en avant . . . etc.[2]

Or Note 23, tending to disprove the suggestion that Montaigne, in his later years, had moved away from Christianity:

> Pourtant nous lisons, au chapitre IX, du Livre Troisième: 'Tout au commencement de mes fièvres et des maladies qui m'atterrent, entier encore et voisin de la santé, je me reconcilie à Dieu par les derniers offices chrestiens, et m'en trouve plus libre et deschargé . . .'[3]

The presence of such notes helps one to understand why Gide, rereading the *Essai*, should have thought that 'je m'y suis montré soucieux de ne rien forcer'.[4]

The difficulty of forming a picture of Montaigne in which conflicting features are understood in their relation to one another and each accorded its proper weight is such that one is bound to rely on those scholars whose long experience of the *Essais* entitles them to a respectful hearing. Gide deserves to be tested against a

[1] *O.C.*, t. XV, p. 66.
[2] loc. cit.
[3] *O.C.*, t. XV, p. 67.
[4] *Journal*, p. 911.

worthy partner, our own role being that of an observer. In the case of scholars who have written about Montaigne after 1929, the encounter has, of course, already taken place, with here and there a fleeting mention of the outcome: Thibaudet admiring a study in which 'Gide tire son auteur à lui, nullement en le dénaturant'; Friedrich, not explicitly commending, but occasionally citing Gide as a valuable witness; Frame linking Gide with Sainte-Beuve as among the 'most brilliant readers' of Montaigne. But there is no satisfaction in simply drawing up a list of tributes, nor do they carry much conviction as a form of argument. What we must do is to lay two versions of Montaigne side by side, and see whether that of Gide can sustain the comparison.

Which aspects of Montaigne capture Gide's attention? Above all, the autobiographical:

> Qui supprimerait tous les passages où Montaigne parle de lui, diminuerait d'un tiers le volume . . . Pour moi, c'est ce tiers précisément que surtout je voudrais garder. Dans les deux autres, que de bavardage![1]

It follows that he is interested especially in the 1588 edition of the *Essais* and the Third Book, by which time, 'Montaigne, parfaitement maître, non de lui-même . . . mais de son sujet, ne tâtonne plus'.[2] The message he discovers there is one of self-assertion, if in this one term we may gather up the various elements of self-knowledge, self-acceptance, self-confidence. Two formulas convey this message, one of them a characteristically Gidean invention: he imagines Montaigne answering the question 'What is truth?' in the words of Christ: 'JE suis la vérité', the sense of the remark being profane, entirely human and different from the original. This situates the new gospel in relation to the old, in a way which reflects Gide's understanding of his own intellectual development and that of European man, and it seeks to invest humanism with the prestige of Christianity. The other formula is Montaigne's own which Gide suggests might serve as

[1] *O.C.*, t. XV, p. 43.
[2] ibid., p. 6.

epigraph and key to the *Essais*: ' "l'estre veritable est le commencement d'une grande vertu" '.[1] If there were such an epigraph, would it commend intellectual honesty, or individualism, or only the preliminaries of heroism: *reculer pour mieux sauter*? Gide would be happy to let us speculate.

According to Gide, Montaigne considers that education and convention pose as much of a threat to the true self as do the passions. The effort of penetration required to discover behind the social man 'l'être humain . . . authentique' is one that has to be undertaken in every age:

> A chaque époque de l'histoire, une figure conventionnelle de l'humanité tente de recouvrir cet être réel. Montaigne écartera ce masque pour atteindre à l'essentiel; s'il y parvient, c'est par l'effort assidu d'une perspicacité singulière; c'est en opposant à la convention, aux croyances établies, aux conformismes, un esprit critique toujours en éveil . . .[2]

Montaigne's great merit is to have revealed himself 'pareil à nous et ordinaire'.[3]

Prominent among the 'croyances établies' which Montaigne contests is the notion of the soul's pre-eminence:

> . . . sans doute admet-il la division de l'âme et du corps; mais non point que l'on oppose l'un à l'autre;[4]

or again, changing one term of the antinomy:

> Pour Montaigne, le corps importe autant que l'esprit . . .[5]

Montaigne's reliance upon nature in his later years follows directly from the attack on reason in his period of greatest scepticism. 'Volupté' and 'plaisance' constantly recur as value criteria, while his comments on a form of Christian aspiration to saintliness are at best equivocal. Gide quotes, as we should expect him to do in

[1] *O.C.*, t. XV, p. 5.
[2] *Les Pages immortelles de Montaigne*, pp. 10–11.
[3] *O.C.*, t. XV, pp. 5–6.
[4] ibid., p. 23.
[5] *Les Pages immortelles de Montaigne*, p. 11.

this connection, those sentences from *De l'expérience* on which Molière was to dwell, and in which it has been suggested that we should see the meaning of *La Porte étroite*:

> 'Ils veulent se mettre hors d'eux et eschapper à l'homme. C'est folie; au lieu de se transformer en anges, ils se transforment en bestes; au lieu de se hausser, ils s'abattent.'[1]

Besides accommodating sensual man, Montaigne acknowledged the diversity of human motive and of action, the variability of the human soul:

> J'estime que c'est une grande force de Montaigne, d'avoir su accepter en lui-même les inconséquences et les contradictions.[2]

He would have us believe that, in this aspect of human behaviour, Montaigne perceived more than mere 'inconstance'; that he knew that the conception of man held forth by 'les bons autheurs' – 'des amoureux qui (sont) tout amoureux, des avares . . . complètement avares' – was less than the truth. The most forceful statement of Gide's opinion on this point comes in the preface:

> C'est peut-être par les quelques subtiles clartés qu'il nous apporte inopinément et comme sans le vouloir, sur les incertaines frontières de la personnalité et sur l'instabilité du *moi*, que Montaigne me paraît le plus surprenant et qu'il s'adresse le plus directement à nous.[3]

---

[1] *O.C.*, t. XV, p. 25.

Is Gide correct in representing this opinion as anti-Christian? We would refer the reader to an acute and tantalizing paragraph in *Mimesis*, where Auerbach discusses the passage of *De l'expérience* in which these sentences occur:

'. . . (Montaigne) might easily have added considerably to the number of Christian testimonies in support of his view. Above all he might have called upon the incarnation of the Word itself for support. He did not do so, although the idea undoubtedly occurred to him; in this connection it could not but force itself upon anyone brought up a Christian in Montaigne's day. He avoided the allusion, obviously intentionally, for it would automatically have given his statement the character of a profession of Christianity, which was far from what he had in mind. He likes to keep away from such ticklish subjects. But the question of his religious profession – which, by the way, I consider an idle question – has nothing to do with the observation that the roots of his realistic conception of man are to be found in the Christian-creatura. tradition' (op. cit., translation Willard R. Trask, Princeton, 1953, p. 306).

[2] *Les Pages immortelles de Montaigne*, p. 21.

[3] ibid., p. 23.

On the other hand, he declines to dwell on a related theme to that of 'inconstance': Montaigne's insistence on the vanity of man, the 'côté Pascal' of the *Essais*. Montaigne's avowed purpose in studying himself – 'apprendre "à se mespriser" '[1] – no longer greatly interests a modern reader.

Gide makes it clear that the views which he attributes to Montaigne are not to be found continuously expressed throughout the *Essais*. They are the harvest of experience, gathered as the result of a sustained process of observation and self-criticism. They belong to the richest, but not the final phase of a development. (In the Bordeaux text, Gide discovers 'réticences, explications, ratiocinations inutiles et affaiblissement'.)[2] In particular, they were views which Montaigne was able to arrive at only after freeing himself from the influence of La Boétie:

> . . . c'est ce *'négligemment'* que nous aimons dans Montaigne. Sous les yeux de La Boétie, Montaigne se drapait quelque peu à l'antique. Sincère encore ici, comme toujours, car il est épris d'héroisme; mais il n'aime pas, il aimera de moins en moins, que l'homme se guinde et craindra de plus en plus qu'il ne lui faille se rétrécir pour se hausser.[3]

Gide quotes with approval Montaigne's late remark: 'Je me laisse aller, comme je suis venu . . . etc.', and regrets that he should have died before he had the possibility of reading *Don Quixote* (1605):

> C'est aux dépens de Don Quichotte que, peu à peu, grandit en lui Sancho Pança.[4]

At the same time, Gide argues against any tendency to exaggerate the amoralism of Montaigne. For on the one hand, 'Montaigne, en qui l'on se plaît trop souvent à ne voir qu'un égoiste, est soucieux du bien public'.[5] He correctly believed that the service which he rendered by writing the *Essais* was greater than

---

[1] *O.C.*, t. XV, p. 9.
[2] ibid., p. 7.
[3] ibid., p. 16.
[4] ibid., p. 53.
[5] ibid., p. 8.

during his period of public office. Doubt is in no way cast on their utility by the fact that the modern reader discovers in them a different message from the one explicitly intended. And on the other hand, Montaigne's ethical teaching, in the last analysis, does not discourage an exacting attitude toward onself:

> Décidément je vois, dans l'éthique de Montaigne, recherche et exigence plutôt que simplement laisser-aller. Tout à la fois il lui plaît de céder à lui-même, et il redoute, dans cette complaisance envers soi, tout ce qui risque de compromettre la liberté et la droiture de son jugement. Il me semble que c'est là ce que proprement il appelle: vice.[1]

It is this concern for intellectual honesty which makes the *Essais* possible. To achieve his aim of self-knowledge, 'la seule vertu qu'il exige, c'est "la fidélité" '.[2] Montaigne is quite prepared to be indiscreet or indecent if it serves his larger aim, and those parts of the *Essais* which have sometimes given offence Gide interprets not in terms of the author's lack of modesty but as 'une certaine protestation contre la bienséance':

> 'Je dy vray, non pas tout mon saoul, mais autant que je l'ose dire; et l'ose un peu plus en vieillissant.'[3]

In the later preface, while continuing to emphasize the value of honesty with regard to self, Gide pitches more strongly what he has to say about its importance in our dealings with others:

> Ce que Montaigne nous enseigne surtout, c'est ce que l'on appela beaucoup plus tard le *libéralisme* et il me paraît que, de nos jours, c'est la plus sage leçon que nous puissions tirer de lui . . . 'Aus dissensions présentes de cet Etat, mon intérest,' dit-il, 'ne m'a faict mesconnaître ny les qualitez louables en mes adversaires, ny celles qui sont reprochables en ceux que j'ay suivi.'[4]

That the new emphasis is owed to Gide's unhappy experience as a

---

[1] *O.C.*, t. XV, p. 21.
[2] ibid., p. 7.
[3] loc. cit.
[4] *Les Pages immortelles de Montaigne*, p. 39.

critical friend of Communism is confirmed by a diary entry of 6th of January 1938 (at which time he is preparing the anthology): he quotes Montaigne on the Aristotelian for whom ' "la touche et reigle de toutes imaginations solides et de toute vérité, c'est la conformité à la doctrine d'Aristote" ', and he comments:

Ceci soit dit pour nombre de marxistes aujourd'hui – ou de catholiques.[1]

Finally, Gide shows Montaigne in possession of the serenity to which he aspires, regretting nothing, repenting nothing, rejecting nothing. Increasingly, he puts his trust in 'le seul conseil de la nature'. Like Goethe, he now requires that virtue, to be worthy of the name, should be 'sociable et souriante'. And if in wisdom, duty, virtue, it is pleasure which he seeks, his concern is still not one of simple egoism,

(puisqu'il) comprend de quel enseignement, de quel conseil, peut être pour l'humanité tout entière le seul exemple d'un homme heureux.[2]

And again, Gide quotes:

'Pour moy donc, j'ayme la vie et la cultive telle qu'il a pleu à Dieu nous l'octroier.'[3]

Death is a part of the scheme which Montaigne can accept as calmly as the rest: nowhere is the development of his thought more evident than here.

These are, we believe, the main ideas expressed in Gide's criticism of Montaigne. Are they superficial and idiosyncratic, or do they represent the nucleus of a genuine understanding? Those who are versed in Montaigne will form their own opinion. And indeed, we wonder whether, with a question of this kind, there is any substitute for the total response of the informed individual. What kind of proof is possible? What kind of proof is not possible? It would certainly be pointless to ransack a series of

[1] *Journal*, pp. 1294–5.
[2] *O.C.*, t. XV, p. 23.
[3] ibid., p. 24.

Montaigne critics with a view to assembling fragments of a picture which would coincide with Gide's. But perhaps there is room for an appeal to some single individual who commands the range of material thrown up by modern scholarly investigation, his own included. We have chosen Donald M. Frame, and in particular his study: *Montaigne's Discovery of Man. The Humanization of a Humanist*.[1] In no sense is the choice inevitable, but we imagine that it is one which might meet with fairly general approval.

The unfolding of Montaigne's thought, says Professor Frame, may be understood as a 'progressive liberation from apprehension and tutelage'.[2] Small wonder that Gide should have been attracted, or considered himself ideally placed to provide a commentary! From his friendship with La Boétie, Montaigne derived:

> an admiration for stoical humanism that was not quite natural to him and that he had to fight in order to become fully himself.[3]

The development of the essayist is the subject and dictates the form of Frame's study, as can be judged from the chapter titles: 'The Young Hedonist', 'The Apprehensive Humanist', 'The Skeptical Revolt', etc. The scale and the manner of treatment is such that, where Gide could only allege a development and attempt to characterize it in a striking image – Don Quixote to Sancho Panza – Frame can describe and explain it. Thus, the famous *Apologie* takes its place as a necessary link in a chain, instead of being rejected, as it is by Gide, on aesthetic grounds: 'fastidious' in its composition, and hence unrepresentative.

In some respects, however, what Frame has to say on the *Apologie* corroborates Gide's brief remarks. For on the one hand he suggests that Montaigne's scepticism here can best be seen as 'an intellectual game',[4] in which case Gide's neglect is less reprehensible:

---

[1] New York, 1955.
[2] op. cit., p. 7.
[3] loc. cit.
[4] Donald M. Frame, op. cit., p. 61.

. . . ce scepticisme n'est point ce qui me plaît dans les *Essais*, ni la leçon que surtout j'y puise.[1]

And on the other, while rejecting a view of the *Apologie* as 'a covert but thorough undermining of Christianity and all dogmatic religions'[2] (a view which he attributes to Gide as well as to Sainte-Beuve), he admits that, as a 'declaration of complete intellectual independence',[3] it shows Montaigne freeing himself from Christianity as a way to goodness.

After the *Apologie*, the pursuit of universal truths by rational means no longer interests Montaigne. He turns to what he has some hope of attaining: self-knowledge, and through self-knowledge, happiness. Not the manner of a man's death but the manner of his life is now seen as the challenge and test of his philosophy.

How are we to live? In the Introduction, Frame tells us that Montaigne's constant rule is to follow nature. Later, in discussing *Des cannibales*, he shows Montaigne handling the contrast between the spontaneous and the affected in a more subtle way; envisaging a form of conduct which is neither natural nor artificial, but a manifestation of 'a higher human naturalness that is beyond art'.[4] Here is the counterpart of Gide's debate as to whether Montaigne advocates 'recherche et exigence plutôt que . . . laisser-aller'.[5]

As we should expect, there is agreement with Gide that, for Montaigne:

> the basic fact of man's nature is that he is made up of body and soul. And his basic deduction is that these two are equal.[6]

There is agreement, too, on Montaigne's account of the soul, although Frame is able to explain, as Gide was not, the connection

---

[1] *O.C.*, t. XV, p. 4.
[2] Donald M. Frame, op. cit., p. 58.
[3] ibid., p. 77.
[4] ibid., p. 100.
[5] *O.C.*, t. XV, p. 21.
[6] Donald M. Frame, op. cit., p. 143.

between the essayist's theme of the vanity of man and his optimism. But even the Voltairean *parti pris* which causes Gide to neglect the destructive side of the *Essais* can seem justified in view of the confidence in man expressed, for example, in *De l'institution des enfans*.

Of Montaigne's alleged decline (alleged by Gide, that is), there is no mention. The last stage observed by Frame in the development of Montaigne is rather what he calls 'The Discovery of Others', one which tends to confirm Gide's arguments in favour of his altruism. His sympathies expanding, his sense of human solidarity increasing, Montaigne progressed from an aristocratic ideal to one which was more broadly based: the *honneste homme* replaced the *gentilhomme*.

> Wisdom, for Montaigne, consists entirely in knowing how to live. This involves four things: knowing ourselves, accepting ourselves and our life, learning what to expect of ourselves, and learning our duty to ourselves and others.[1]

'Wisdom, for Gide . . . involves four things . . .' Is the statement less true with the name changed? Perhaps, after all, it is not surprising that what Gide discovers in the *Essais* coincides at many points with what a scholar can discover, employing an 'objective' method.

In respect of one important matter – Montaigne's religious beliefs – there is, however, no coincidence. Hitherto, we have mentioned only indirectly Gide's view of Montaigne's Christianity. This was not because we wished to disguise a weakness of his criticism, but because the most controversial aspect seemed to merit separate discussion. We begin with a summary which properly belongs with the outline offered above of Gide's principal ideas on Montaigne.

Montaigne's Catholicism, according to Gide, is formal and expedient. It draws its strength from his political conservatism:

> Ce qui lui plaît, dans le catholicisme . . . c'est l'ordre et l'ancienneté . . . La religion de l'Eglise, la religion française, il la

---

[1] Donald M. Frame, op. cit., p. 149.

veut garder telle quelle; non point tant parce qu'il la croit seule bonne, que parce qu'il croit mauvais d'en changer.[1]

He professes lack of competence in theology and evinces lack of interest. He is doctrinally confused.[2] His ethical teaching is at odds with Christian ethics. He takes a positive view of human nature and its possibilities. He knows the meaning of repentance, but is without enthusiasm for the practice. Sometimes he expresses admiration for saintly virtues; elsewhere he questions our ability to rise to them and indicates that he personally is disinclined to try. 'Tout le long des *Essais*,' says Gide, 'la souriante liberté de sa pensée païenne est manifeste.'[3] Given their general tenor, how can we interpret the various expressions of orthodox opinion, often later additions in conflict with the surrounding text, except as 'paratonnerres', or as Gide more modishly puts it:

comme ces étiquettes de sirop ou de limonade, sur les bouteilles de whisky, en temps de régime sec aux États-Unis?[4]

Gide, for his part, inclines to adopt the formula of Sainte-Beuve:

'Il peut bien avoir paru très bon catholique, sauf à n'avoir guère été chrétien.'[5]

Montaigne was aware of this, and in his professions of orthodoxy we detect *prudence, cautèle, malice, hypocrisie.*

It is here that, in effect, Gide would seem to have exposed himself to the objection: 'd'avoir à l'excès acéré les idées de Montaigne'.[6] Not in the matter of the dissimilarity between the ethics of Montaigne and of Christian teaching, but in the suggestion that Montaigne's religion had more to do with politics than with belief. Gide was not the first, nor the second either, to have difficulty in imagining how such freedom of thought could be

---

[1] *O.C.*, t. XV, p. 21.
[2] Cf. Gide's remarks on *Des prieres*: ibid., pp. 40–41.
[3] *O.C.*, t. XV, p. 61.
[4] ibid., p. 20.
[5] loc. cit.
[6] *O.C.*, t. XV, p. 31.

combined with orthodox belief, but he was not any the less mistaken for having company. We know of no reason to dispute the following assessment:

> . . . though Armaingaud and Gide consider him an unbeliever, the prevailing and the soundest opinion seems to be that of such Montaigne scholars as Villey, Plattard, Lanson and Janssen, who regard him as a sincere believer, but somewhat inconsistent or at least unorthodox by modern standards.[1]

Frame might have added the name of Alan M. Boase to the list of authorities who disagreed with Gide, and perhaps his testimony is the most conclusive, since what is extremely difficult to prove solely on the strength of the text of the *Essais* becomes an overwhelming probability when the intellectual history of the period is invoked. To some extent therefore it would be fair to say that Gide's error in this matter exposes the shortcomings of his method – neglecting, as a matter of principle, '(le) souci de considérer chaque auteur dans ses rapports avec son temps'.[2] But while his ignorance of the historic role of fideism no doubt made it easier for him to persist in a mistaken view, it was, we believe, a different failure which led Gide to adopt that view at all.

For the fact is that, whatever arguments for unbelief or an unbelieving Montaigne have in the past been drawn from the *Apologie*, Gide makes scarcely any attempt to repeat or to exploit them. He does not appreciate the *Apologie*. He does not especially appreciate the scepticism. He talks very little about either of them. The burden of his argument in favour of an unbelieving Montaigne is to be found, not in the paragraph which makes the

---

[1] Donald M. Frame, *Montaigne in France*, 1812–1852 (New York, 1940), p. 82. n.

[2] *Tableau de la Littérature française* (Paris, 1939), p. 7; and compare, *The Fortunes of Montaigne* (London, 1935), p. xiii:
'Is M. André Gide correct when he sees in that natural conservative, Montaigne, the prototype of his own contemporaries Barrès and Maurras – "the first Catholic who was not a Christian"? It is my purpose, first of all, to show that there is no longer an enigma . . . that if we will replace him in his own historical setting, this enigma disappears.'

implicit comparison with Maurras and mentions scepticism,[1] but here in the image of a man for whom the notion of sin, repentance, resurrection, held no meaning:

> . . . devant les autorités ecclésiastiques, quelle curieuse soumission que la sienne! alors que, tout le long des *Essais*, la souriante liberté de sa pensée païenne est manifeste.[2]

It is not the sceptic but the sage, the 'humanized' humanist, the serene Montaigne, whom Gide cannot imagine as a Christian. For this resistance to be overcome, we should have to confront Gide, not with the evidence of how the fideist system worked and of its popularity in the second half of the sixteenth century, but with what Professor Boase calls the 'ideology' connected with fideism and which is present in the *Essais*: Montaigne's insistence on the vanity and misery of man. It is clear that in these tragic themes the emotional basis of faith is potentially present. Gide knew that they were there, but turned his back on them, with the result that Montaigne's religious position became incomprehensible:

> . . . rien ne nous est devenu plus étranger . . . que ce plaidoyer de Pascal pour établir la misère de l'homme . . ., tout ce que résume admirablement cette phrase de Montaigne . . .: 'Ce sont les pieds du paon qui abbatent son orgueil.'[3]

There can be no question here of a failure of method: the error is wilful. Like Bernard in *Les Faux-Monnayeurs* – 'Le "mol et doux oreiller" de Montaigne n'est pas fait pour ma tête . . .'[4] – Gide had made up his mind which intellectual options he was prepared to countenance.

From this it does not follow that the Montaigne criticism is vitiated by subjective bias. This is true neither of the whole, nor

---

1 'Montaigne est le premier de ces catholiques non chrétiens, qui font profession de se rattacher à Rome et qui pourtant ignorent le Christ. Et l'on s'explique dès lors son hostilité à l'égard des protestants . . . Le parfait scepticisme de Montaigne ne peut s'accommoder de devoirs envers Dieu qui impliquent évidemment une croyance en Dieu . . . etc.' (*O.C.*, t. XV, p. 43).
2 ibid., p. 61.
3 ibid., p. 56.
4 *Romans* (Bibliothèque de la Pléiade, 1958), p. 1090.

of the greater part. Any such conclusion is merely extravagant, particularly where we know at what point and for what reason Gide's account is wide of the mark. What follows is rather a question about the value of the *Essai* for the light it sheds on Gide. And here we come upon a difficulty which has not always been sufficiently remarked. Suppose we agree that 'Gide tire Montaigne à lui', where does that leave Montaigne? If we decide that Gide has fashioned Montaigne in his own image, what, then, is Montaigne like? In which of his Protean manifestations shall we assume that Gide has been arrested? With the statement: 'Tel que je suis, je le prends tel qu'il est',[1] it is clear that discussion as to *comment il est* can centre on either part.

Gide himself formulates, in respect of the *Essais*, the sort of question which now we want to ask of him, and he outlines a possible answer:

> Sans doute est-il intéressant de chercher à travers les confidences de Montaigne, s'il est toujours bien pareil à ce qu'il croit être, ou si seulement il le devient: 'Je sens ce proffit inesperé de la publication de mes meurs . . . qu'elle me sert aucunement de regle. Il me vient par fois quelque consideration de ne trahir l'histoire de ma vie. Cette publique declaration m'oblige de me tenir en ma route, et à ne desmentir l'image de mes conditions.' Si naturel qu'il soit (ou plutôt encore: qu'il se veuille), il s'est un tantinet fabriqué.[2]

That Gide stands in a similar dynamic relationship to his publications is a critical commonplace. The decision to publish *Corydon* affords only the most striking example of his using his writing to strengthen the resolve with which he pursues a particular course of action. What we have here is the Wildean paradox: nature following art,[3] put on an active footing. Instead of being com-

---

[1] *O.C.*, t. XV, pp. 3–4.
[2] ibid., p. 6.
[3] Cf., for example, the diary entry for the 10th of February 1929:
' . . . je crois, avec Wilde, que les plus importants artistes ne copient point tant la nature qu'ils ne la précèdent; de sorte que c'est eux au contraire que la nature semble imiter. Je crois, de plus . . . que l'immense majorité des êtres humains se contentent de sentiments de convention . . .' (*Journal*, p. 913).

pelled by images to which he can offer no alternative, the writer submits voluntarily to an image of his own choosing. It is in this light that we should see the *Essai sur Montaigne*: as an expression of Gide in 1929, it has more to do with volition than description.

In what respect was the *Essai* the projection of an ideal rather than the actual Gide? Above all, in respect of what, for Gide, was the main lesson of the *Essais*, the one embraced in the formula: ' "JE suis la vérité".' A part of the gloss which follows reads:

> De là cette extraordinaire défiance, dès qu'il raisonne; de là *cette confiance, cette assurance, dès qu'il s'abandonne à lui-même* et qu'il résigne à lui ses visées.[1]

Assuming that this is an accurate description of Montaigne, transferred to Gide would it meet with general acceptance? It is in the 1920s, with the publication of *Corydon*[2] and *Si le grain ne meurt*,[3] that Gide asserts most vehemently his right to be himself, 'qu'il s'abandonne à lui-même'. Yet the idea that this period, in which the public *démarches* are so decisive, is a period of great inner confidence, will scarcely bear examination.

It is belied above all by the evidence of *Les Faux-Monnayeurs* (1926). The fascination of the aesthetic problems raised by the book cannot disguise its autobiographical character. Nor is there any conflict between this view and the remarks of Thibaudet which Gide welcomes in the last entry of the *Journal des Faux-Monnayeurs*:

> Le romancier authentique crée ses personnages avec les directions infinies de sa vie possible . . .[4]

We are not tempted to identify Gide with any one of the various projections of his private problematic contained in the novel, but we are in no doubt that the private problematic is at the centre. Jacques Lévy understood this perfectly, and made it the basis of a brilliant and eccentric study:

---

[1] *O.C.*, t. XV, pp. 4–5; my italics.
[2] Anonymous, limited edition, 1920; *première édition dans le commerce*, 1924.
[3] 2 vols., 1920 and 1921.
[4] *O.C.*, t. xiii, p. 62.

> On n'a pas l'impression d'un entremêlement de destins, mais au contraire celle d'un destin unique qui se poursuivrait tantôt sous une forme, tantôt sous une autre . . .;[1]

and again:

> Le véritable sujet serait le rapport des personnages avec l'auteur, et le livre tout entier serait le produit d'une sorte de mythologie spirituelle.[2]

If this interpretation is correct, and *Les Faux-Monnayeurs* is 'l'histoire d'une conscience', then the conscience reflected in the characters is far from being quiet and assured. In Passavant, the dissembling pederast, exposed and humiliated by Strouvilhou and Cob-Lafleur. In Vincent, who absorbs into himself the hellish person of Lady Griffith: 'se croit possédé par le diable; ou plutôt il se croit le diable lui-même . . .'[3] In the *ménage* La Pérouse, where we recognize, via such signs as the letters from the old man's brother of which his wife is jealous, a statement of personal tragedy. In the relationship between Boris and Bronja, mirroring that of Gide and Madeleine as children and ending in the death of both.[4] In Armand, a victim, like Vincent Molinier, of the divorce of intellect and sensibility. Jacques Lévy thought that the key to the book was to be found in the death of Boris, understood as the death of the soul. 'L'atrocité de cette mort,' he wrote, 'me semblait un crime collectif pesant sur tous les personnages.'[5] Almost certainly, he exaggerates the negative and tragic aspects of the novel. This we would not wish to do. We do not overlook the fact that Olivier is rescued; that his love-affair with Édouard ends in happiness; that Bernard's emancipation leads to maturity and not corruption; that the final paragraph, with all its Gidean irony and promise of new departure, speaks of reconciliation, tolerance,

---

[1] Jacques Lévy, *Journal et correspondance* (Grenoble, 1954), p. 42.
[2] loc. cit.
[3] *Romans* (Bibliothèque de la Pléiade, 1958), p. 1233.
[4] Cf. *Si le grain ne meurt*: 'C'est alors que survint l'angélique intervention que je vais dire, pour me disputer au malin . . . etc.' (*Journal 1939–1949*, p. 430).
[5] op. cit., p. 35.

a society reconstituted. But the fact remains that whatever confidence emanates from such a character as Bernard, it is matched by the hesitations, regrets, misgivings expressed in the other figures.

A reading of the novel which finds in it the expression, if not of *une âme en peine*, at any rate of *une âme qui cherche, et qui n'a pas trouvé, l'équilibre*, is supported by the fact that the period of composition of *Les Faux-Monnayeurs* coincides with the period covered by the *Journal intime*, the part of Gide's diary concerning his relationship with Madeleine.[1] The diary entries show Gide to be profoundly unhappy and suffering from the illusion which, in *Les Faux-Monnayeurs*, he attributes to La Pérouse:

> 7 *août* (1922) '. . . il me semble que je suis déjà mort et que je ne vivais que par elle';[2]
> 11 *juillet* 1923 'Il me semble souvent que j'ai déjà cessé de vivre';[3]
> *Début de janvier* 1925 'Je n'ai plus vécu, depuis, qu'une existence quasi posthume, et comme en marge de la vraie vie'.[4]

It would be a mistake, no doubt, to imagine that such impressions haunted Gide continually: 'La joie, en moi, l'emporte toujours . . .' he tells us in *Si le grain ne meurt*.[5] Nevertheless, it is certain that, in his period of most uncompromising self-assertion, from the *affichage* of his liaison with Marc Allegret to the publication of *Les Faux-Monnayeurs* and after, Gide was a prey to recurrent and acute self-doubt.

Are we intent on rediscovering in Gide the *inquiétude* which it seemed to him his Catholic friends and former friends were

---

[1] First published in 1947, together with *Et nunc manet in te*. The first entry in the *Journal des Faux-Monnayeurs* is dated 17th of June 1919, while at the end, in 1925, we read: 'Hier, 8 juin, achevé *Les Faux-Monnayeurs*' (*O.C.*, t. xiii, p. 62). In the *Journal intime*, the entry concerning the destruction of Gide's letters by his wife – the event which marks the collapse of their relationship – is dated 21st of November 1918. Subsequent entries are made at intervals until 1927, after which there is a long silence until the death of Madeleine, in 1938, prompts three further entries.
[2] *Journal 1939–1949*, p. 1155.
[3] ibid., p. 1156.
[4] ibid., p. 1157.
[5] ibid., p. 494.

perversely anxious to observe?[1] Not necessarily so. Our point is simply that the serene individualist of the *Essai sur Montaigne* was not the actual Gide. He was a tribute to the hedonistic imperative which Gide and Montaigne both acknowledged – ' "Il faut estendre la joye, mais retrencher autant qu'on peut la tristesse" '[2] – paid at a time when Gide was not himself conspicuously happy.[3] Gide's purpose was not to endorse his humours but to combat them – as he strove to do ten years later, after the death of Madeleine:

> *Paris.* 21 *Août* (1938). '. . . Depuis qu'elle n'est plus, je n'ai fait que semblant de vivre . . .';[4]
>
> 26 *au soir.* '. . . Si je ne parviens pas à rejoindre la sérénité, ma philosophie fait faillite. Il est vrai, j'ai perdu ce "témoin de ma vie" qui m'engageait à ne point vivre "négligemment", comme disait Pline à Montaigne . . .; mais, de même que je ne laissais pas son amour, durant sa vie, incliner dans son sens ma pensée, je ne dois pas, à présent qu'elle n'est plus, laisser peser sur ma pensée, plus que son amour même, le souvenir de cet amour.'[5]

W. M. L. Bell

[1] Cf. *Journal*, p. 901: 'Ils m'ont longtemps reproché ce qu'ils appelaient mon inquiétude; puis, lorsqu'ils ont commencé de comprendre que cette inquiétude n'était pas la mienne, mais celle des êtres que je peignais . . ., ils m'ont reproché d'avoir trouvé le calme et cette sérénité qui précisément me permettait de produire . . . . etc.'

[2] *O.C.*, t. XV, p. 46.

[3] Cf. Louis Martin-Chauffier's description of the diary entries of 1928:
'Cette morne année 1928, ce ne sont point tant les sombres pensées sur le vieillissement et la mort qui lui donnent son caractère; mais la brièveté même des notes, leur abandon . . . A la recherche d'un équilibre qui le fuit du dedans; ou plutôt dans la vaine poursuite d'un cadre qui lui rendra quelque vitalité. Il cherche à s'abuser, s'évade pour s'éviter, mais partout se traîne avec lui' (*O.C.*, t. XV, pp. xi–xii).

[4] *Journal*, p. 1310.

[5] ibid., p. 1315.

Rabelais: Menippean Satirist
or Comic Novelist?

❯❯❯ ❯❯❯ ❯❯❯ ❯❯❯ ❯❯❯ ❯❯❯ ❯❯❯ ❯❯❯ ❯❯❯ ❯❯❯ ❯❯❯ ❮❮❮ ❮❮❮ ❮❮❮ ❮❮❮ ❮❮❮ ❮❮❮ ❮❮❮ ❮❮❮ ❮❮❮ ❮❮❮ ❮❮❮

NOW (TO FORBARE for ever solittle of Iris Trees and Lili O'Rangans), concerning the genesis of Harold or Humphrey Chimpden's occupational agnomen (we are back in the presurnames prodromarith period, of course, just when enos chalked halltraps) and discarding once for all those theories from older sources which would link him back with such pivotal ancestors as the Glues, the Gravys, the Northeasts . . . or proclaim him offsprout of vikings who had founded wapentake and seddled hem in Herrick or Eric, the best authenticated version . . . has it that it was this way . . .[1]

Tres illustres et tres chevaleureux champions, gentilz hommes et aultres, qui voluntiers vous adonnez à toutes gentillesses et honnestetez, vous avez n'a gueres veu, leu et sceu, les *Grandes et inestimables Chronicques de l'enorme geant Gargantua* et, comme vrays fideles, les avez creues tout ainsi que texte de Bible ou du sainct Evangile . . .[2]

MY OBJECT in beginning with these two quotations is not to compare Joyce's creative method with Rabelais's, his word-play, his spinning of rhyme, rhythm and sense-associations into a cosmos of fantasy and reality where his characters are superhuman or mini-human. It is rather to see Joyce and Rabelais both working

---

[1] James Joyce, *Finnegans Wake*, London (1966), p. 30.
[2] I have used the critical edition by Lefranc *et al.* for *Gargantua* and *Pantagruel*, the critical edition of *Le Tiers Livre* by M. A. Screech, and the edition of *Le Quart Livre* by P. Jourda. The last part of the phrase cited was in the first edition by Claude Nourry (1532), and was omitted later for religious reasons. See Lefranc, *Pantagruel*, p. 3.

29

in a fictional world: Joyce with his tracing of a narrative skeleton, Rabelais with his parody of romance. For in this early extract from *Finnegans Wake*, and in Rabelais's first Prologue, one is immediately aware of a *persona* speaking: that is, a created author, or the author's second self, who chooses his standpoint as a novelist irrespective of the real author's ideas. Joyce and Rabelais are consciously, indeed self-consciously, writing a comic and parodistic book: the language is both ironical and comic, the tone of entertainment is there and both extracts are suffused with jest and censure.

Throughout this essay I shall be concerned only with the created author, the *persona* as it appears in Rabelais's work and, in particular, with the question of how it works as a fictional device. One becomes aware when reading *Don Quixote*, for instance, that Cervantes is building up multiple perspectives: for example, the pretence of using the Arabic chronicler Cide Hamete Benengeli to suggest that the fiction is history.[1] One is similarly aware of the various devices that Rabelais has used to create the same effects: for instance, at the beginning of *Gargantua* a *joly livret* is introduced where the *antiquité et geneallogie* and the whole story of the giants have to be translated.[2] Cervantes, of course, winds his story around a knight who is himself constantly moving to and fro between fiction and reality, so that the author can stand back and as it were abdicate responsibility for the various tricks of perspective he has used. So much so that Albert Cook can argue that Cervantes is creating vertical worlds of illusion and reality (fictional reality, that is) around his characters, while Rabelais extends his fictional world horizontally in a more complicated – though not in a more novelistic – way.[3] Is there, then, no line to

---

[1] Cervantes, *Don Quixote*, translated by J. M. Cohen, London, part I, ch. ix.

[2] At certain times Cervantes mentions deeds he himself did, for example I, xl, when in slavery, but the effect is yet another perspective on the fantasy of the novel in that the 'truth' of real life is brought in. When Rabelais in the *Quart Livre*, ch. 27, names people close to Guillaume du Bellay on his death, one of whom is Rabelays, there is no connection between the real author and the *persona* of the fiction.

[3] Albert Cook, 'The Beginning of Fiction: Cervantes', *Journal of Aesthetics and Art Criticism*, vol. XVII (1959), pp. 463 ff.

guide the reader through the vast satirizing and transmogrifying catalogue of Rabelais's fictional world? Is the narrative line merely a tool of satire? Let us look a little more closely at the *persona* Rabelais creates for himself, to see whether this is the main device that will give shape to the vast range of narrative *techniques* in the fiction.

Obviously the short breaks in a chapter, for mock assurances of truthfulness from the first person to the readers (a *you* singular or plural), are a standard technique in satiric writing from Seneca's *Apocolocyntosis* onwards. So, too, are the intrusions of a chapter or more where the *persona* plays in a mocking or self-mocking way with parodies of philosophy as in Lucian, epic tales as in Petronius, or romances as in Folengo. But in Rabelais, who is more than a satirist, the *persona* is more complex: for instance, what is the effect when the *persona* splits up into a host of narrative voices? These voices may be those of Alcofrybas or a pseudo-chronicler, who tell the story for a time and seem to be jostling for the dominant place. The *persona* is easiest to look at first without introducing characters, for we may find that this technique does, in fact, affect or alter the author's view of his fictional world.

If we look back at the first Prologue we observe that apart from the burlesque satire the author also gives us a thumb-nail sketch of one voice: 'C'est des horribles faictz et prouesses de Pantagruel, lequel j'ay servy à gaiges dès ce que je fuz hors de page jusques à present. . . .' Not only are we already inside the fictional world but the *persona* has another voice – Alcofrybas his pseudonym – whose relationship with the giants is very different from the *persona*, for he is a *humble esclave* to *mon maistre Pantagruel*. Furthermore, in the Prologues to the first four books there is built up between the *persona* and his readers a line – satiric or comic – which looks at human affairs without getting emotionally attached to the story at all, but can, quite detachedly and intellectually, approve or disapprove of any action or discussion. Finally there is the sharp irony of 'ces tant veritables contes', or the self-mockery of 'ce livre seigneurial',

31

which hint at a multiplicity of dimensions in Rabelais's fiction.[1]

In the first chapter of *Pantagruel* there is the introduction of another voice: the pseudo-chronicler. Everything he says is turned by the *persona* into a comic commentary. The title of the chapter (and this is true of every chapter in the four books) makes us expect a fifteenth-century romance, with a straight and linear directive from the chronicler. But here the chronicler is mixed up with the *persona*: 'ce ne sera chose inutile . . . vous ramentevoir', to give you information about Pantagruel; *but* a dig at all good historiographers follows: 'non seulement des Grecz, des Arabes et Ethniques mais aussi les auteurs de la sainte escripture comme monseigneur sainct Luc mesmement, et sainct Mathieu'.[2] A fifteenth-century device like 'Il vous convient doncques noter que' is followed by a *fantaisiste*, *persona*-type embroidery: 'au commencement du monde (je parle de loing, il y a plus de quarante quarantaines de nuyctz, pour nombrer à la mode des antiques Druides)'. This is not straight chronicling, but the comic intermingling of two voices, and will carry on throughout the fiction. This is clearly like Lucian or Sorel, who use a first person singular for satiric purposes: for example, Sorel will give in his *Francion* similes which are *merveilleux*, and then comment on them – to make them even more fantastic.

The *persona* also acts in the third person in a neutral omniscient way, with no comments or intrusions – to present a comic view. In the third chapter of *Pantagruel*, for example, there is the *reductio ad absurdum* of rhetoric by Gargantua which puts us outside the reach of sympathy and makes us laugh at the perpetual see-saw of the argument.[3] The comic level is established at once here through similes and comparisons which reduce the stature of the giant to an animal or robot, and there is a quick little aside from the *persona* on midwives at the funeral service: '(où sont elles?

---

[1] See my article on 'Rabelais' Prologues', which is to appear shortly in *Modern Language Review*.

[2] In the early editions only.

[3] For another interpretation of the Gargantua dilemma, see M. A. Screech, *The Rabelaisian Marriage*, London (1958), p. 25.

bonnes gens, je ne vous peulx veoyr)', to reinforce the comic distance at which we are set.

Then there is the voice of Alcofrybas. How does this fit into the pattern? We may take a well-known episode – the author in the giant's mouth (ch. 32) and see whether it is different from the *persona*'s voice. At first we have exactly the same technique in both: the ironical assurances of truth, with the reader's detachment increased by a Folengo-like intrusion: 'Mais, ô Dieux et Déesses, que veiz je là?' But when we enter the story the dialogue, for instance, between the cabbage-planter and Alcofrybas transports us to a world of fantasy which is none the less depicted as a close-up of something extremely real and ordinary. In one sense the make-believe is exactly like the non-sense of nursery rhymes. There is one in Welsh which is very close to the situation here:

> *Ar y ffordd wrth fynd i'r Bettws*
> *Gwelais ddyn yn plannu tatws;*
> *Gof'nais iddo beth o'n wneud,*
> *Plannu tatws, paid a deud.*[1]

The comic is brought out by juxtaposing the two phrases – 'I saw him planting – but had to ask'; similarly *je* is *tout esbahy* and is forced to ask: 'Mon amy, que fais tu icy? Je plante (dist-il), des choulx.' The author here, by creating two or three worlds inside the giant's mouth, is laughing at every level of reality. He has so dislocated our eyes and our customary reactions that we have something very comic created out of everyday events. Alcofrybas is a dramatized narrator who can recount scenes and happenings with great fullness, and yet his role is overlaid with the *persona* detachment of the Olympian creator. We could contrast this with Cervantes: the chronicler Cide Hamete Benengeli stands with the intermediary translator on one level, and Cervantes' *I* on another,

---

[1] An English translation:
> *On the way to Bettws*
> *I saw a man planting potatoes;*
> *I asked him what he was doing,*
> *Planting potatoes, but tell no one.*

but you do not get another *I* created to give a further dimension to the story. Alcofrybas's *je* participates in the story (though rather inconsistently at first), can give shifting perspectives on characters, or can be used as in this episode to break down completely our intellectual views of the world.

In *Gargantua* there is an increase in the use of the *persona* – both as a tool for satire and as a fictional device. Thus, for instance, in the birth scene, the emphasis may be seen to be 'Si ne le croyez, je ne m'en soucie'; that is, there might be religious satire here, but it may be viewed through the Olympian telescope of the *persona*. As a fictional device the *persona* is much more in control of the whole book: from the 'vos seigneuries', through the translating of 'je (combien que indigne)' of the story which was found in a 'gros, gras, grand, gris, joly, petit, moisy livret', through the mocking throwing off large gestures: 'Qui vous meut? Qui vous poinct?' through the leitmotiv of 'Vous vous mocquez du vieil beuveur', to frere Jan's closing words on the enigma, the author/ reader relationship is quickened by highly developed, racy and impatient dialogues.

In the *Tiers Livre* the *persona* line is interesting, since here it is an outer frame that encloses the comic frame. Thus in chapter 1, the famous one on colonization, there is the intermingling of the third-person-neutral narrator with the *je* of the *persona*, and the effect is a detached and burlesque commentary of an Olympian narrator. For instance, there is the leitmotiv of drinking: 'Noterez doncques icy, Beuveurs', there are the realistic views on colonization; at the same time, our attitude to Pantagruel, the prince, is being outlined. In the second chapter the author extends his summing up of him from the first book to 'Je vous ay ja dict et encores rediz que c'estoit le meilleur petit et grand bon hommet que oncques ceigneit espée'. This is still the outline view of Pantagruel; but what follows is a combination of Stoic ideas and common-sensical themes, expounded without a hint of irony or parody. Pantagruel has grown up since the first book of *Pantagruel*, and is now going to be the norm for a highly amusing comedy. At the end (ch. 49 onwards), when the comedy is over, there is a return to the *persona*, which has the effect of distancing us from the comedy and from Pantagruel. Thus, for instance, in comparing the *herbe Pantagruelion* to Pantagruel, the line: 'Car, comme Pantagruel a esté l'Idée et exemplaire de toute joyeuse perfection', is immediately followed by this parenthesis '(je croy que personne de vous aultres, beuveurs, n'en doubte)', which takes us back again to the first chapters of the book. Pantagruel has diminished in size, or rather he has turned into a fabulous giant once more. In the narrative there is a constant turning to the reader, and a highly rhetorical flavour to the *persona*'s speeches: 'Croyez la ou non, ce m'est tout un. Me suffist vous avoir dict verité.' It is as if the created author has arranged for every point of view to be brought out and in fact chooses none of them; it is up to us, readers, to make the choice.

Now in the *Quart Livre* we have yet another dimension: the voice of *nous* which is Alcofrybas again, a member of the company, who will give us reports of his master Pantagruel, participate more consistently in various episodes (e.g. the *Paroles Gelées*) and, what is in fact a new extension, speak for the company. Let us look at this *nous* acting in one important episode: chapter 28, the description of the death of Pan. The narration is handed over to Pantagruel: he interprets it as the death of Christ; all through we are in intellectual sympathy with him – perhaps, as Professor Screech has argued, quite consciously so.[1] But at the end there is a change of narrative viewpoint; when Pantagruel has finished he is deeply moved: 'ce propous finy, resta en silence et profonde contemplation'; and immediately after we move outside Pantagruel, and we have the grotesque tone of *nous*: 'Peu de temps après, nous veismes les larmes decouler de ses œilz grosses, comme œufs de austruche.' The *nous* narrator is detaching himself from the story, and viewing it as a gigantic act. Furthermore the *persona* comes in (just to make sure we know that it is nothing but a fantastic tale) with 'Je me donne à Dieu si j'en mens d'un seul

[1] M. A. Screech, 'The death of Pan', *Bibliothèque d'Humanisme et Renaissance*, vol. XVII (1955), pp. 36ff.

mot'. So that here we can see the first step: taking us from Pantagruel to the *nous*, and the second step: from the *nous* to the *je* of
the *persona* – the whole thing done so quickly that the reader is
thoroughly jolted by the transition. We are thus once again seeing
things through the Olympian telescope, close up yet far away.
This *nous*, then, is sometimes the servant of the giants whose tale
it is telling, and at other times it is made into one of the devices
which prevent us from becoming closely attached not only to the
characters but also to the story. What indeed follows this Pan
episode, the cluster of chapters on 'Quaresmeprenant' (ch. 29–
35) drives us out of sympathy altogether: the *persona* enters and
invites us to regard this fight as 'merveilleux'. Take, for instance,
chapter 34, where the *persona*'s voice is heard throughout: 'Vous
nous racontez aussi d'un archier Indian' . . . until at last we are
bursting with admiration for the marvellous Pantagruel, and ready
for the phrase 'Le noble Pantagruel en l'art de jecter et darder
estoit sans comparaison plus admirable'.

There is thus a situation in which, while the *persona* remains in
control throughout the four books, its narrative line splits up
into a host of different voices, which enable us to watch the story
from different vantage-points, but at crucial times dissolve back
into the single *persona*. In the light of all this, what can one now
observe about the characters? Northrop Frye, in his *Anatomy of
Criticism*, classes Rabelais as a Menippean Satirist, for good satiric
reasons; but all satirical writers are concerned with mental attitudes and with stylized characters who must be mouthpieces of
the real author and not people who can be disengaged from the
satiric narrative.[1] And this is precisely the point at which
Rabelais parts company with Menippean Satire. For in his works
we find comic characters, comic episodes and comic language
being used poetically. This is very different from the way in which
Swift uses language to satirize, for instance in his name for the
Emperor in Lilliput: 'Golbasto Momaren Evlame Gurdilo Shefin
Mully Ully Gue' – although Rabelais, too, uses this technique

[1] Northrop Frye, *Anatomy of Criticism*, Princeton (1957), pp. 223–39.

often enough. What we cannot be so sure about is Rabelais's handling of the comic throughout the first four books. So what I shall do now is to pick out some details from the *persona* line, and indicate their possible importance for the work as a whole.

To begin with, how does this multi-layered technique work when it comes to creating characters? Let us take Panurge as our example.[1] In *Pantagruel I* he is introduced in chapter 9 by the omniscient narrator: his entry on to the stage is gloriously funny, semi-picaresque, actively comic, where his mighty thirst and hunger, and his revelling in languages existing and non-existing, make him as it were dance round and round the rather immobile Pantagruel. The first Spanish picaresque anti-hero Lazarillo de Tormes, from the novel written around 1525 and published in 1554, comes to mind here, with his equally ravenous hunger and thirst. But its form being autobiographical (very important for the development of the picaresque novel in Spain and France), it has no *persona* line, no intermediary at all; we are invited to see the story entirely from the viewpoint of Lazarillo himself. Panurge is coming from adventures, with all the outward appearance of the worst possible time, but he is still 'elegant, beau de stature', and Pantagruel 'falls' for him precisely because of these reasons. The omniscient narrator, in this first scene, is keeping us laughing with Panurge: Pantagruel is brought to life in a comic guise (quite different from his burlesque-comic of previous scenes): for instance, he slips in a phrase like 'Mon amy, je n'entens poinct ce barragouin; pour tant, si voulez qu'on vous entende, parlez aultre langaige', and restarts Panurge, who is delighted by his own inexhaustibility.

But this is not the only perspective one has on Panurge. For in chapter 17 the Alcofrybas voice takes us to another part of the observation platform, and we watch both of them stealing money in church. Alcofrybas comments: 'De ma part je n'en gaignoys plus; mais luy . . .'; after a certain hesitation, he refuses to be

---

[1] Frere Jan in *Gargantua* would be an equally good example, for in the first two books Rabelais has one anti-hero plus a giant as raw materials to work on.

further involved – 'car tu seras une foys pendu,' he says, and quick as a flash Panurge replies: 'Et toy . . . tu seras une foys enterré . . .' Now this episode heightens our awareness of fictional reality, takes us around the character in order to have more than one view of him; and what is more, it is quite detached from the scenes where Pantagruel joins in the fun with Panurge. In the counterpoint of these two characters we have the beginnings of 'novelistic' threads: from parody or imitation the author steps into fiction, once he perceives that in the noble 'enfant terrible' of Panurge he has an anti-hero, and in Pantagruel a genial companion. In Pantagruel (who is also, of course, a mouthpiece of satire), we observe once more the same technique of playing with voices, so that at every point where we might be siding with him there is an entry of the *persona* or Alcofrybas to remind us just where we stand. For example, the satire of Thaumaste is in itself a mini-satire of Pantagruel: the *persona* sidles in with 'Messieurs, vous qui lisez ce present escript, ne pensez que jamais gens plus feussent eslevez et transportez en pensée que furent, toute celle nuict tant Thaumaste que Pantagruel.' If we take the last chapter as an Epilogue, and discount all the things that he promises to do but will change his mind about, we find an interesting editorial elaboration from the *persona*: it is clear that we have been reading a prose fiction with two main characters – Panurge and Pantagruel – and our appetite is whetted for more adventures, both grotesque and fantastic, involving the giant and the semi-*picaro*. In fact, we can see hints of further developments which will make Rabelais a 'comic novelist'.

Consider Panurge's role in the *Tiers Livre*. We have seen that the whole book is in the hands of the *persona*, and most readers would agree that the deepest level of comedy is established here. In particular let us look at the second chapter: Pantagruel gives Panurge Salmiguondin – 'Et se gouverna si bien et prudentement Monsieur le nouveau chastellain, qu'en moins de quatorze jours il dilapida le revenu certain et incertain de sa chastellenie pour troys ans.' Here there is an intermingling of the *persona* with the narrator: the choice of the word *Monsieur*, the juxtaposition of

fourteen days and three years, and the irony of 'si bien et prudentement'. By using the same verb at the beginning of the next
sentence: 'Non proprement dilapida . . .', we are still in the
realm of reality; but by the time the sentence closes we are sailing
away on the wings of fantasy. The first half sets out what he could
do to spend his income in fourteen days, but did not do, and the
second half by contrast details what he *did*, in fact, do: he starts
with 'abastant boys', and ends with 'mangeant son bled en herbe'.
The comic of language here makes him highly *sympathique* to the
reader, and his delight with words is set against the seriousness
and moderation of Pantagruel. Pantagruel presents one side of the
comedy – the norm – and the other half comes from Panurge.
'Mangeant son bled en herbe' is the first step in a comico-poetic
voyage: suspension of old habits of looking at the world by giving
back to an expression its concrete origins. Panurge's embroidery
around the basic power of giving life to a metaphor makes him
stand out as the merry jester, and what is more earns from
Pantagruel in chapter 8 the phrase 'depuys les dernieres pluyes tu
es devenu grand lifrelofre, voyre, diz je Philosophe', where the
first qualification means he is a good drinker and the second a sly
dig at philosophers, with the toleration and good humour that
Panurge calls out from him throughout the book. Where Pantagruel presents one half of what critics call Rabelais's Pantagruelism,
the other half comes from Panurge: 'Aviez vous en soing pris me
faire riche en ce monde? Pensez vivre joyeulx, de par li bon Dieu
et li bons homs.' Panurge is given an archaic form of expression
which is reminiscent of the prologue to Pantagruel. In other words
it is the *persona* that is implicitly in control here, too, and we have
the comic character counterpointing the rather staid Pantagruel,
as an inner frame for the larger frame provided by the *persona*.

Furthermore, the inner frame encloses the other characters,
too: for instance, frere Jan and Panurge together provide a lot of
the comic, with their talk of sexual virility and adventures around
women, but frere Jan and Pantagruel provide a foil to Panurge's
folly; the comedy which starts as a duologue between Panurge and
Pantagruel becomes a complete social comedy with the 'publique

opinion' there from chapter 14 onwards.[1] The re-entry of Gargantua heightens the norm as he holds forth about moderation at a moment when Panurge is at his worst and funniest; in chapter 36 he says: 'Je ne voy goutte, je n'entends rien, je sens mes sens tous hebetez, et doubte grandement que je soye charmé.' At the end Panurge's language spins into inarticulate nonsense and he proposes a voyage which will be the *Quart Livre*.

Where in the *Tiers Livre* the inner frame was one of comedy, the *Quart Livre* reverts to a narrative technique, with the story of the voyage providing a thin holding-together of the incidents.[2] I shall take just one example to show the *persona* forming the outer frame: the Panurge and Dindenault debate (ch. 5–8). We don't know anything about Dindenault: it is like a picaresque novel, with figures of cardboard entering and then disappearing – offering their fun to the reader and to the characters. Dindenault has one joke in his head – that Panurge is a cuckold, while he himself is a splendidly married man with a stupendous wife. Panurge picks up the superlatives with which the merchant scatters his speech, in a verb of sexual coinage: 'si . . . j'avoys sacsacbezevezinamessé ta tant belle, tant advenente, tant honeste, tant prude femme'. The *persona* slips in a remark about rusty swords at sea, Panurge tells frere Jan and Epistemon to retire and watch the fun; the dialogue is beautifully told by the narrator only, to dissolve finally in the comment made by the *persona*: 'Soubdain je ne sçay comment, le cas feut subit, je ne eus loisir le consyderer, Panurge sans aultre chose dire, jette en pleine mer son mouton criant et bellant.' With the result that we are invited to laugh with Panurge, against the doltish character of Dindenault, and the stupid nature of sheep, from the Olympian author's distance. Thus in this episode the larger fictional frame is that of the *persona*, with the inner frame being a narrative context, and the Alcofrybas voice being fused with the *persona*.

[1] I hope to publish an article on the social comedy of the *Tiers Livre*, where a number of these points will be discussed.
[2] A. C. Keller, *The Telling of Tales in Rabelais. Aspects of his Narrative Art*, Analecta Romanica (1963).

Now what about the giants, and in particular Pantagruel? If we accept that the *persona* is in ultimate control throughout the four books, we are still left with many aspects which Pantagruel takes seriously – the religion, the Stoic philosophy, the peaceful, lovable prince who hates war, etc. Is this where the fictional frame breaks down completely, and one has to see Pantagruel as expressing Rabelais's own personal ideas – as in Menippean Satire, in fact? So long as the *merveilleux* is the framework for Pantagruel, it gives rise to comic situations created by him. But once it recedes, as it does in the *Tiers Livre*, do we have emotional sympathy with Pantagruel, or are we rather sympathizing intellectually with him? He could be compared with Don Quixote, who as the novel goes on becomes more sane, more discreet, and is the spokesman of Cervantes on a number of topics. Here the response of the reader is that of affectionate reprobation. With Pantagruel, the response to him as a fictional character, as a mouthpiece for satire and as a spokesman for Rabelais's ideas, is rather ambiguous: always likeable, always tolerant, always overlaid with physical and mental exuberance, in many senses the congenial companion who forms an opposite to Panurge and frere Jan, but always, as the novel goes on, more and more abstract as a character. Where Cervantes dissolves all the intermediaries, to bring all his characters in together, in a jovial apostrophe: 'Oh, most celebrated author! Oh, happy Don Quixote! Oh, famous Dulcinea! Oh, droll Sancho Panza! May each one and all of you live infinite centuries', Rabelais can also dissolve all the narrative devices into the *persona*, into the disruptive role of a self-conscious narrator. This is like the author's second self; any successful novel makes us believe in an author as narrator, distinct from the author as a person existing apart from his work.

In the *Tiers Livre* the outer line is provided by the *persona* and Pantagruel gives us the other one – the norm of a social comedy. The ideas he is made to carry belong to a society which is Erasmian in orientation – that is, intellectual and enlightened, yet very religious. So that the angry attack of Gargantua on priests who will marry a couple without the consent of parents is an

41

audacious passage, whilst the divination chapters seem, four centuries later, less than bold. As readers accepting a norm, we have in these passages to make up our own mind – outside Pantagruel. The *persona* line around the giants means that ultimately they are stamped with the *oui et non* world of Rabelais's fiction – the *merveilleux*, the grotesque, the bouffonnerie and the serious all included together – so that we cannot believe in them very much as characters. They are merely the pivots around whom much of the action in the story takes place. Rabelais's technique is like a camera shifting about to give us several views of a person and above all of his comic vision of the world. Where both Cervantes and Rabelais start with a parody, Cervantes takes the reader deeper into the truth and reality of characters, while Rabelais's world takes the ideas and attitudes of characters; he shows them to us in every frame and extends them in a horizontal line by his language and narrative devices. He does not make truth and reality around his characters, but around the whole world.

Dorothy Coleman

Flaubert and the Authors of the
French Renaissance[1]

FLAUBERT WOULD have been the first to look with a sardonic eye at this title. Evidence on his reading is necessarily incomplete, and any mind tinged with his own encyclopaedomania will be aware of the gaps in what we can deduce. Moreover, a critical discussion of his sporadically adumbrated reactions could not but have appeared *HHHénaurme* to one who so often scarified the profession of the critic. From his early notebook ('Voici les choses fort bêtes: 1° la critique littéraire quelle qu'elle soit, bonne ou mauvaise')[2] or the first *Education* to *Bouvard et Pécuchet*, there echoes the theme of the insufficiency of aesthetic theories: because first, they use abstract terms in undefined or tautological ways; second, they lay down 'norms' to which every work of art must be fitted; third, they concentrate either on peripheral circumstances or sweeping parallels, rather than on investigating what is irreductibly individual; finally and above all, they cannot explain the genesis of a masterpiece: Bouvard, in his search for the creative principle, is driven back to the fundamental advice: 'inventez des ressorts qui puissent m'attacher', and retorts with the naive but still more basic question: 'Comment inventer des ressorts?' To Flaubert, in fact, past criticism serves mainly to

---

[1] References will be to the Conard edition unless otherwise stated. I have adopted the abbreviation C for the nine volumes of the *Correspondance* and CS for the four volumes of supplement. Place of publication in references is Paris unless otherwise stated.

[2] *Souvenirs, notes et pensées intimes*, ed. L. Chevalley Sabatier (1965), p. 97.

provide instructive and amusing evidence of the frame of mind of the times in which it was written. He would certainly have read with joy the article in which A. M. Boase analyses through anthologies of poetry 'the whirligig of taste'.[1]

Yet Flaubert, on this as on most problems poised between opposite urges, had his own plans for critical works. Two lay in his own century: the preface to the works of Bouilhet, and the introduction to the *Dictionnaire des Idées reçues*. His other main critical projects refer to three sixteenth-century authors: Ronsard, Rabelais and Montaigne. In 1838 he writes:

> Je lis toujours Rabelais et j'y ai adjoint Montaigne. Je me propose de faire plus tard sur ces deux hommes une étude spéciale de philosophie et de littérature (C I 29),

and in 1853:

> Nous relisons du Ronsard et nous nous enthousiasmons de plus belle. A quelque jour nous en ferons une édition. [. . .] J'y ferais une préface [. . .] Je dirai l'histoire du *sentiment poétique en France* (C III 139; see also III 321).

Except for the very early article on Rabelais (*Oeuvres de Jeunesse* I 144–56), no sixteenth-century plan was carried out, but this trinity of authors recurs at intervals throughout his lifetime among the *livres de chevet* which have in different ways been 'convertis en sang et nourriture'.

Of detailed knowledge of other early or late Renaissance authors in France, there is little proof. We may too easily today assume a general reassessment of sixteenth-century poets from the 1830s onwards, after Sainte-Beuve's *Tableau*, Nerval's anthology, and the enthusiasm of individual romantics; scholastic syllabuses continued to make the classical seventeenth century the focus of literary studies, and earlier reading must largely have remained a matter for personal enterprise.[2] Flaubert provides brief mentions

---

[1] 'Tradition and Revaluation in the French Anthology, 1692–1960', in *Essays presented to C. M. Girdlestone*, Durham (1960), pp. 49–63.
[2] A. M. Boase, art. cit., p. 62, remarks that as late as the Crépet anthology of 1861–2 'it is striking to realise with what serious reservations of the Pléïade are still represen-

of Marot, Régnier, Saint-Amant; the preface to Bouilhet's *Dernières chansons* remarks that Bouilhet was annotating Du Bartas; there are allusions to d'Aubigné and Brantôme, and the joyful discovery, among the later non-classics, of Cyrano de Bergerac.[1] As one might expect, there is nothing on the poets so rewardingly restored to the canon of our own day (Scève, Sponde or others); more surprisingly, perhaps, I have found no mention of Du Bellay.

The present article will first briefly sum up the evidence on Flaubert's reading in the three great authors,[2] and will then dis-

---

ted [. . .] The prejudices of academic "good taste" [. . .] are revealed as still deeply entrenched in attitudes to the Renaissance'. I possess a delightful *Course of French Literature containing a Critical Review of all the French Authors of Eminence*, by A. D. Doisy, Dublin (1832) – out of 423 pages it devotes two to Rabelais and Montaigne together; one line is given to Marot, and no other sixteenth-century poet is mentioned. (But La Fontaine is surprisingly well analysed in detail.)

On Flaubert's school programmes J. Bruneau, *Les Débuts littéraires de Gustave Flaubert*, provides interesting material. It would be useful to have further studies of syllabuses and textbooks as a background to nineteenth-century authors.

[1] Marot is quoted in *Mémoires d'un Fou* (p. 521), mentioned in the *Voyage aux Pyrénées*, 1840 (pp. 392 and 395), and given as evidence of how tastes change in *Par les Champs*, 1840 (p. 74). As J. Bruneau points out (op. cit., p. 246) the quotation may come from the Ledentu edition of Rabelais which Flaubert possessed. For Saint-Amant see *Education sentimentale* of 1845 (p. 262); Preface to Bouilhet's *Dernières chansons* (in *Œuvres*, ed. Lemerre, 1880 p. 297); Letter to the Municipalité de Rouen (L'Intégrale edition of Flaubert, 1964, II, p. 765); and C V 153, VII 71. Régnier is among Flaubert's *livres de chevet* in 1844 (C I 153), is quoted in a letter of 1846 (C I 370), and mentioned in *Par les Champs* (p. 74), Preface to Bouilhet, p. 294 and C IV 83. In 1853 he has read of D'Aubigné only *Le Baron de Foeneste*, long since and with difficulty (C III 392; see also C VIII 373 and *Education* of 1845, p. 257). For Brantôme see *Education* of 1845 (pp. 161 and 257); C VI 405. For Cyrano de Bergerac C II 449, 455, III 4, 34; here there is clearer evidence of enthusiastic reading – 'C'est énorme de fantaisie et souvent de style'.

[2] A number of critics have treated excellently certain aspects of the subject. The present article will attempt a synthesis, will use some details from works either not available at the dates when previous studies were published, or not used in them, and will, I hope, have its own focus. For previous discussions see particularly: J. Boulenger, *Rabelais à travers les âges* (1925); D. M. Frame, *Montaigne en France, 1812–52*, New York (1940); the following articles in the *Revue des Etudes rabelaisiennes*: H. Patry, 'Rabelais et Flaubert' (1904); L. Larose, 'Rabelais et Flaubert' (1910); J. Plattard, 'Flaubert lecteur de Rabelais' (1912). See also the relevant passages in A. Coleman, *Flaubert's literary development in the light of his 'Mémoires d'un Fou', 'Novembre' and 'Education sentimentale' (version of 1845)* (1914); H. Frejlich, *Flaubert d'après sa*

45

cuss what Flaubert's remarks on these 'pères nourriciers'[1] reveal of the mainsprings of his own temperament: of the interplay of satirical scepticism, absorptive enthusiasm and rigorous self-discipline from which his art is wrought.

First, the facts. Ronsard is mentioned in *Par les Champs* (p. 74) of 1840, and in 1842 is being read, with Horace and Rabelais, 'mais peu et rarement, comme 'l'on fait de truffes' (C I 116); a year later Flaubert is again reading 'un peu de Ronsard, de mon grand et beau Ronsard' (C I 145). The stage of prolonged reading and enthusiasm comes in 1852–3; he writes triumphantly:

> J'ai un Ronsard complet, 2 vol. in-folio,[2] que j'ai enfin fini par me procurer. Le dimanche nous en lisons à nous défoncer la poitrine. Les extraits des petites éditions courantes en donnent une idée comme toute espèce d'extraits et de traductions, c'est-à-dire que les plus belles choses en sont absentes. [. . .] Quel poète! quel poète! quelles ailes! [. . .] Donc nous avons encore pour deux ou trois mois de dimanches enthousiasmés. Cet horizon me fait grand bien et de loin jette un reflet ardent sur mon travail (C II 369).

There are frequent references between now and 1854,[3] including a letter (not in the Conard *Correspondance*) of March 14th, 1853,[4] relating that 'nous avons hier passé trois heures à lire les hymnes de Ronsard'; at the end of March comes Bouilhet's plan for an edition to which Flaubert would write the Preface, for:

> il y a cent belles choses, mille, cent mille, dans les poésies complètes de Ronsard, qu'il faut faire connaître, et puis j'éprouve le besoin de le lire et relire dans une édition commode (C III 139).

---

correspondance (1933); E.-L. Ferrère, *L'Esthétique de Flaubert* (1913) (pp. 97 ff.); and for the early years the very full study by J. Bruneau, *Les Débuts littéraires de Gustave Flaubert, 1831–1845* (1962), with his full bibliography.

[1] Expression used of Montaigne, C IV 33.
[2] This is not the edition mentioned by Bruneau, op. cit., p. 35, as existing in the Croisset library.
[3] C II 426, III 18, 68, 264, IV 32 (and others discussed below).
[4] Published by Jacques Suffel in *Figaro littéraire*, 11 August 1962.

After 1854 there is little evidence until 1872, when Flaubert is associated with plans for a monument in Vendôme;[1] he sub-scribes, intends to write a speech for the opening ceremony, but in a period of strain is too weary to complete it, and finally, at the thought of those who would be his travelling-companions, decides not to attend.

The Preface to Bouilhet's *Dernières Chansons* instances Ronsard as among the outstanding examples of reversal of reputation, for:

> la gloire d'un écrivain relève non pas du suffrage universel, mais d'un petit groupe d'intelligences qui à la longue impose son jugement.[2]

And to the end of Flaubert's life attitudes to Ronsard obviously remain a kind of litmus-paper test of literary judgement; in appreciating an article of Maupassant on French poetry in 1877 he regrets that there is no proper praise of Ronsard (C VIII 9), and in the same year he writes of his stay at Chenonceaux:

> Mme Pelouze est une personne exquise et très littéraire. On y apporte *Ronsard* à la table, au milieu du dessert! (C VIII 44)

Montaigne is quoted by the truculent adolescent in the *Moralité* of *Un Parfum à sentir* of 1836: 'Cecy est un livre de bonne foy: je donne mon advis, non comme bon mais comme mien', and the 'Que sais-je?' of Montaigne and 'Peut-être' of Rabelais are cited in the provocative *Moralité* to *Rage et Impuissance*.[3] The project for a special study of Montaigne and Rabelais occurs in September 1838, but the real burst of enthusiasm comes in October 1839: 'Je me recrée à lire le sieur de Montaigne dont je suis plein; c'est là mon homme' (C I 57). Much later he recalls this period 'Je m'en suis bourré [de Montaigne] toute une année à 18 ans, où je ne lisais *que*

---

[1] C VI 382, 384, 390; CS III 9, 32, 33, 35. Flaubert mentions Blanchemain as 'mon ami', but is unaware that he no longer lives in Paris. The desire to discover which towns commemorate their great men by statues recurs at intervals, not only when the Bouilhet monument is being discussed.

[2] See also *Par les Champs*, p. 74: 'le mauvais goût du temps de Ronsard, c'était Marot; du temps de Boileau c'était Ronsard', etc.

[3] For Balzac's *La Peau de Chagrin* as a possible source cf. A. Coleman, op. cit., p. 69, and J. Bruneau, op. cit., p. 120.

lui' (C III 379). The *Voyage aux Pyrénées* (1840) tells how he handled the manuscript of Montaigne with religious veneration (p. 352) and discusses (p. 391) the shift in Renaissance spirit from the wild and gigantic fantasy of Rabelais to the clarity, humanity and consciousness of style in Montaigne. From now on references, brief discussions and scraps of quotation proliferate.[1] Montaigne is above all a recourse in times of distress: he comes to mind in a fit of student wretchedness in 1843 (C I 137), is among the *livres de chevet* in nervous strain in 1844 (C I 153) and is the author read as Flaubert watches for the night by the body of his dead sister (C II 3). In February 1853 he sets out to 'relire Montaigne en entier. C'est une bonne causerie, le soir avant de s'endormir' (C III 102); this remains his bedside book through April (III 184) and into October:

> C'est singulier comme je suis plein de ce bonhomme-là [. . .] Je suis ébahi de trouver l'analyse très-détaillée de mes moindres sentiments! Nous avons mêmes goûts, mêmes opinions, même manière de vivre, mêmes manies. Il y a des gens que j'admire plus que lui, mais il n'y en a pas que j'évoquerais plus volontiers et avec qui je causerais mieux. (C III 379)

It is in 1854 that Montaigne is called 'mon père nourricier' (C IV 33). As years go on, he is held up to Flaubert's correspondents as 'un homme dont vous devriez vous nourrir, et qui vous consolerait'; his works are made part of the education of Flaubert's niece.[2] Finally, in 1876, shut off from the outer world, Flaubert is reading each evening Montaigne and La Bruyère 'pour me retremper dans les classiques' (C VII 367).

Quotations from Rabelais, as from Montaigne, chosen to be

---

[1] *Par les Champs*, p. 15. *Souvenirs, notes et pensées intimes*, ed. L. Chevalley Sabatier (1965), pp. 64, 70, 80, 107 (the enigmatic remark on p. 70: 'L'esprit de Montaigne est un carré; celui de Voltaire un triangle', may be illuminated by the passage on p. 106 on the geometry of dramatic art: 'le sublime dans Corneille et dans Shakespeare me fait l'effet d'un rectangle'). See also an unpublished letter quoted by J. Bruneau, p. 285; the epigraph to *Novembre*; C I 57, 62, 98, 116, 119, 317, 353, 385–6, II 236, 414, 434, III 228, 341, 358, 409, IV 122, 239, V 197, 250, VI 47, 154, 160, VII 8, VIII 112, 255; CS II 307, CS complémentaire 19, as well as the other passages discussed below.

[2] C IV 185, 197, V 167, 206, 208, 209.

provocative, are used in the adolescent works of 1836–7.[1] In 1838 a youthful letter remarks:

> Vraiment je n'estime profondément que deux hommes, Rabelais et Byron, les deux seuls qui aient écrit dans l'intention de nuire au genre humain et de lui rire à la face (C I 29);

a month later Flaubert is nearing the end of his reading and

> Mon Rabelais est tout bourré de notes et commentaires philosophiques, philologiques, bachiques, etc. (C I 33).

From this stage presumably dates the youthful essay on Rabelais. As J. Bruneau points out (op. cit., p. 263), Rabelais specialists have treated this severely for its enthusiastic and derivative generalizations.[2] Bruneau defends its 'admiration sincère et assez bien motivée' for Rabelais; but it is worth calling special attention to how, at this very early age, Flaubert has through Rabelais shaped an embryo programme for the different sides of his own future work. Rabelais's enigma, crammed with the trivial, the crude and the comic, showing how

> l'humanité[. . .] dépouillée de ses robes de parade et de ses galons mensongers [. . .] frémit toute nue sous le souffle impur du grotesque

at the same time provides

> les aperçus les plus fins sur la nature de l'homme, les nuances les plus délicates du coeur, les analyses les plus vraies.

Imaginative inventiveness and skill with dialogue combine with 'le comique des caractères' and with 'la phrase si bien ciselée en relief'. Other possible attitudes to the human condition (bitter, openly personal, meditative) are compared with the great gust of laughter. Rabelais's successor in a modern age will find his subject in 'cet éternel gouffre béant que l'homme a en lui'; provided he

---

[1] On the corruption of monarchs preceding *Un secret de Philippe le Prudent*; *Moralité* to *Rage et Impuissance*; epigraph from *Gargantua* to *La Dernière Heure*.

[2] I am not, however, sure that the Gargantua, Sancho, Falstaff comparison is as closely derived from the Philarète Chasles article only as J. Bruneau assumes.

can achieve detachment, 'se dépouiller de toute colère, de toute haine, de toute douleur! [. . .] son livre serait le plus terrible et le plus sublime qu'on ait fait'. In clumsy but suggestive formulations Flaubert is groping for the detached technique which might treat Romantic despair with Renaissance scale and vigour, might combine satirical sting with subtle analytical insight.

In the next years references and quotations are frequent.[1] Letters from Alfred Le Poittevin show how to both friends Rabelais is a household word, and culminate in a sardonic vision of what it would be like if both ever qualified as pillars of justice: 'Ce serait à désirer que Rabelais revînt, pour faire un nouveau roman.'[2] In 1852–3 the constant discovery of new riches in Rabelais is reiterated (C III 49, 92, 312). He is the Sunday reading, along with *Don Quixote*, towards the end of 1852 (C III 53 and Preface to Bouilhet's *Dernières chansons*). Other dates when Flaubert goes back to reread 'le sacro-saint, immense et extra-beau Rabelais', 'patriarche de la littérature française depuis trois cents ans' (C VII 319) are September 1861 (C IV 452) and November 1867 (C V 341). When Caroline visits Chinon in 1876 she is to greet Rabelais's supposed house with his 'pensée de respect et d'adoration' (C VII 317); Flaubert is reading him yet again. In his last years, wishing to praise a contemporary, he will write 'Il y a là un souffle à ranimer Rabelais du tombeau', or, consoling Maupassant for accusations of immorality, will recall 'Rabelais, d'où découlent les lettres françaises'.[3]

Flaubert certainly first came to the Renaissance through highly coloured and impressionistic generalizations. From the beginning he attributes to this period four sides deeply rooted in his own

---

[1] *Par les Champs* pp. 28, 38; *Education* of 1845, p. 257; C I 62, 98, 115, 151, 152, 267, 368 (with misprint 'Panurge fuyait les loups' for 'coups' – cp. Index), II 450, III 39, 41, 149, 157, 322, 325, 332, 349.

[2] See Alfred Le Poittevin, *Une Promenade de Bélial et Oeuvres inédites*, ed. R. Descharmes (1924), p. 177, and also p. 170.

[3] For other references see C III 69, 98, 157, 332, 333, 347, 442, IV 22, 33, 96, 422, VII 141, VIII 101, 372; CS II 159.

nature: a violent demolition of set social and religious systems; a mighty grasp of encyclopaedic detail, ranging from the trivial to the epic; a frank and rich expression of the world of the senses; and finally a vital spirit which, whether through revolt, scepticism, stoicism, hedonism or sheer sense of the comic, moulds a positive reaction to permanent problems.[1]

The spirit of opposition plays a joyous part in his choice of authors. Du Camp speaks of Flaubert's reading while at school: 'lectures que ses maîtres n'eussent pas approuvées, s'occupant plus de Ronsard que de Virgile et plus de Brantôme que de Fénelon'.[2] Letters tilt at the poor taste of the French who prefer to Ronsard 'un pédant comme Malherbe ou un pisse-froid comme Boileau'[3] (C I 145), note that 'Béranger sera toujours plus lu' (C III 139) and scorn Villemain's phrase 'la diction grotesque de Ronsard' (III 264). His projected preface was to be an attack on the stereotyped and orthodox French taste in poetry; the speech for the Ronsard ceremony in 1872 would have been 'une protestation contre le Panmuflisme moderne' (C VI 382; C. S. III 33). In the Preface to Bouilhet's *Dernières chansons* Ronsard is the poet of the few, and in the *Dictionnaire des Idées reçues* the stock view of Ronsard is laconically summed up: 'Ridicule avec ses mots grecs et latins.'[4]

Rabelais in the early article is the great demolisher whose gale of laughter has a destructive force equivalent to that of Luther in the realm of religion or of the French Revolution in the realm of action. 'Mes lectures de Rabelais se mêlent à ma bile sociale'

---

[1] Brief general passages on the Renaissance occur in the Rabelais article, the *Voyage aux Pyrénées*, pp. 390 ff., *Par les Champs*, pp. 287 ff., and *Education* of 1845, pp. 257 ff. If early 'morceaux de bravoure' on the Renaissance highlight its picturesque and passionate aspects, by the first *Education* the artist-hero has learnt to look beneath the purely picturesque, to mistrust all formulae, to investigate in each individual author the ways in which general and particular are combined to make originality, and to wish to make his own art profit from what is best in all periods.

[2] Quoted in preface to L'Intégrale edition, p. 19.

[3] Other letters will express admiration for Boileau.

[4] Gustave Flaubert, *Dictionnaire des Idées reçues*, Edition diplomatique des trois manuscrits de Rouen par Lea Caminiti (1966), p. 110.

(C III 94). His 'robustes outrances' are set against the petty wit or salacious innuendo of nineteenth-century taste (C II 451 ; III 31, 39). Like Ronsard, he is unappreciated by the crowd:

> D'où vient qu'on est toujours indulgent pour la médiocrité dorée? et qu'on sait Béranger par cœur et pas un vers de Saint-Amant, pas une page de Rabelais? (C V 153)[1]

He provides a fine contrast to contemporary cant, whether in an early comment on a Belgian expurgator (*Par les Champs*, p. 28), in a sardonic aside about what would have been Rabelais's views on Queen Victoria (C IV 227) or in comments on the Préfet of scandalous personal life who banned public lectures on his work (C VII 71, 85, 104).

Montaigne's destruction of conventional beliefs goes still deeper:

> Je suis de l'avis de Montaigne . . . il me semble que nous ne pouvons jamais être assez méprisés selon notre mérite. J'aime à voir l'humanité et tout ce qu'elle respecte ravalé, bafoué, honni, sifflé. La torpeur moderne vient du respect illimité que l'homme a pour lui-même (C IV 33).[2]

Montaigne lays bare man's presumptuousness, shows how he 'bêle après l'infini' (C II 414), refuses him heroism in face of physical pain, being 'homme à me mettre sous la peau d'ung veau pour l'éviter' (C III 358) and finds that 'toutes nos vocations sont farcesques' (C VIII 112).[3]

---

[1] See also CS II 159: 'Fr. Baudry, qui a déjeuné chez moi . . . m'a avoué que la littérature française était en décadence depuis le XIIe siècle et que Rabelais avait une mauvaise syntaxe. Vous voyez que les idées *chic* ne sont pas mortes en France.' The *Sottisier* contains Lamartine's remark 'Rabelais, ce boueux de l'humanité' (G. Bollème, *Gustave Flaubert: le second volume de Bouvard et Pécuchet* (1966) p. 90). Flaubert might have wished to add the few lines that dispose of Rabelais in the work of A. J. Doisy (1832) mentioned above: 'Rabelais abused his talent, and the gaiety which seems to have been his principal characteristic, by turning all his contemporaries into ridicule; . . . nothing, however sacred, escaped his sarcasm' (p. 7).

[2] Cf. *Souvenirs, notes et pensées intimes* (1965) p. 64: 'Me parler de la dignité de l'espèce humaine c'est une dérision, j'aime Montaigne et Pascal pour cela.'

[3] See also C V 197 on 'cette délicatesse qui est au giron de la mélancolie'.

But there is a good deal more in these likings than the joyous opposition to stock literary taste or to illusions about the human condition. Had Flaubert written his prefaces, he intended to make them a safety-valve, a means of exorcising his furies so that no passionate didacticism would intrude into his own literary works (C III 139–40). We have seen the need for detachment posited in the call for a successor to Rabelais;[1] Montaigne is early made its symbol in this vision of him at the States-General of 1588:

> Assis à l'écart . . . sans doute qu'il remâchait en lui-même quelque passage de Salluste ou quelques vers de Lucain que les circonstances présentes lui remettaient en mémoire. Sans passions au milieu de toutes ces passions hurlantes, sans croyances à côté de tant de convictions violentes, il était là comme le symbole de ce qui reste à côté de ce qui passe (*Par les Champs*, p. 15).

The Renaissance offers lessons not just in detachment but in delight. Delight first in the sensuous detail of the physical world. As a blessed contrast to the aridities of legal terminology the young Flaubert quotes from Ronsard the stanza:

> *Quand au lit nous serons*
> *Entrelasséz, nous ferons*
> *Les lascifs, selon les guises*
> *Des amants, qui librement*
> *Pratiquent folâtrement*
> *Dans les draps cent mignardises* (C I 116)

and in the *Mémoires d'un Fou* he recalls Marot's

> *Tetin refaict plus blanc qu'un oeuf,*
> *Tetin de satin blanc tout neuf.*

A letter to Taine in 1865 discusses the abstract images of the seventeenth century ('appuyons les soupirs', 'couronner la flamme') and asks:

---

[1] 'Qu'il puisse se dépouiller de toute colère, de toute haine, de toute douleur' (*Oeuvres de Jeunesse*, II 156).

Pourquoi n'y a-t-il pas une image fausse dans les poètes du XVIe siècle – et peut-être pas une précise ou originale dans ceux du XVIIe? La rage de l'*idée* leur avait enlevé tout sentiment de la *nature*. Leur poétique était anti-physique (C S II 44–5).

To read Ronsard aloud was to experience intense physical sensations:

une pièce qui m'a fait presque mal nerveusement, tant elle me faisait plaisir. C'est comme si l'on m'eût chatouillé la plante des pieds (C II 369).[1]

From Montaigne he recalls 'un [des baisers] dont parle Montaigne (les âcres baisers de la jeunesse, longs, savoureux, gluants)' (C I 317). The epic treatment of appetite constantly rejoices Flaubert; the passage on Maître Gaster is one he early picks out in Rabelais (C I 33) and he remarks with gusto that 'les héros sont de terribles mangeurs'.[2] Gastronomic images to describe the chosen authors are frequent: he prefers Rabelais to *Gil Blas* because:

J'aime les viandes plus juteuses [. . .] les styles où l'on en a plein la bouche (C III 98)

and of Montaigne he writes:

C'est là mon homme. En littérature, en gastronomie, il est certains fruits qu'on mange à pleine bouche, dont on a le gosier plein, et si succulents que le jus vous entre jusqu'au coeur (C I 57; cf. I 116 on Ronsard).[3]

For he is constantly drawn by a sense of untrammelled vitality. In poetry:

Depuis la fin du XVIe siècle jusqu'à Hugo, tous les livres, quelque beaux qu'ils soient, sentent la poussière du collège (C III 367). Il n'y a peut-être que Ronsard qui ait été tout simplement un poète, comme on l'était dans l'antiquité et comme on l'est dans les autres pays (C III 68)

[1] Cf. Baudelaire on the physical effect of his first reading of Gautier (Pléiade edition, vol. II, 1961, p. 690).

[2] One remembers J. P. Richard's opening sentence: 'On mange beaucoup dans les romans de Flaubert' (*Littérature et sensation*, 1954).

[3] Cf. *Souvenirs, notes et pensées intimes* (1965), p. 64: 'Montaigne est le plus délectable de tous les écrivains. Ses phrases ont du jus et de la chair.'

Both Rabelais and Montaigne pursue things to the extreme:

> Pour être durable, je crois qu'il faut que la fantaisie soit monstrueuse comme dans Rabelais. Quand on ne fait pas le Parthénon, il faut accumuler des pyramides (C III 31);

while Montaigne takes self-analysis to a pitch where only the most exceptional nature could succeed in his gigantic task (C I 385–6). The Flaubert who signed letters 'l'Excessif' rejoices in a world both of epic stature and of infinite detail, and in writers who were 'des encyclopédies de leur époque' (C IV 52).

But it is precisely these *écrasants livres* of superhuman stature (C III 149) which provide a particular problem for the artist:

> Une chose triste, c'est de voir combien les grands hommes arrivent aisément à l'effet en dehors de l'Art même. Quoi de plus mal bâti que bien des choses de Rabelais [. . .] Mais quels coups de poing subits! [. . .] Vouloir imiter les procédés de ces génies-là, c'est se perdre (C III 143). Ils n'ont pas besoin de faire du style, ceux-là; ils sont forts en dépit de toutes les fautes et à cause d'elles. Mais nous, les petits, nous ne valons que par l'exécution achevée [. . .] Les très grands hommes écrivent souvent fort mal, et tant mieux pour eux. Ce n'est pas là qu'il faut chercher l'art de la forme, mais chez les seconds (Horace, La Bruyère) (C III 31–2).

To learn one's craft one must turn to close study of a 'génie complètement différent de celui qu'on a, parce qu'on ne peut le copier' (C III 228; cf. II 353 and *Education* of 1845, p. 256): for this he turns from the exuberance of Rabelais to the controlled precision of La Bruyère. Even so, one must still steep onself in the greatest works, for 'cela s'infiltre à la longue . . . le talent se transmet par infusion' (C III 228). They are no guides to technique, but a means to gradual forming of substance:

> Il faut savoir les maîtres par cœur, les idolâtrer, tâcher de penser comme eux, et puis s'en séparer pour toujours.[1]

---

[1] One remembers Chénier on the ancients:

> *Faire en s'éloignant d'eux avec un soin jaloux,*
> *Ce qu'eux-mêmes feraient s'ils vivaient parmi nous*

and, of course, the Pléiade discussions of imitation.

Above all, they are a means of living on a particular level.
Loving the qualities of demolition or exuberance, Flaubert still
stresses that the artist transforms them into a strange but pervasive serenity. At its barest, this comes from the refusal of
illusion:

> Lisez Rabelais, Montaigne, Horace ou quelque autre gaillard qui ait
> vu la vie sous un jour plus tranquille, et apprenez une bonne fois pour
> toutes qu'il ne faut pas demander des oranges aux pommiers [. . .]
> du bonheur à la vie (C I 98).

In Rabelais 'rire est le propre de l'homme' and no mere destructive gale of angry satire. Even the very early article, con-
centrating on the demolition of prejudice, underlines the
frank and healthy force of this reaction to human ills, contrasted
with bitterness, melancholy or disillusion, and adds the suggestion
that behind denunciation and farce 'il a [. . .] que sais-je, entrevu
peut-être un monde politique meilleur, une société tout autre'.
Later, laughter will be defined as 'le dédain et la compréhension
mêlés, et en somme la plus haute manière de voir la vie' (C IV
33). And as with the other authors, whose works are pitiless,
complex and infinitely troublous in implications, there is yet in
Rabelais a prevailing serenity:

> Cela est sans fond, infini, multiple. Par de petites ouvertures on
> aperçoit des précipices; il y a du noir en bas, du vertige. Et cependant
> quelque chose de singulièrement doux plane sur l'ensemble! C'est
> l'éclat de la lumiére, le sourire du soleil, et c'est calme! c'est calme!
> (C III 323)

But Montaigne particularly provides the means to calm:[1]

> Je vous recommande d'abord Montaigne. Lisez-le d'un bout à l'autre,
> et, quand vous aurez fini, recommencez (C IV 197). Je ne connais
> pas de livre plus calme, et qui dispose à plus de sérénité (C III 184).[2]
> Lisez Montaigne, lisez-le lentement, posément. *Il vous calmera.* Ne

[1] He is quoted on 'l'homme[qui] bêle après l'infini' and on 'il nous faut abestir pour
nous assagir' (C II 414, I 137).
[2] 'Le chapitre de Démocrite et Héraclite . . . le dernier paragraphe' is singled out.

lisez pas [. . .] pour vous amuser, ni [. . .] pour vous instruire. Non, lisez *pour vivre* (C IV 197; cf. 195).

The letter on the night spent watching by the body of his sister (C II 3) analyses without complacency or sentimentality what such reading can offer. From personal anguish, physical decay, and snoring husband and priest, he turns to reflect on his reading and on the calm splendour of the distant stars through the open window:

> Je lisais du Montaigne, [. . .] et je me disais, en contemplant tout cela, que les formes passaient, que l'idée seule restait, et j'avais des tressaillements d'enthousiasme à des coins de phrase de l'écrivain.[1] Puis j'ai songé qu'il passerait aussi;

the stars, too, will pale and disappear, 'tout sera dit; et ce sera plus beau encore'.[2] Whether in face of personal suffering or a wider sense of metaphysical impermanence there is the same recourse:

> Rappelle-toi l'arrière-boutique de Montaigne [. . .] et tâche de t'en faire une. Est-ce que l'Art ne doit pas consoler de tout? (C I 119)[3]

As a tailpiece to the theme of literature as a way of life, one thinks of the days in May 1877 when Ronsard was read over dessert in the Château de Chenonceaux, this shared enjoyment of one of 'mes chers anciens' taking up across the centuries, in a Renaissance background, Ronsard's own delight in the reading of the ancients in his own countryside.

Flaubert's three sixteenth-century admirations would have to be seen against a wider background than can properly be discussed here. By the side of Shakespeare there are times when all the rest seem dwarfs, and *Don Quixote* 'que je savais par cœur avant de

---

[1] E-L. Ferrère, op. cit., p. 101, presents Flaubert as oddly interested in the man rather than the writer. But here, at a moment of heightened tension, it is the expression that strikes home. D. M. Frame, op. cit., gives a more balanced summing up.

[2] One remembers the 'Et ce fut tout' of the second-last chapter in *L'Education sentimentale*.

[3] No slick pronouncement; Flaubert immediately adds 'Ce qui est facile à dire' . . .

savoir lire' he finds at the root of his whole literary experience; when he recalls it, three aspects predominate which we have seen in his love for the French Renaissance authors: the theme of man's baffled but creative dreams ('cette perpétuelle fusion de l'illusion et de la réalité qui en fait un livre si comique et si poétique'); its sharp sense of everyday physical detail – dusty roads in the sun and the smell of onions; and its final tone of the 'gaîment mélancolique'. On the side of abundance or excess would be set his views on Homer, Apuleius, Aristophanes, Sade, Goethe, Chateaubriand, Hugo; on that of clarity or craftsmanship Horace, La Bruyère, La Fontaine, Boileau, Buffon, Voltaire, Montesquieu. Modern authors are often associated in odd parallels or contrasts with those of the Renaissance. Byron, later to be outgrown, is initially seen as the modern form of Montaigne's self-analysis. To Michelet, whose works Flaubert devoured with enthusiasm in youth, and both admired and sharply criticized later, he writes in 1861: 'je vous serre les mains dans la haine de l'*anti-physis*' (IV 430);[1] in his love of suggestive paradox he is said to have claimed Sade as 'l'incarnation de l'*Antiphysis*, le dernier mot du catholicisme, la haine du corps'.[2] Musset and Béranger are held up with scorn against the touchstone of Rabelais; Hugo, that force of nature, full of flaws and greatness, is frequently compared with the spirit of the Renaissance.

Can any direct results of his 'fréquentation des grands hommes' be traced in Flaubert's own works? Other critics have investigated some aspects in detail; I add only one or two brief suggestions. Ronsard would seem to have been a personal enjoyment rather than of immediate importance to his own art.[3] Montaigne, as the

---

[1] Many passages in letters summing up what he admired in Michelet are very close in tone to those evoking Rabelais.

[2] Reported by the Goncourt, quoted by J. Bruneau, op. cit., p. 33.

[3] Flaubert does note as a discovery a point familiar to any student today: 'il y a dans la poétique de Ronsard un curieux précepte: il recommande au poète de s'instruire dans les arts et métiers, forgerons, orfèvres, serruriers, etc., pour y puiser des *métaphores*. C'est là ce qui vous fait, en effet, une langue riche et variée' (C IV 52).

epitome of self-examination and of scepticism (but also as, through the destruction of illusion, finding the personal calm of his *arrière-boutique*) was obviously a permanent 'père nourricier'. If the self-confession of Flaubert's early works is often closer to more romantic models, yet a letter of 1846 (C I 386) shows how closely Montaigne's self-analysis is associated with the urge to draw a great work from direct expression of personal substance, and with the reasons (both of personal humility and of aesthetic purpose) which gradually turn Flaubert to different means of expression.[1] The contribution of Montaigne's mind and style is obviously both pervasive and difficult to pinpoint.[2]

It is Rabelais's influence which is most openly, and often intentionally, to be seen and enjoyed; pastiche, parody, and transposition into modern terms weave deliberate variations on his themes and technique. Early letters elaborate fashionable coruscations around his style; mocking remnants of this mode among the intellectuals of Flaubert's youth will persist in the Hussonnet of *L'Education sentimentale*.[3] The comic aggrandizement of the most trivial material object to make it hold an epic significance is one of Flaubert's main delights, reaching its pitch of virtuosity in a letter where the spirit of each century is with a fine fantastic logic symbolized in the rich detail of its different footwear; in *Madame Bovary* a subtler network of variations will be woven on how the shape, material or state of upkeep of this humble object reflect character or mood.

Rabelais's technique of inserting into epic fantasy the details of a comic pseudo-precision has obviously captivated Flaubert's interest in playing with different tones and levels of artistic illusion. Where Rabelais mainly starts from gigantic and fantastic feats, then parodically 'authenticates' them through solemn and exact

[1] A. P. Coleman, op. cit., pp. 12–15, examines some detailed parallels.

[2] *Par les Champs*, p. 287, evokes 'Rabelais qui rit, Shakespeare qui voit, Montaigne qui rêve', three key-points in Flaubert's own art.

[3] Scraps of pseudo-sixteenth-century language recur throughout the letters, too numerous to list. Balzac's *Contes drolatiques* were no doubt a contributory influence. See C III 72–5 for a developed piece of this style (discussed by H. Patry in art. cit.). See also VII 337.

location and numeration, Flaubert often reverses the effect, setting out from factual precision to produce a crescendo of detail which almost imperceptibly culminates in epic fantasy. On the cab journey of Emma and Léon through Rouen, exact details of streets, squares, docks, parks are strung together in a labyrinthine concatenation widening into a sense of the infinite complexity of the city and the frenetic fulfilment of desire.

Rabelais's amassing of a horde of characters in one festive gathering, where they rub shoulders, declaim paradoxes, and bring alive in vastly heightened form an age and its problems, was, of course, handed on to the nineteenth century through the scene in *La Peau de Chagrin* in which Balzac deliberately sets out to rival the 'propos des Beuveurs' in contemporary terms. Flaubert's equivalents will be many, from the wedding-feast or the *comices agricoles* in *Madame Bovary*, through a series of contrasted celebrations in *L'Education sentimentale*, to the receptions at which Bouvard and Pécuchet entertain their neighbours. The arrival of the carriages for the wedding feast in *Madame Bovary* shows a Rabelaisian delight in developing to the last degree the enumeration of every type of current wheeled vehicle, in caricaturing these odd conveyances and their occupants, stylized into stiffened and clumsy puppets by Sunday clothes, cropped hair and razor-slashed skin; they participate in a gargantuan provincial feast, bedecked with nineteenth-century pretentiousness and provincial prettification; cliché and crude jest seethe; then all finishes in an epic *débandade* as unreined vehicles crazily rocket with their drunken owners across the countryside into the night. In *Madame Bovary* the puppet-show with epic extensions is restricted to a provincial background; in *L'Education sentimentale* it spreads over the political experience of a key generation in the capital; the use of precise and trivial detail to culminate in a vertiginous heightening of obsession or ineptitude reaches its epitome in Frédéric's prolonged pursuit of the ever-absent Regimbart from café to café, and in the mad manœuvres at the Club de l'Intelligence.[1] Finally,

---

[1] I have left aside *Salammbô* and *La Tentation* where the multiplicity of sources would require a different kind of discussion.

Bouvard and Pécuchet involve themselves in a wild emulation of the Rabelaisian desire to become 'un abîme de science'. The outcome proves them no giants; the mocking sympathy directed towards them[1] has perhaps a certain affinity with the presentation of the all-too-human Panurge in face of his recurrent dilemmas.

On the sixteenth century Flaubert is obviously neither scholar nor critic proper, though his scattered remarks might well fit Baudelaire's desire for criticism: 'partiale, politique, et qui ouvre le plus d'horizons'. What he says is suggestive much less for its analysis of the authors than for what it reveals of his own mind and art, and of the fruitful contact of minds and forms across the centuries. In this context, his personality shows some of its most positive and generous impulses. If, set against complacency and apathy, 'haïr et admirer sont deux rares vertus'[2] (CS IV 208), yet 'la postérité rira de nos dénigrements plutôt que de nos admirations' and 'Comme ça fait du bien d'admirer' (Preface to Bouilhet's *Dernières chansons*, and C III 91). Whatever his scepticism, there is one unwavering conviction:

> Je ne permets pas qu'on touche à mes chers anciens. Cela m'a rappelé Montaigne disant 'insulter Seneca, c'est m'insulter moi-même' (C VII 185).

Finally, he writes of the difference between the authors one respects, those one enjoys in general, and

> ceux qui nous prennent à la fois par tous les bouts, et qui nous semblent créés pour notre tempérament. On les hume, ceux-là; on s'en nourrit, ils nous servent à vivre (C IV 416).

---

[1] I have discussed some aspects of this in an article on 'Flaubert et la conscience du réel', in *Essays in French Literature*, No. 4 (University of Western Australia Press, 1967).

[2] Saint-Simon, in his Mémoires, discussing a weakling unable to hate, remarked that 'le nerf et le principe de la haine et de l'amitié . . . est le même' (*Selections*, ed. A. Tilley, Cambridge, 1920, p. 203).

Those whose profession and pleasure has been to transmit to successive generations a response to the mind and art of the Renaissance can find in Flaubert an *amateur* who conveys in his own terms the stimulus of personal delight and the renewal of lasting tradition.

Alison Fairlie

Ramond and the École Centrale
des Hautes-Pyrénées

BY THE DECREE on public instruction of Brumaire 3, Year IV
(October 1795), the Convention, just before its dissolution, had
ordained *inter alia* that an *école centrale* should be set up in each
department. The old universities had been suppressed; Napoleon's
Université de France was still to come; the *école centrale* was to provide a half-way house between what we call today secondary and
higher education. The experiment was to be short-lived; when it
was given up not every department had received its *école*. Picavet's
Les idéologues describes several of these schools, but hitherto no
one has paid much attention to that set up in Tarbes.

During its short life the École Centrale des Hautes-Pyrénées
acquired some lustre from the fact that Louis-Elisabeth Ramond
(1755–1827) taught natural history there and that Dangos the
astronomer, a friend of Dolomieu, held the Chair of Mathematics.[1] In 1795 Ramond was nearly forty-one. His youthful plays
and poems were forgotten; for the public he was the author of
two highly esteemed books on the Alps and Pyrenees. He had
spent seven years in the service of Cardinal de Rohan and had represented Paris in the Assemblée Législative, in which he had
been one of the principal speakers. He had left the capital in July
1792 and had been living in Barèges and near Argelès, except for a

---

[1] It may be added, though no lustre accrued therefrom, that the ex-constitutional
Bishop of Cher, Torné, then living in penury in his native town, was given the post of
Librarian and held it till his death in 1797.

period of captivity at Tarbes during the Terror. In 1795 he had taken up his abode at Bagnères-de-Bigorre with his sister and brother-in-law Borgella. He was influential in securing an *école centrale* for Tarbes and in February 1796 he was appointed Professor of Natural History there.

The *écoles centrales* had neither traditions nor curricula; everything had to be improvised. At Tarbes there was not even a building. In the later years of its short life the École Centrale des Hautes-Pyrénées came to occupy the former college of the Christian Doctrine Brothers which had been the city's chief educational centre before 1790; the college had been used as an emergency prison in 1793–4 and Ramond himself had lain there. Under Napoleon it was to house the Lycée, which today incorporates the original building.

At first the school's different departments were scattered about the town. As late as April 1797 Ramond still had to teach in 'deux salles basses où nos élèves ne s'enrhument pas moins à nous entendre que nous à leur donner des leçons'.[1] There was no boarding accommodation for staff or students; he lived half the *décade* in an inn and the other half at home.

The school was declared open in July 1796 and Ramond composed a pompous oration which a mishap in the mountains prevented him from delivering. Natural history comprised, of course, zoology, botany and mineralogy – that is, geology. The teaching was to begin in the autumn of 1796. Neither school nor professor was ready; Ramond, whose first spell of teaching this was, called himself 'un vieux écolier obligé de passer maître' without having the time to effect the transformation properly.[2]

> Quel embarras pour un écolier subitement devenu maître et forcé de composer et dicter des cours sur les trois parties de l'histoire naturelle quand les plus grands génies en ont à peine possédé une ou deux![1]

The lack of resources was total for the school and almost total

[1] Letter to Picot-Lapeyrouse, Germinal 20, V.
[2] Letter to Gouan, Vendémiaire 9, VII.

for Ramond, who had brought very few books away with him from Paris. Observing without instruments and studying without books, he said, he had learnt little, but that little had stuck.

Goodwill and an infinite capacity for muddle were about equal in the Hautes-Pyrénées administration. Early in 1796 Ramond was consulted on the choice of a site for a botanical garden, the creation of which was one of his dearest wishes; he hoped to found a kind of Pyrenean annexe to the Jardin des Plantes. He was offered, first, a garden of about the right size, but with a bad aspect; next, one with a magnificent aspect, but a water-logged soil; the site he himself selected was refused him. Above all, he needed a gardener who was also a botanist, for the local 'planteurs de choux' were useless until they had been trained by someone competent.

One must remember the degree of internal disorganization in France under the Directoire, to understand the situation. Travelling was perilous, communications uncertain; the countryside was harried by Royalist bands and ordinary highwaymen. Tarbes was isolated and Ramond had to rely on his Toulouse colleague, Picot-Lapeyrouse, for information which today we obtain almost without noticing it. Had the second part of Saussure's *Voyages autour du Mont-Blanc* come out? What book should he use for 'les vers nuds et les testacés'? For crystallography, would it be enough to boil down R. J. Haüy's lectures?[1]

The utter lack of technical assistance also seems astonishing. Ramond had to prepare not only his lectures but also his specimens of animals, birds and rocks. Having decided to begin his course with the birds, he had to stuff and mount them himself; he did so to his own satisfaction, 'assez proprement', but he could not manufacture glass eyes and begged Lapeyrouse to send him some.[2]

When the young Léon Dufour called on him at Barèges he found him busy pinning and setting the insects he had collected for

[1] Letter of Vendémiaire 15, V.
[2] Letters of Prairial 13, V, and Vendémiaire 15, VI.

the school; Ramond at once claimed a handsome stag-beetle, *cerambyx alpinus*, which the youth had caught and stuck in his cap.[1]

For lack of books and illustrations he had to make drawings of mountain views and engrave them himself. Again he appealed to Lapeyrouse, because, though he had the means to engrave, his 'misérable département' would provide neither copper plates nor press. Could plates be had in Toulouse, he asked, and could a press be made there 'à bon compte', consisting of two cylinders ten to twelve inches long?

> Si je pouvais me procurer cet attirail, il me servirait à tirer moi-même et corriger mes épreuves, après quoi je les livrerais à un imprimeur pour la main d'œuvre du tirage en grand que je lui aurais bientôt enseigné.[2]

How maddening this Heath Robinson equipment must have been, especially as he had also the actual courses to get up from scratch!

All the summer of 1796 he was doing field-work in the mountains and, although the school opened in September, he put off his own lectures till October 15th in order to take advantage of the last fine days. This is how he sums up the situation in December: nothing ready, no encouragement, not the most rudimentary garden or cabinet; a library useless for his purpose and 'dans le *Tohou-bohou* de la Genèse'; a dozen birds, several hundred insects, a caseful of stones.[3] Fortunately, he still has in Paris 'un très petit cabinet de minéralogie' and three quite large herbaria for which he has sent.

At least he was his own Board of Studies, Faculty and Senate, and could arrange his syllabus as he pleased. He decided to run courses of one year only, not merely 'pour attirer une jeunesse qui n'est point faite à l'étude', but also because he expected many fresh students when he began botany in his second year.

---

[1] Léon Dufour, *Souvenirs d'un savant français à travers un siècle (1780–1865)*, Paris (1888), p. 19.
[2] Letter to Lapeyrouse, Prairial 29, VI; letter to Gouan, Nivôse 17, VII.
[3] Letter to Lapeyrouse, Frimaire 23, V.

He had to point out to the administration, to whom it was not obvious, that the time-table must allow every student to choose his course without fear of clashes;[1] many students of eighteen to twenty, he considered, needed to follow all the courses. Lectures were given daily except on *quintidi* and *décadi*, between eight and five, with a lunch break of an hour and a half. The syllabus included every day one hour each of ancient languages, mathematics and drawing, and every other day one hour of 'législation' or history, 'grammaire générale' or *belles-lettres*, and physics or natural history. Ramond gave four lectures a *décade* from half-past ten to noon.

In his first semester he took mineralogy, botanical nomenclature and plant physics, alternating all three for the sake of variety. He began with thirty-five to forty students; Dangos had forty-five to fifty. His teaching combined speaking and dictating.

> Je parle d'abondance, j'explique et je me rends le plus clair que je puis. Ensuite lorsque je me vois compris, je me résume et je dicte un résumé clair, simple, précis qui fait le cahier des élèves.[2] Je n'ai trouvé que cette façon de leur apprendre à entendre et à extraire . . . Enfin de temps à autre j'interroge tantôt les plus diligents pour les faire connaître, tantôt les plus paresseux pour les punir, tantôt ceux qui ont besoin d'explication pour établir une petite controverse qui éclaircit les idées de tous.[3]

It was by the sole light of nature that he had devised this method.

It stands to reason for us that all scientific instruction should be given in the vernacular. It was still not always so at the end of the eighteenth century and Ramond felt he must justify his choice of French as his medium.

---

1 'Sans en être empêché par la rencontre de deux leçons à la même heure.' Having over many years asked in vain French colleagues for the equivalent of 'clash' in this context, I am grateful to Ramond for having answered my question one hundred and seventy years ago.

2 Such a 'cahier' has been preserved in the family of one of his students and published by F. L. Ydrac in the *Bulletin de la Société Ramond*, 1935, pp. 53–70.

3 Letter to Lapeyrouse, Frimaire 23, V.

Il est d'autant plus nécessaire d'instruire en français que beaucoup d'élèves entendent fort peu le latin.[1]

Like every true pedagogue, he hoped his students would acquire not merely 'science' but 'le désir et la manière d'apprendre'.[2] Unlike many of his contemporaries, he had come to science through outdoor observation as much as through books, first in his native Vosges, then in the Alps and Pyrenees; he was the reverse of a *savant de cabinet* and set great store by making his students work in the field during the long summer vacation. He was contemptuous of scientists who did not undertake labour in the bosom of nature. Those who do, he says, recognize at once their colleagues whose knowledge comes only from books and whose botanical descriptions 'ne font trouver une plante que dans les livres'.[3]

The *écoles centrales* were a hybrid conception and from the start they were threatened with suppression. As early as June 1797 their continued existence seemed unlikely.[4] Cries of alarm arose and petitions were addressed to the highest levels from the towns fortunate enough to possess them. In November 1797 Ramond wrote to Marie-Joseph Chénier and Fourcroy to enlist their support.[5] In November 1798 the beginning of term at Tarbes was celebrated with pompous publicity, comprising a military and civic procession, and speeches, including one by Ramond on 'L'utilité de l'instruction publique', a defence of modern studies which were constantly under fire. Nevertheless, the Tarbes school was wound up in 1800.

Ramond seems to have been a painstaking, stimulating and approachable teacher. In his three years as professor he won the lasting friendship of several of his students, among whom two

[1] Letter to Antoine-Laurent de Jussieu, Prairial 28, V.
[2] Letter to Lapeyrouse, Frimaire 23, V. A desire expressed also by Condorcet in the first of his five *mémoires* on public instruction.
[3] Letter to Gouan, Brumaire 23, V.
[4] Letter to A. L. de Jussieu, Prairial 28, V.
[5] Letters of Frimaire 5, VI. The letter to Fourcroy is lost, but a copy of Fourcroy's answer is in the Dossier Ramond in the archives of the Académie des Sciences. The letter to M. J. Chénier was published in *Pyrénées*, 1952, p. 212.

were to become distinguished: the horticulturist and park designer Massey and the botanist and future academician Brissot de Mirbel, both of whom joined in his expeditions to the Brèche de Tuquerouye in August and September 1797.

His duties as teacher terminated at the end of 1799, but he remained interested in education. In 1801 Destutt de Tracy sent him his *Observations sur le système actuel de l'instruction publique* and Ramond's comments on it prompted the author to declare that, of all those who had spoken of the little work, it was he who had best understood its basic ideas.[1]

During his tenure of office as Prefect of Puy-de-Dôme (1806–13) the Lycée of Clermont was completed and was formally opened by him on February 8, 1808. His speech, in which he expounded his views on public instruction, is one of his weightiest occasional writings and it will be interesting to dwell on it, for, although his opinions agree in the main with those of the *idéologues*, there are some differences in emphasis.[2] Moreover, they are still of topical interest.

The ex-professor and legislator turned administrator places his subject in a historical setting, as indeed he did with almost everything he studied, whether scientific or humanistic, and his opinions are borne on a stream of political judgements of which those on the Revolution are particularly impressive.[3]

His speech is a profession of the pedagogical faith which underlay his service at Tarbes and took shape during his three years of teaching. The object of public instruction, he says, is not to produce geniuses; that is nature's task and no educational system can claim to know her secret. It is to train the ordinary men who make up society to grow up useful to themselves and to others – that is, to be good citizens. To succeed in this, both its object and its form must be in harmony with the life to which those who receive it are destined. This harmony existed in antiquity, but

[1] Ramond's letter is lost, but a copy of Destutt de Tracy's, dated Messidor 30, IX, is in the Dossier Ramond in the archives of the Académie des Sciences.
[2] The speech, published at the time in Clermont-Ferrand, has never been reprinted.
[3] Cf. Sainte-Beuve, *Lundis*, September 18, 1854. Ramond is ignored by Picavet.

has gradually vanished and ever since the Renaissance the best minds have advocated a closer concordance

> entre la nature de l'instruction et son objet, entre sa partie dog-matique et sa partie usuelle, entre le genre de savoir inculqué à de jeunes esprits et le genre de connaissances qui, dans l'âge de la maturité, constitue l'homme utile et le vrai citoyen.

By the end of the eighteenth century the divergence between 'l'université'[1] and society was due to the former's inability to keep up with the advance of knowledge and the consequent changes in the structure of society.

> Toujours plus tentée de restreindre le savoir à sa propre mesure que d'accorder sa doctrine avec les lumières du temps, elle semblait s'éclairer plus lentement que la nation qu'elle-même avait éclairée et avouer à regret les succès dont elle était la première source. Bientôt on sut beaucoup plus de choses qu'elle n'en enseignait et elle n'enseigna qu'une partie de celles qu'il importait d'apprendre.

With the upheaval of the Revolution came the opportunity to remedy this deficiency and to 'rendre à l'instruction première ce caractère de généralité qui seul peut l'approprier à tous les besoins de l'État et des particuliers'.

The two foundations of instruction are letters and science, and the quarrel of prestige between them is absurd. Such rivalry, he says optimistically, is now obsolete.

> On rit aujourd'hui des disputes de prééminence qui s'élèvent entre le littérateur qui ne sait pas l'arithmétique et le savant qui ne sait pas l'orthographe,

an opposition still not unknown today and which it is easy to express in modern terminology.

The justification for a literary grounding is that

> apprendre à parler, c'est apprendre à penser. En s'occupant de l'arrangement des mots, on est forcé de mettre de l'ordre dans les idées.

[1] Which, of course, included colleges imparting what we call secondary as well as higher education.

But letters are insufficient and Ramond has no difficulty in establishing an equal claim for 'les sciences de calcul et d'observation' which constitute 'une philosophie plus analogue aux lumières acquises et à l'état actuel de la science'. His insistence on the importance of science in contemporary society is a measure of the resistance which scientific teaching was encountering.

> Les mathématiques introduisent aux sciences exactes comme les lettres aux sciences conjecturales: elles complètent donc l'instruction élémentaire.

Enriched by these two streams of knowledge, able to 'dire des choses utiles et de les bien dire', the pupil is fitted for positions honourable to himself and useful to the State. And, looking further afield, the Prefect exclaims: 'Notre siècle n'est pas à nous: il est à l'Europe entière' – at that date, of course, Europe was almost an extension of France.

Descending from the heights of theory, he turns to the teachers themselves, warning them that they will not be judged only by the parents of their charges.

> Vous n'en êtes pas quittes pour la sentence des pères; au sein de vos classes se prépare la sentence de leurs enfants. En eux la postérité commence.

Drawing on his own experience, he reminds them that it is not enough to work on their intellect; the teacher must also attach himself

> aux mouvements les plus secrets de leur âme. Suivez-les non seulement dans leurs études mais dans leurs jeux, mais dans leurs rapports mutuels, mais dans l'essai qu'ils font entre eux des relations sociales, mais dans les premiers développements de ces passions qui n'attendent que la direction qui va leur être donnée pour prêter leur emportement au vice ou leur énergie à la vertu. Ce n'est pas seulement l'homme instruit; c'est l'homme de bien et de sens que vous avez à former.

Such an ideal makes an even greater demand on the teacher's

character than on his learning. 'Que la morale soit chez vous en action plus qu'en maximes, et dans votre conduite plus que dans vos discours.' To be worthy of directing others, he must be constantly questioning and searching himself. His aim must be to 'faire aimer le savoir à de jeunes esprits et la sagesse à de jeunes cœurs', and this calls for treasures of wisdom and patience, for justice, for 'un cœur droit, un esprit libre, une âme ferme'. Need one apologize for what appears commonplace in the prefect's ethical exhortations and reflect that this ideal, so familiar to our own pedagogy, is still beyond that of some lycées where one hears expressed the ancient dogma that the function of the school is instruction, while moral upbringing and character building should be left to the home?

Ramond concludes with a comparison in keeping with his biological interests. A pupil, he says, is like a tree; if tree and pupil grow up badly, teacher and gardener should be ready to blame themselves.

> L'ignorant jardinier s'étonne de ce que son arbre ne prend pas spontanément la forme qu'il lui destine, et s'offense de ce beau luxe de la végétation, dont la prodigalité, cependant, fournit à tous les caprices de la culture. Votre élève est cet arbre. En lui réside la perfectibilité de l'homme. Mais, indifférent à la forme, il eût été Spartiate à Lacédémone, il serait Chinois à Pékin et sauvage sur les bords de l'Ohio. Le moule est dans vos mains: faites-en un bon Français. Si le succès ne répondait pas à votre attente, je serais moins tenté de m'en prendre à lui qu'à vous.

The Revolution and Empire are often accused of excessive abstraction. It is good to qualify this accusation and to recognize that sanely pragmatic views of the teaching vocation were also held. Ramond is, of course, in line with earlier theorists like the Abbé Pluche, who, in his *Spectacle de la nature*, had urged as much natural history as rhetoric, as well as with the father of universal instruction in France, Condorcet, and some of his *idéologue* contemporaries. But over most of these he had the advantage of having both organized teaching and carried it out during his years of struggle at Tarbes, and it is this that gives so modern a ring to the advice which he lavished in 1808 on the Lycée teachers at Clermont-Ferrand.

Note: Ramond's letters to Picot-Lapeyrouse are in the Muséum d'Histoire naturelle; those to Jussieu in the archives of the Académie des Sciences; those to Gouan in the British Museum.

Cuthbert Girdlestone

The *Heptaméron* Reconsidered

⇛ ⇛ ⇛ ⇛ ⇛ ⇛ ⇛ ⇛ ⇛ ⇛ ⇛ ⇚ ⇚ ⇚ ⇚ ⇚ ⇚ ⇚ ⇚ ⇚ ⇚ ⇚ ⇚

DESPITE THE considerable amount of erudition expended on the *Heptaméron* in the past eighty years, Félix Frank's edition of 1879, in three volumes, has remained not only the starting-point for most serious research, but in many ways the finishing-post as well. Thanks to M. François[1] we now have an edition soundly based on MSS., which includes the main variants and alternative stories; thanks to P. Jourda[2] a good deal of Marguerite's biography is now much clearer; thanks to E. V. Telle[3] and L. Febvre[4] we can see Marguerite's religious and psychological ideas in something like the proper perspective. The work of all these, and other scholars, deserves acknowledgement, but it is no exaggeration to say that some of the basic problems of the work have yet to be solved. R. Ritter[5] is almost the only recent critic to have queried some of the facts so long accepted on trust by others, but even he has not gone far enough. The series of interlocking problems involved is perhaps insoluble in the same way as those affecting any other unfinished work, but there are some questions which should have been asked long ago and some answers which should never have been given.

The first question concerns the status of the work. According

---

[1] *L'Heptaméron*, ed. M. François, Paris (1943). Throughout this article page references to this edition are given in brackets.

[2] P. Jourda, *Marguerite d'Angoulême*, 2 vols., Paris (1930).

[3] E. V. Telle, *L'Œuvre de M. d'Angoulême et la querelle des femmes*, Toulouse (1937).

[4] L. Febvre, *Autour de l'Heptaméron*, Paris (1944).

[5] R. Ritter, *Les Solitudes de M. de Navarre*, Paris (1953).

to the Prologue, the author is rather belatedly realizing a project already mooted at Court, by producing a French *Decameron* to rival that which Antoine Le Maçon had been engaged on translating for a dozen years or more at her instigation. From the start certain rules are laid down: all the stories must be true, or at least given some authenticating details; they must be original, and not of literary provenance; they must be told by amateurs. The purpose of the exercise is to offer the King and his Court a collection to divert them as the work of Boccaccio had done. It should at once be stressed that it is the stories, and nothing else, to which the Prologue refers; the Prologue itself, together with the rest of the framework narrative and discussion, is neither explicitly nor implicitly part of the enterprise, but purports to be a simple record of its progress.

As far as the stories are concerned, the great majority formally obey the conventions of the game as agreed, being 'quelque histoire que [chascun] aura veue ou bien oy dire à quelque homme digne de foy' (10), and M. Jourda has shown in detail that a good number (a score or more) of the seventy-two extant tales have a verifiable basis of fact. From the first the tales themselves have naturally attracted most interest, and some editions and translations simply omit the framework narrative. Since Frank attention has certainly been paid to the context of this framework, but scholars have tended, as is their wont, to concentrate on sources, analogues, or techniques of the stories rather than on the work as a whole.

In this connection a word must be said on the problem of authenticity. Changes made by Gruget for the first complete edition of 1559 are relatively minor, consisting almost entirely of omissions, whether of proper names or of religious views judged to be too audacious. More serious is the substitution of a completely different and quite lengthy dialogue for that found in the MSS. after tale LV, and though this only occurs once on so large a scale, it must be admitted that Gruget's version not only looks genuine but is actually more effective than Marguerite's original. Her style is neither very distinctive nor distinguished, and the sort of dialogue which serves only to link tales could be inserted by any skilful editor without arousing suspicion, but sustained exchanges such as follow the alternative tales given in M. François's Appendix (published by Gruget in place of XI, XLIV and XLVI) pose a real problem. In style and content these passages are as much in character as the tales in question, and though in the nature of things it is hard to prove, it looks very much as if they were drafted by Marguerite, who then changed her mind about where or whether to insert them. Modern methods of stylistic analysis might resolve any lingering doubts, and should certainly be tried, but fortunately this particular problem of authenticity affects only a small part of the work, and the MS. tradition is conclusive for the rest.

The seventy-two extant stories bear a curiously ambiguous relationship to the rest of the book, and it is obviously much less trouble to treat them like any other collection of tales devised for entertainment than to relate them to any deeper purpose or more complex plan. Yet there are grounds for supposing that the book is quite different from others which it apparently resembles.[1] Frank made the interesting comment in 1879: 'C'est l'Anglais Chaucer, contemporain de Boccace, qui dans ses *Contes de Canterbury*, laissés inachevés, fournit le prototype le plus voisin des entretiens de *l'Heptaméron*,'[2] but he spoils the effect of this insight a few pages later where he writes: 'Elle accepte de toute main ce qui lui agrée pour l'œuvre rêvée: de Boccace . . .; de Sabadino . . .; de Masuccio . . .; de Chaucer la forme d'entretien qui anime le commentaire, avec la diversité des interlocuteurs.'[3] It is certainly true that the *Canterbury Tales* offer points of comparison with the *Heptaméron*, but there seems to be no evidence that the *Tales* were known at all in sixteenth-century France, or indeed that they were translated in whole or in part until quite recent times. It is none the less helpful to think of Chaucer's aims

[1] The best discussion of the conventions involved is in W. Pabst, *Novellentheorie und Novellendichtung*, Hamburg (1957), pp. 163–230.
[2] Vol. I, p. LXIII.
[3] ibid., p. LXVII.

and methods even if his influence can be discounted; Frank was right to note the affinity.

Critics have given some very odd answers regarding the status of the Prologue. M. Febvre is typical of those who have seen in the assembly at Serrance an event as plausible as that of the pilgrims at the Tabard Inn: 'Marguerite a travaillé à créer une illusion topographique parfaite; elle y a réussi'.[1] M. Ritter, living in the shadow of the Pyrenees, has exposed in detail the errors of his predecessors for whom topography apparently means toponymy, with no regard for the lie of the land. He proves quite conclusively[2] that neither Marguerite nor anyone else could have made the journeys described, and M. Febvre's perfect illusion does not survive a course in basic map-reading. As for the encounters with brigands, bears and things that go bump in the night, everyone has recognized this to be the purest fantasy. The adventure (but not necessarily the discussion) in the Prologue is thus an additional story, with no claim to veracity.

The next question concerns the status of the author. The second sentence of the Prologue begins 'Ma fin . . . la matière que je veulx escripre', and there are other occasional lapses into the first person, as in the penultimate sentence of the Fourth Day 'je pense que . . .', though they are rare. All are agreed in identifying Marguerite with Parlamente in the framework narrative, and in the tales themselves she quite often appears under one of her titles (Duchesse d'Alençon, Reine de Navarre) or (if we are to believe Brantôme) thinly disguised beneath the anonymity of this or that noble lady. While to some extent the character of Parlamente is a self-portrait, it is visibly adapted to the needs of the story-telling game as the presentation of the historical Marguerite is not, but there is no real clash, because Parlamente does not comment on Marguerite, any more than the 'je' of the narrator comments on Parlamente, except in the most general terms. This triple level is unusual, however, and remarkably well handled.

[1] op. cit., p. 183.
[2] op. cit., pp. 123–8.

The status of the other characters is a very difficult question, and inevitably bound up with the question of their identification. The only characters specifically related to each other are Parlamentc and Hircan, who constantly refer to each other as husband and wife. Internal evidence has been taken to establish the fact that Ennasuitte is married to Simontault and Nomerfide to Saffredent, but in fact more emphasis is laid on the extra-marital interests of the various characters than on their official relationships. Each at one time or another speaks of husband or wife, but never by name and never in direct address, as is constantly the ease between Parlamente and Hircan. Moreover, Geburon, who is certainly not accompanied by his wife, refers to her several times, and Longarine, whose husband perishes in the Prologue, talks just as much about love and marriage as any of the others. This vagueness about their marital status is almost certainly intended by the author, for she is equally vague about other relationships (for example, parent and child), though it is reasonable to suppose them to exist. Indeed, the only reference of this kind is when Parlamente addresses Oisille in the Prologue: 'Madame, . . . vous . . . qui maintenant à nous, femmes, tenez lieu de mere', and Oisille replies: 'Mes enfans . . .' (6–7). Such deliberate imprecision makes it easier to preserve the convention of equality in the story-telling game, to which Hircan alludes in the last lines of the Prologue ('au jeu nous sommes tous esgaulx'), but tends somewhat to blunt the point of the numerous allusions to unofficial attachments within the group. To some extent the characters are individuated by external features, such as age, widowhood and so on, though not by rank or profession (there is no hint that Dagoucin is in orders), and inasmuch as they emerge as individuals it is mainly through a marked attitude to life. Any comparison with the diversity of Chaucer's pilgrims is, however, quite misleading, above all for social reasons, and whatever may be the acceptable identification of Marguerite's circle the ten come much closer to the homogeneity of interest and experience of Boccaccio than the variety of Chaucer.

So far as the game goes, each character provides his own story, which can, of course, be at second hand, in which case it is generally acknowledged as such, but as none of the stories is told in the first person, the relationship of narrator to story-character must depend on at least tentative identification. There is, however, some evidence that stories assigned to a given narrator have, for the most part, common provenance. It can hardly be an accident that all the tales told by Saffredent, Parlamente and Oisille (with the exception of two undated) are set in the period before 1531, or that the first four of Nomerfide's tales are set in the west of France (Alençon, Thouars, Mayenne, Niort) or that Hircan tells a tale set in Pampelona, capital of the lost kingdom of Navarre. There is at least one tale by Longarine (LXII) which almost certainly refers to Marguerite, describing 'une dame du sang roial, accompaigné d'honneur, de vertu et de beaulté', which one can hardly imagine Marguerite writing of herself, but which it would be perfectly proper of her to report from someone else. The best working hypothesis is that Marguerite collected rather than composed the majority of her tales, which she first heard orally and then edited as she wrote them down. Tales LXX and LXXII reinforce this view, for the former is offered by Oisille exceptionally as from a written source and the latter is stated by Dagoucin to have come from Marguerite herself; such comments would have little point unless the other tales really had been related orally by the pseudonymous narrators.

Much of the foregoing is obvious, but it is necessary to repeat it if the right causes are to be linked to the right effects. By putting herself and her husband into the fictional situation of the Prologue Marguerite was not committing herself, but by participating with him under the most transparent disguise in discussions on love, morality and religion she clearly was. Whether she eventually intended to publish the book or not (and her attitude to all her works is not readily discernible), she certainly would have circulated the *Heptaméron* among her friends at the Courts of France and Navarre. All critics now agree that the other eight characters represent people known to Marguerite and each other, and presumably to both courts, and this in itself would explain why she takes no trouble to fill in the *état civil* of persons known to her readers. It also means that we are not here dealing with one of those imaginary dialogues of which the Renaissance, following antiquity, was so fond, but with a discussion between the author, her husband and eight once identifiable friends on subjects of major importance, and often of the most controversial nature. For all the work of recent critics it is by no means clear what they think Marguerite was doing, or trying to do, apart from presenting stories with a moral set in a superficially realistic background.

The plan of the composition repays study. It soon becomes evident that the rules of the game require a gay (and short) story to follow a serious (and longer) one, that a man follows a woman, that each narrator nominates the next, and each has the right to begin only one day. Though the arguments printed at the head of each day are misleading and not by Marguerite, M. Telle has shown in a long analysis of the work the continuity of theme in the first four days, with some slackening in the next. Such continuity is affected by various recognizable devices which show something of her working methods; thus the first story told by Parlamente on the Third Day explicitly refers to a second story to follow (XXI and XL), while Ennasuite says that she will keep for the following day the serious story (XXXVI), as she has an amusing one ready (XXVII). This proves that Marguerite arranged these two Days at the same time, and all the indications are that the composition of the first four, and perhaps five, Days followed continuously and fairly quickly after the Prologue, so that the first fifty tales were conceived as an articulated whole.

Days Six to Eight are linked by similar structural devices, for at the end of Six Saffredent is detailed by Oisille to begin the next Day, despite the fact that he had earlier begun Five, which means that a woman (in the event Parlamente) has to redress the balance by also beginning a second Day. This odd breach of the simple enough rules is only one of several details which suggest hasty work and a certain change in procedure. Thus, the discussion over the beginning of the Eighth Day leads Dagoucin (who has not yet begun one) to relinquish his right in favour of Saffredent, which leaves Hircan as the only man still to begin, no doubt the Ninth Day, but then Nomerfide also resigns in favour of Parlamente, having already had her turn on the Second Day, whereas it should have been either Longarine or Ennasuite who stood down. There is a muddle over the authorship of LVIII, which is told by Dagoucin, but subsequently attributed to Simontault, who has already told LII (it certainly suits him better, and Gruget makes him tell both). There is also a perceptible charge in the dating of the tales: the two most recent stories in the whole book, indeed the only ones precisely dated after 1540, are LXVI (after 1544) and LXVII (1548), while the only one of the last twenty-two to go back to the previous century is LVII, told by Parlamente herself, whereas a large number of the first fifty had brought in the more distant past (e.g. XLVI, XLIX); LXX is the only story presented as from a written source, long before living memory. It is only now that Marguerite includes tales set in Béarn (LXVIII in Pau and LXIX in Odos), and perhaps most significant, she is herself involved by name in LXI and LXVI, anonymously in LXII, she relates LXIV and LXXI, tells us that LXX is known only to her (Parlamente) and Oisille, and is given by Dagoucin as his source for LXXII. In other words more than half of the last dozen stories are directly associated with her, which marks so clear a break from her earlier practice as to demand explanation. The impression of haste, of making the most of suddenly limited material, is inescapable.

These phenomena must be seen in the light of external as well as internal evidence. It is generally accepted that Marguerite began her Prologue on her return from Cauterets in autumn 1546, continuing throughout the winter and spring until she had finished perhaps half her task. The most natural moment for a break in composition would be in April 1547, when she learnt at Tusson of her beloved brother's death, and this would correspond with the break after the Fifth Day. It is not at all clear when she resumed work, but certain that she was not more than half-way through the Seventh Day when she related the incident set in late 1548 (LXVI). From what has already been said it looks as though she normally composed more than one Day at a time, and that the last twenty-two tales were provided with their framework narrative in one continuous period of composition, for which the most natural starting-point would seem to be Jeanne's second marriage in October 1548.

A feature of the introductions to Days Six, Seven and Eight confirms this view, and reinforces the impression that with François's death she came to conceive her enterprise in rather different terms. She could hardly have begun the work without at least a provisional idea of what she was going to put in the Epilogue. and as we follow the discussion it becomes more and more apparent that it would have led up to a conclusion of some profundity as they all prepare to resume their everyday lives. M. Ritter shrewdly observes[1] that Marguerite was no doubt keeping a Parthian shot for the avaricious abbot whose guests they were, but this could be only incidental. As each day goes by the companions learn more about themselves and each other, and some comment on their final attitude to their relationships and obligations must have been intended to close the work. Already in the Prologue their daily routine is foreshadowed by their monastic surroundings and Oisille's addiction to Scripture reading. Each of the first five Days begins with the Bible reading and commentary, followed by mass in the abbey church, but on the Sixth Day for the first time we are told what she read: the First Epistle of Saint John. What makes this detail so significant is that then, and only then, we are told, as if as an afterthought, that the preceding five lessons had been from the Epistle to the Romans. The Seventh Day begins with a reading from the beginning of Acts, followed by a mass of the Holy Spirit – the only time any detail of the monastic liturgy is given – and on the Eighth and last Day we are told that Oisille took rather longer than usual over her reading, because she wanted to finish St John's Epistle.

One literary implications of this stands out at once: although each Day succeeds the preceding one directly, it is only after six that Marguerite seems to remember that even in a Pyrenean

[1] op. cit., p. 181.

monastery beset by floods, Sunday comes round once a week. There is admittedly no mention of Sunday as such, but the break between the two readings from I John caused by the reading from Acts is too striking to be accidental. It is particularly odd that Marguerite shows herself so indifferent to the passage of time, because the Prologue is quite detailed on that score: the travellers arrive at Cauterets on 1 September, stay rather more than three weeks, meet an old monk coming back from his annual visit to Serrance for the feast of the Virgin's Nativity (8 September) and so on; and more to the point, Boccaccio had set a clear example. Already at the end of the Second Day of the *Decameron* the newly elected queen proposes a two-day adjournment, as the next day is Friday, a day of abstinence, and on Saturday many of the ladies have special devotions to offer to the Virgin, so that they in fact resume on Sunday (without hearing mass). Whether from inadvertence or not, Marguerite seems only to have become concerned to mark the passage of time after allowing five days to pass without comment. This lends support to the view that there was a break in composition after the first fifty tales, and that the remainder were put together in a continuous operation.

Though the mass of the Holy Spirit is not indicative in itself of any one liturgical season (if it is just a votive mass), in conjunction with the reading from the beginning of Acts it inevitably recalls Whitsuntide rather than the autumn of the narrative. It is noteworthy that each of the last three Days specifically mentions the Holy Spirit in the introduction, where no such reference occurs earlier. In this connection it is a suggestive coincidence that Marguerite's first visit to Cauterets in September 1546 is agreed to have inspired her Prologue, but that she paid another visit there with her newly remarried daughter in May 1549. She actually wrote a poetic epistle from there dated Ascension Day (30 May) and only just missed spending Whitsun there before returning to Pau in early June. It could well be that the season may have subconsciously been reflected in her resumed work.

Much more important is the Scriptural point. Her selection is not accidental and fits in well with the time available: the sixteen chapters of Romans (the last being largely composed of personal greetings) would provide roughly three chapters for each of the first five readings, and the five chapters of I John with the beginning of Acts (a natural break would be after ch. iii) would similarly occupy the next three. Romans was a favourite with the reformers because of its teaching on faith and works; I John, as Marguerite herself says, provides the key text on Christian love, and the opening chapters of Acts are our principal authority for the teaching on the Holy Spirit and the beginnings of the Church, so that the lessons are entirely appropriate for a group with Evangelical leanings. It can scarcely be doubted that she had by this stage decided on the lessons for the last two Days, and for once conjecture seems reasonably certain. The direction of the previous Days' discussions, the relationships of the characters one to another and their impending return to the world make I Peter the obvious choice. It is the right length (five chapters, like I John) and chapter iii, with its rehearsal of the duties of husbands and wives, is so apposite to their situation that she must have thought of it at once. The Epilogue would probably have woven together the message of the Scripture reading, the stories and their discussion into some final homily on love, sacred and profane.

The consequence of this tardy introduction of a planned programme of Scripture reading, retrospectively applied to the first five Days, is inescapable: the tales and succeeding discussions take on much more of the role of the traditional exemplum, and the rather vague piety and moral lessons of the first half of the book give way to a much closer relationship between religion and the story-telling game. A notable, and rather incongruous, illustration of this is the *De Profundis* said by the monks at the end of the Seventh Day for the lovers of LXX. Whatever Marguerite's initial intentions, the death of François seems to have inspired this change of emphasis. Hircan's last words, on the last extant page, are significant: 'Taisez vous,' he says to his wife; 'encores n'est pas finée la tragédie qui a commencé par rire' (427). M. Telle has pointed out that Oisille's lessons bear fruit: 'Elle est d'ailleurs très écoutée, si l'on en juge par l'attitude de Saffredent, de Hircan, de Simontault, qui à partir de la quatrième journée adoptent le ton édifiant des nouveaux pasteurs évangéliques.'[1] He might have gone on to say that in the light of the evidence we have just considered we should expect their improvement (conversion is perhaps too strong a word) to go on developing to the end. This indeed seems to have been Marguerite's final intention, and is what distinguishes her work from others of superficially similar character.

With this interpretation of her intentions the question of identifying the characters other than herself and her husband becomes acute, for all ten are now seen to be involved in something of a very different nature from what we find in Boccaccio or other models. As M. Jourda says: 'Il ne semble pas que l'exactitude de ces identifications "importe peu" et qu'il suffise de savoir que le petit groupe est formé d'intimes de Marguerite', and 'Nous nous trouvons en présence d'un véritable cénacle . . .; qui sait même si nous n'avons pas affaire à tel ou tel personnage qui fournit à Marguerite, oralement, bon nombre de ces récits?'[2] One can only agree with such views, but, in common with all critics of the past eighty years, he follows Frank's identifications without checking them critically and without Frank's consistency. Frank saw that by identifying Oisille with Louise de Savoie, who died in 1531, he had to make the others members of Marguerite's circle between 1527 (when she married Henri) and 1531, for otherwise the cenacle would include at least one ghostly member. His position is admirably clear: 'Ainsi, il faut voir dans les *devisants* de l'*Heptaméron* . . . des commensaux, des compagnons du même foyer et de la même heure',[3] and he thinks that she simply added the recent Pyrenean décor of the Prologue to her memories of happier days, 'rêvant ainsi d'immortaliser et l'automne et l'été de sa vie avec la mémoire de ses meilleurs amis et de sa mère si tendrement aimée'.[4] To that end he thinks all the characters are meant to

[1] op. cit., p. 140.
[2] op. cit., vol. II, p. 762.
[3] op. cit., vol. I, p. CLXX.
[4] ibid., p. XLVII.

have the age they would have had about 1530. The great merit of this theory is its consistency; all the others admit that the picture of Louise as Oisille is highly idealized, and, if they advert to the question at all, regard her presence in a cenacle described at the end of Marguerite's life as fictional licence.

The tone of the conversations, and the nature of the relationships within the group, certainly give the impression of a real circle of friends, and since the concept of rivalling the *Decameron* is presumably linked with Marguerite's request to Antoine le Maçon to translate it some time after 1531, it seems on the face of it pointless to make Louise one of the interlocutors. Even in life she can have spent only a few weeks at most with Marguerite and Henri, taking into account the couple's long journeys, Marguerite's confinements and so on, and by 1546 her memory must have been somewhat faded. The tendency must be resisted always to make everything mean something, to discover just how many children Lady Macbeth had, but there is more at stake than amateur detection in this case. The advantages of replacing the defunct Louise by a live one (for the anagram is sound enough) are obvious enough to justify the attempt, and there happens to be a strong candidate: Louise de Daillon, Madame la sénéchale de Poitou, doyenne of Marguerite's household and her constant companion from about 1535 to the end.

Oisille is identified as the oldest of the group, and much is made of her years and infirmity, yet, though a sick woman, Louise de Savoie was only fifty-five when she died, just the age of Marguerite when she began the *Heptaméron*. Louise de Daillon, on the other hand, was at least as old, and perhaps older, and by 1546 would have been about seventy, a very great age for those times. She survived Marguerite, though her date of death is so far unknown, and was an indefatigable story-teller, as her grandson Brantôme amply proves. She is the one person who would beyond all doubt have formed part of any intimate circle around Marguerite. Frank actually considered her as a candidate, but rejected her, largely on the grounds that all the others call her 'Madame', which he thinks would only suit the King's mother. This is to ignore both the respect due to a person of such great age and out-standing character (François Ier is known to have had the highest regard for her) and the conventions of their game, in which rank has no part, as Hircan reminds us at the end of the Prologue. Little is known of her later years, except Marguerite's great affection for her, but death had struck so often at her family, most of the men dying in battle, that she may well have turned to religion in her old age, though no proof is at present available. It is at any rate natural that her age would make the other women regard her as mother (to quote Parlamente's words in the Pro-logue) and lead her to recall the same period as Louise de Savoie would have done if she had lived. Moreover, the comments passed by Oisille on Madame la Régente (Louise de Savoie) after tale LXI would sound misplaced in the mouth of the subject herself.

Acceptance of this identification means that we can regard the book not as set in the fixed and arbitrary past, but as reflecting the changing attitudes of a real group of persons both present in the dialogue and supplying a good many of the tales. Above all it makes possible a much closer relationship between Marguerite's real occupations in her last years and her work, though this is not to deny the strong element of idealization and stylization present in any literary composition written in accordance with established conventions.

It is only too easy to spend a great deal of time on the other identifications, but it is probably best to accept Frank's conclusions, even if some of his alleged anagrams and pseudonyms defy credulity. Geburon, for example, is so unconvincing an anagram of Burye, that if the man in question had not, in fact, been in Marguerite's circle from about 1540 one would be tempted to look for some connection with the important Norman fief of Neubourg, near Evreux, held by the families of Harcourt and Coësme. For the rest, the pattern is logical with one glaring exception: Longarine as the widowed baillive de Caen, Aimée Motier de la Fayette, dame de Longray, Dagoucin as Nicolas Dangu, successively Abbot of Juilly and Saint-Savin, then Bishop of Séez and finally Mende, Ennasuite as Anne de Vivonne, daughter of the sénéchale and mother of Brantôme, Simontault as François de Bourdeilles, her husband, and Geburon as Charles de Coucys, seigneur de Burye and sometime Lieutenant-General in Guyenne, were all members of the same circle in the last years of Marguerite's life, and for the most part for many years before, but the identification of the remaining couple can be proved wrong.

From the very questionable form 'Fidemarcon' or 'Fiedmarcon' Frank evolved the equally questionable anagram Nomerfide, and has been followed, sometimes a little gingerly, by everyone since in identifying the last couple as Françoise de Fimarcon (the usual spelling) and her husband (Saffredent) as Jean Carbon de Montpezat (not, incidentally, a nickname from his dark complexion, but a common family name in that part of the south-west). This involves so many errors that it is worth correcting once and for all. In the first place it is simply not true that this couple were closely linked with Marguerite, who only once or twice refers to Carbon in her letters, usually in a military context. Then his wife was Françoise de Lomagne, whose father and grandfather were seigneurs de Montagnac. The title Fimarcon passed from her great grandfather, Odet de Lomagne-Fimarcon, to his elder son Jacques, who died in 1505, leaving his daughter Anne as sole heir. She married in 1499 Aimery de Narbonne, and henceforth the title Fimarcon passed to that family. If the imperfect anagram still encourages consideration of a Fimarcon, the only reasonable candidate would be Anne's daughter, also Anne, who married in 1535 the famous Jean-Jacques d'Astarac, seigneur de Fontrailles (died 1552), whose son, Bernard, became Jeanne's Lieutenant-General in Béarn, but her claim is slender.[1]

If by analogy with the others one looks for the most prominent member of Marguerite's entourage not so far included in the identifications, choice falls at once on Jean (or Gensane) de Bourbon, vicomte de Lavedan, head of her household and *gouverneur* to Jeanne from 1542, as well as Henri's right-hand man. It is most unlikely that Saffredent is an anagram at all, and it looks like a nick-

[1] See P. Anselme, *Histoire . . . de la Maison de France*, Paris (1726), vol. II, pp. 623, 676.

name from 'safre', which meant variously 'greedy, lively', together with 'dent'. There may be a play on the sound as well as the sense of Lavedan, for heavy drinking is one way of washing one's teeth, but it is prudent to keep one's imagination in check. A corroboration of this theory is to be seen in the fact that Saffredent is the only one, apart from Hircan, to set a story in Pampelona, and his (XXVI) is actually about Gabriel d'Albret, seigneur d'Avesnes, whose aunt, Louise, was Lavedan's grandmother and Henri's great-aunt. Lavedan died in 1549, but we are not told when, and it was probably he, rather than his son and heir by his first marriage, Anne, who is the vicomte de Lavedan in charge of Marguerite's funeral. This in itself indicates how odd it would be if he were not in the circle of narrators.

After losing his first wife, he married secondly Françoise de Silly, daughter of the baillive de Caen (Longarine), and widow of Frédéric de Foix.[1] She stands high on the list of Marguerite's household from her second marriage in 1539, and as her family came from Alençon had been known to Marguerite since she was born. She is a good candidate for Nomerfide, being much the youngest of the group, and it is natural that her first four stories should be set in the west of France where she was brought up. The rather uncharacteristic setting of XLIV at Sedan further confirms this, for Louise d'Albret, sister of the Gabriel just referred to, had married into the Croy family in 1495, and there would be no reason for anyone not in the family to locate such an anecdote so precisely.

The name Nomerfide remains a mystery, but it is only honest to report that it makes an almost exact anagram of I[sabeau] de Fremond, a founder member of Marguerite's Alençon household in 1512 and as demoiselle in 1524 more than half-way up the salary scale. She disappears after 1524, but a Julienne de Fromond (a perfectly feasible variant spelling) appears with a similar salary from 1539, and was by then married to Marguerite's secretary, Guillaume Lesné (or L'Aisné), seigneur de Torchamps (Orne).

[1] ibid., vol. I, pp. 368–9, and vol. VI, p. 213.

The anagram would be unaffected (the initial is the same) and it may well be the same person known under different first names (or even a misreading), but the discovery is probably more intriguing than significant.[1] Everything points to Lavedan, and if Saffredent is meant to be married to Nomerfide (which is not quite certain), Françoise de Silly must be our choice.

In connection with these identifications, no one seems to have considered the significance of the fact that François de Boudeilles (Simontault) made his will in 1546 and his wife is described as a widow in a document of April 1549.[2] Even setting aside Lavedan's death in 1549, one must take this loss into account both in explaining the unfinished state of the *Heptaméron* and the talk of death at the end. It is remarkable that by 1549 all the pseudonymous ladies of the book should have been widowed at least once.

If all these proposals can be accepted, the *Heptaméron* takes on a somewhat different, and much more interesting, aspect. Merely by identifying Oisille with Louise de Daillon one can see the work as originating from real discussions among real people in the 1540s. The project of a French *Decameron* could then well have been sponsored in 1546, perhaps at Cauterets, by the very group behind the pseudonyms. Marguerite almost certainly began by extracting a certain number of stories from her friends, with promises of more, and Gruget's alternatives suggest that some contributed more than their bare quota. Then, after François's death, and perhaps about the time of Jeanne's second marriage, she went back to the work, this time clearly intent on introducing a religious pattern, and making the time scheme explicit. The death of Bourdeilles, separation from her husband and daughter in July 1549, her own failing health, would explain why she manipulated the rules to give Parlamente a second Day to begin (and motivated this change by giving Saffredent the previous Day). References to recent events, and to Béarn for the first time, in the

---

[1] For details of Marguerite's household see H. la Ferrière-Percy, *M. d'Angoulême, son livre de dépenses*, Paris (1862), and A. Lefranc et J. Boulenger, *Comptes de Louise de Savoie* . . ., Paris (1905).

[2] L. Lalanne, *Brantôme, Vie et Ecrits*, Paris (1896), p. 7.

concluding Days, the exceptional choice of a written source for LXX, the unusually high proportion of tales in which she plays a part, all suggest that she was hurrying to finish as much as she could in the absence of some of her friends and with limited material up to a short time before her death. Except for Nomerfide's announced but missing story at the end, it seems most unlikely that she had completed more than has come down to us, though it is perfectly possible that odd stories, without linking narrative, may yet turn up. In any case few of the original company survived to see the first printed edition of 1559, and there can have been little incentive for anyone else to complete it.

What the pilgrims said and did at the martyr's shrine in Canterbury, what Parlamente and her companions said and did as they crossed the repaired bridge on their way home, is a mystery as impenetrable as the song the sirens sang. Perhaps, however, closer study of the *Heptaméron*, especially the last twenty-two tales, on the lines set forth in these pages may yet bring a clearer understanding of a remarkable, and perhaps unique, document which is very much more than a literary exercise.

A. J. Krailsheimer

The Amorous Tribute: Baudelaire and
the Renaissance Tradition

Je veux te raconter, ô molle enchanteresse!
Les diverses beautés qui parent ta jeunesse . . .
(Le Beau navire)

➤➤➤ ➤➤➤ ➤➤➤ ➤➤➤ ➤➤➤ ➤➤➤ ➤➤➤ ➤➤➤ ➤➤➤ ➤➤➤ ➤➤➤ ⬅⬅⬅ ⬅⬅⬅ ⬅⬅⬅ ⬅⬅⬅ ⬅⬅⬅ ⬅⬅⬅ ⬅⬅⬅ ⬅⬅⬅ ⬅⬅⬅ ⬅⬅⬅ ⬅⬅⬅

THE SIMPLEST way of writing a love poem to a lady is to particularize, admiringly, her charms. This highly traditional form of
tribute may be either comprehensive or selective; in the latter
case it may, as in the *blasons anatomiques* of certain sixteenth-century French poets, be narrowed down to an obsessive fetishism.[1]
Or again, the tribute to the lady's physical beauties may be linked
to the celebration (more frequently, the idealization) of her moral
qualities, her qualities of mind and heart; the mode then becomes
Petrarchan.[2] All these variations on a theme which, in its truly
formalized sense, dates only from the Renaissance, are to be found
in Baudelaire's love poems – but adapted, and in some cases transformed, to fit the exigencies of a 'modern' lover: complex,
sophisticated, self-doubting, often perverse.

Perhaps the most complete example of the genre is *Le Beau
navire*. Here, from the outset, Baudelaire declares his intention of

---

[1] See in this connection – as also for an excellent discussion of the *blason* genre in
general – the recent book by D. B. Wilson, *Descriptive Poetry in France from blason to
baroque*, Manchester University Press (1967), pp. 6–99.
[2] Cf., for examples (taken from Petrarch himself as from his French disciples) of
both 'moral' and 'physical' types of portrait, M. Piéri, *Pétrarque et Ronsard, ou de
l'influence de Pétrarque sur la Pléiade française*, Marseilles (1896), pp. 109–19.

describing the varied beauties of his mistress (Marie Daubrun, in this instance):

> *Je veux te raconter, ô molle enchanteresse!*
> *Les diverses beautés qui parent ta jeunesse;*
> *Je veux te peindre ta beauté,*
> *Où l'enfance s'allie à la maturité.*[1]

The effect of a rounded picture of the lady's (rounded) charms, is enhanced by the devices of repetition on which Baudelaire draws. Thus each of the first three stanzas is repeated at different points of the poem. The opening stanza recurs as the fourth, and this, after two intermediate verses evoking the grace of her carriage and head movements, has the effect of recalling to the reader's mind the idea of a *diversity* of charms – as if to whet his appetite for those still to be described. So, too, with the second quatrain of the poem:

> *Quand tu vas balayant l'air de ta jupe large,*
> *Tu fais l'effet d'un beau vaisseau qui prend le large,*
> *Chargé de toile, et va roulant*
> *Suivant un rythme doux, et paresseux, et lent.*

When these lines reappear towards the end of the poem their image of the girl's indolent, majestic gait (the title-metaphor of the fine ship putting out with full canvas to sea) leads by a natural transition into a line conveying the bold movement of the 'nobles jambes' beneath the wide, flounced skirt. The third stanza, finally, is repeated at the very end of the poem; the line 'Tu passes ton

---

[1] For a specific analogy of some interest, with a Renaissance poem of 'amorous tribute', cf. these lines with which Ronsard, for his part, opens his *Élégie à Janet, Peintre du Roy*; one must, of course, allow here for the difference of context (the 'portrait' is presumed to be entrusted to a painter-friend, rather than undertaken directly by the poet himself): 'Pein moy, Janet, pein moy, je te supplie,/Sur ce tableau les beautez de m'amie/De la façon que je te les diray' (*Œuvres complètes*, ed. G. Cohen, Pléiade [1965], vol. I, p. 105). All verse citations from Baudelaire, be it here noted, are to the 1861 edition of *Les Fleurs du Mal*, as reproduced by J. Crépet and G. Blin, Paris, Corti [1950] (hereafter abbreviated: *FMCB*); prose texts, unless otherwise stated, are quoted from the appropriate volume of the *Œuvres complètes*, Paris, Conard (ed. J. Crépet).

chemin, majestueuse enfant', now perfectly sets the seal on the whole tribute, leaving us with the reminder both of the girl's physical grace, as she glides her way from our view, and of that curious fusion within her, so attractive to her poet, of the child-like and the mature:

> *Sur ton cou large et rond, sur tes épaules grasses,*
> *Ta tête se pavane avec d'étranges grâces;*
> *D'un air placide et triomphant*
> *Tu passes ton chemin, majestueuse enfant.*

As for the other, unrepeated stanzas, these strike an altogether more intimate note. The opulent splendour of Marie's breasts is conveyed through the audacious metaphor (not without its touch of absurdity) of the 'belle armoire', with its rounded 'panels' (likened in their turn to bucklers drawing fire upon themselves), its rich store of 'good things' hinting at deeper 'intoxications' of both mind and heart. The atmosphere of complicity established in these two verses (the fourth and fifth of the poem) is deepened when, a little later, the poet comes to speak of Marie's 'noble legs', and the obscure desires they stir as they move beneath the flinging skirts – a notion markedly weakened, it is true, by the incongruity of the ensuing simile, with its two *witches* busily mixing their 'dark potion' within a tall jar. The final 'beauty' described is that of Marie's splendidly robust arms, with their renewed suggestion of amorous invitation and promise; after which, having with singular felicity fulfilled his declared 'programme': to portray his lady in all the diversity of her charms, Baudelaire returns us, as I have said, to the image of the third quatrain, with its 'majestueuse enfant' pursuing her relaxed and graceful progress through the reader's mind. Here is the complete text, repetitions and all:

> *Je veux te raconter, ô molle enchanteresse!*
> *Les diverses beautés qui parent ta jeunesse;*
> *Je veux te peindre ta beauté,*
> *Où l'enfance s'allie à la maturité.*

Quand tu vas balayant l'air de ta jupe large,
Tu fais l'effet d'un beau vaisseau qui prend le large,
        Chargé de toile, et va roulant
Suivant un rythme doux, et paresseux, et lent.

Sur ton cou large et rond, sur tes épaules grasses,
Ta tête se pavane avec d'étranges grâces;
        D'un air placide et triomphant
Tu passes ton chemin, majestueuse enfant.

Je veux te raconter, ô molle enchanteresse!
Les diverses beautés qui parent ta jeunesse;
        Je veux te peindre ta beauté,
Où l'enfance s'allie à la maturité.

Ta gorge qui s'avance et qui pousse la moire,
Ta gorge triomphante est une belle armoire
        Dont les panneaux bombés et clairs
Comme les boucliers accrochent des éclairs;

Boucliers provoquants, armés de pointes roses!
Armoire à doux secrets, pleine de bonnes choses,
        De vins, de parfums, de liqueurs
Qui feraient délirer les cerveaux et les cœurs!

Quand tu vas balayant l'air de ta jupe large,
Tu fais l'effet d'un beau vaisseau qui prend le large,
        Chargé de toile, et va roulant
Suivant un rythme doux, et paresseux, et lent.

Tes nobles jambes, sous les volants qu'elles chassent,
Tourmentent les désirs obscurs et les agacent,
        Comme deux sorcières qui font
Tourner un philtre noir dans un vase profond.

Tes bras, qui se joueraient des précoces hercules,
Sont des boas luisants les solides émules,
        Faits pour serrer obstinément,
Comme pour l'imprimer dans ton cœur, ton amant.

Sur ton cou large et rond, sur tes épaules grasses,
Ta tête se pavane avec d'étranges grâces;
    D'un air placide et triomphant
Tu passes ton chemin, majestueuse enfant.

Taken as a whole, *Le Beau navire* seems to me something of a *tour de force*, in that it persuades the reader, cajoles him almost, into acquiescing in the poet's entranced and resolute delineation of a type of beauty which in truth verges perilously – in his description at least – on the bizarre; the obsessional fascination exerted on Baudelaire's imagination by the idea of a massive, even gigantic, feminine figure, has here found a yet further outlet.[1] Perhaps the poem owes its success less to the particular images Baudelaire has chosen for his 'catalogue' of Marie's charms than to the pleasingly hypnotic effects of repetition (the repeated verses, the words 'beau', 'belle', 'beauté', imprinting themselves throughout the poem, like a refrain, upon the reader's mind), and to the strongly rhythmical character – so appropriate in a poem which displays its subject always in movement – imparted by the unusual verse-structure: the short, eight-syllabled third line, interrupting and accentuating, by its rapid 'bounce', the measured alexandrine tread of the other three lines of the quatrain.

The metaphor of the fine ship riding the waves reappears in *Le Serpent qui danse*, but in a very different context, and applied to a very different type of beauty: that of Jeanne Duval. As in *Le Beau navire*, the ship image serves to render the particular grace and individuality of the woman's movement – but is here complementary to a whole sequence of descriptive images. The first (announced in the title, but introduced only in the second part of the poem) is of the snake coiling itself, in a sort of dance, around the snake-charmer's stick:

A te voir marcher en cadence,
    Belle d'abandon,

[1] Cf. *La Géante*, passim; *Rêve parisien*, L. 23–4; *L'Idéal*, L. 12–14; *Hymne à la Beauté*, L. 22. For a general comment on B.'s 'gigantisme', in the context of two passages from the *Salon de 1859*, see my article, 'Baudelaire et Kendall', *Revue de litt. comp.*, XXX, 1956, p. 62 and n. 3.

> *On dirait un serpent qui danse*
> *Au bout d'un bâton.*
>
> *Sous le fardeau de ta paresse*
> *Ta tête d'enfant*
> *Se balance avec la mollesse*
> *D'un jeune éléphant,*
>
> *Et ton corps se penche et s'allonge*
> *Comme un fin vaisseau*
> *Qui roule bord sur bord et plonge*
> *Ses vergues dans l'eau.*

'A young elephant'! Only a Baudelaire, perhaps, could convert so apparently unflattering an image into a compliment. . . . But there is already a hint of this strange, quasi-elephantine grace in the poem's opening invocation to the 'chère indolente', which in turn launches the successive tributes to her glittering skin, her dark, luxuriant hair, her cold, jewel-like eyes:

> *Que j'aime voir, chère indolente,*
> *De ton corps si beau,*
> *Comme une étoffe vacillante,*
> *Miroiter la peau!*
>
> *Sur ta chevelure profonde*
> *Aux âcres parfums,*
> *Mer odorante et vagabonde*
> *Aux flots bleus et bruns,*
>
> *Comme un navire qui s'éveille*
> *Au vent du matin,*
> *Mon âme rêveuse appareille*
> *Pour un ciel lointain.*
>
> *Tes yeux, où rien ne se révèle*
> *De doux ni d'amer,*
> *Sont deux bijoux froids où se mêle*
> *L'or avec le fer.*

In the second and third verses, as will be seen, the ship image is applied to the poet himself: it becomes his own vagrant mind, borne away, as if in the freshness of the morning wind, upon the deep and fragrant 'sea' of Jeanne's hair. We encounter here a distinctive feature of Baudelaire's love poetry; the tribute not only to the sensuous but to the *imaginative* potency of the lady's charms – to their capacity to set his imagination in train, to open up limitless vistas in his mind.[1] A similar, if more immediately sensual, expansion of descriptive detail is brought by the final two verses:

> *Comme un flot grossi par la fonte*
> *Des glaciers grondants,*
> *Quand l'eau de ta bouche remonte*
> *Au bord de tes dents,*

> *Je crois boire un vin de Bohême,*
> *Amer et vainqueur,*
> *Un ciel liquide qui parsème*
> *D'étoiles mon coeur!*

While the initial image here, with its incongruous 'glaciers', may not perhaps be of the happiest, the concluding six lines seem to me uniquely memorable – combining, as they do, the vibrant overtones (both sensual and emotive) of the 'liquid sky' scattering the poet's heart with stars, with the sophisticated eroticism of the actual immediate sensation, the taste and wine-like tang of Jeanne's 'conquering' saliva.

In the curiously named *Chanson d'après-midi* (dedicatee unknown), the note of homage and submission, the implicit characterization not only of the woman but of her lover also, are at least as important as the element of pure description. Together with the physical portrait of this strange 'sorceress', with her seductive eyes, her 'wicked' eyebrows, her dark hair with its wild fragrance of desert or forest, her subtly perfumed skin, her languorous and

---

[1] Cf. in this respect my concluding remarks, p. 116, below, concerning the wider role of perfume in Baudelaire's love poetry.

harmonious poses, her silken feet – together with all this, there goes a fuller characterization, no less effective for being suggested only: the capricious frivolity, the alternate moods of gentleness and of 'mysterious' fury, the mocking laughter, the whole vision of abundant warmth, colour and light, irrupting into the Siberian gloom of the poet's mind and compelling his fervent and grateful adoration:

Tes hanches sont amoureuses
De ton dos et de tes seins,
Et tu ravis les coussins
Par tes poses langoureuses.

Quelquefois, pour apaiser
Ta rage mystérieuse,
Tu prodigues, sérieuse,
La morsure et le baiser;

Tu me déchires, ma brune,
Avec un rire moqueur,
Et puis tu mets sur mon cœur
Ton œil doux comme la lune.

Sous tes souliers de satin,
Sous tes charmants pieds de soie,
Moi, je mets ma grande joie,
Mon génie et mon destin,

Mon âme par toi guérie,
Par toi, lumière et couleur!
Explosion de chaleur
Dans ma noire Sibérie!

A final poem giving a 'total' impression of the beloved, *Les Bijoux*, is cast in a very different register. The woman is seen here naked, and in repose: the poet's mood, as he watches her, is one of corresponding, if provisional, passivity. Indeed, the whole description has a curiously static, almost immobile quality, suggesting the techniques of a painter and contrasting strongly with the rapid, 'cinematic' presentation of the loved one in movement, of the three poems previously discussed in this chapter. This 'plastic' quality in the poem should not, I think, be exaggerated; those who have spoken in this context of a suspension or banishment of sensuality have surely ignored the whole tone and implication of the middle stanzas, with their suggestion of a deferred yet expectant amorous fervour.[1] It seems none the less true that in the tranquil retrospect of poetic creation Baudelaire has here viewed his *maja desnuda* above all as an 'art object',[2] summoned up from a moment of the past which had given deep aesthetic as well as sensual satisfaction:

> *La très-chère était nue, et, connaissant mon coeur,*
> *Elle n'avait gardé que ses bijoux sonores,*
> *Dont le riche attirail lui donnait l'air vainqueur*
> *Qu'ont dans leurs jours heureux les esclaves des Mores.*

> *Quand il jette en dansant son bruit vif et moqueur,*
> *Ce monde rayonnant de métal et de pierre*
> *Me ravit en extase, et j'aime à la fureur*
> *Les choses où le son se mêle à la lumière.*

> *Elle était donc couchée et se laissait aimer,*
> *Et du haut du divan elle souriait d'aise*
> *A mon amour profond et doux comme la mer,*
> *Qui vers elle montait comme vers sa falaise.*

[1] Cf. J. Prévost, *Baudelaire*, Paris, Mercure de France (1953), pp. 253, 344–5; M. A. Ruff, *L'esprit du mal et l'esthétique baudelairienne*, Paris, Colin (1955), p. 297. The additional final verse (exact text unknown) which Baudelaire wrote into an autographed copy of *Les Fleurs du Mal*, and in which he reputedly stressed his predominantly 'plastic' intention, may well have been designed as a reassurance to the perhaps prudish recipient, one Saint-Valry; see *Œuvres complètes*, ed. F. Gautier and Y. G. Le Dantec, vol. II, *Les Fleurs du Mal. Documents – Variantes – Bibliographie*, Paris (1934), p. 373.

[2] Baudelaire's own analogy, of course, is with Correggio's *Antiope* rather than with Goya's *Maja*; cf., however, his later and enthusiastic description of the latter painting (or rather, more strictly, of a 'réplique en format réduit' of the Prado original) in a letter to Nadar of May 1859 (*Corresp. gén.*, vol. II, pp. 310–11; P. Guinard, 'Baudelaire, le Musée espagnol et Goya', *RHLF*, LXVII, 1967, p. 327).

Les yeux fixés sur moi, comme un tigre dompté,
D'un air vague et rêveur elle essayait des poses,
Et la candeur unie à la lubricité
Donnait un charme neuf à ses métamorphoses;

Et son bras et sa jambe, et sa cuisse et ses reins,
Polis comme de l'huile, onduleux comme un cygne,
Passaient devant mes yeux clairvoyants et sereins;
Et son ventre et ses seins, ces grappes de ma vigne,

S'avançaient, plus câlins que les Anges du mal,
Pour troubler le repos où mon âme était mise,
Et pour la déranger du rocher de cristal
Où, calme et solitaire, elle s'était assise.

Je croyais voir unis par un nouveau dessin
Les hanches de l'Antiope au buste d'un imberbe,
Tant sa taille faissait ressortir son bassin.
Sur ce teint fauve et brun, le fard était superbe!

– Et la lampe s'étant résignée à mourir,
Comme le foyer seul illuminait la chambre,
Chaque fois qu'il poussait un flamboyant soupir,
Il inondait de sang cette peau couleur d'ambre!

The 'jewels' of the opening two verses (and of the title) lend from the outset an appropriate richness of colour and sound, their 'music' adding as it were a second dimension to the poetic portrait which now assembles before us, as we follow the entranced movement of the poet's gaze, and share the rapt 'calmness' with which he contemplates the woman lying before him: the polished undulation of the limbs; the insidious 'advance' of the belly and breasts; the subtle balance of proportion between bust and hips, pelvis and waist; the colour harmonies of the amber skin, heightened by rouge and deepened to blood-red by the sudden glow of the fire. The studied, 'painterly' composition of this extraordinary and beautiful poem is nowhere better shown than in its final touch, whereby the very background against which the portrait is set (the firelight playing fitfully over the darkened room) is made not merely to harmonize (as in our next poem, *Le Cadre*) with the woman's beauty but to blend into and transform it.

Before passing to more specialized forms of homage, I must mention two poems in which the tribute, though still comprehensive in scope, has a certain distinguishing remoteness. *Le Cadre* is the third of a sequence of four decasyllabic sonnets, *Un Fantôme*, in which the poet, imagining himself to be visited in his loneliness by the memory, or 'phantom', of Jeanne, compares her past beauty to her present sad decrepitude. *Le Cadre* itself is wholly retrospective in its theme: Baudelaire seeks to capture here not merely the sensuous immediacy of Jeanne's former beauty (as in *Les Bijoux*, with its similar pose and setting: Jeanne in her nakedness, among the jewels and furnishings that so enhance her charms) but rather, by some searching analogy, its whole secret and essence:

> Comme un beau cadre ajoute à la peinture,
> Bien qu'elle soit d'un pinceau très-vanté,
> Je ne sais quoi d'étrange et d'enchanté
> En l'isolant de l'immense nature,
>
> Ainsi bijoux, meubles, métaux, dorure,
> S'adaptaient juste à sa rare beauté;
> Rien n'offusquait sa parfaite clarté,
> Et tout semblait lui servir de bordure.
>
> Même on eût dit parfois qu'elle croyait
> Que tout voulait l'aimer; elle noyait
> Sa nudité voluptueusement
>
> Dans les baisers du satin et du linge,
> Et lente ou brusque, à chaque mouvement
> Montrait la grâce enfantine du singe.

The 'frame' within which Baudelaire here places Jeanne does more than merely complement, or set off, her beauty; as in the case of the real painting (and Baudelaire speaks here from the mature and speculative connoisseurship of his final period), it confers a certain enchanted *separateness* from the external world, wherein to contain and concentrate elements of beauty that might otherwise flow away or disperse. In the tercets, this metaphor is varied by others less subtle but more vivid: Jeanne's body (a body 'childlike' not only in the simian litheness of its movements, but in its whole artless, almost rapturous self-delight) now blends amorously into its setting, moulds itself 'voluptuously' to the 'kisses' of satin and linen, with a fluid grace that calls to mind the 'liquefaction' and 'brave vibration' of silks, of Herrick's Julia.

The remoteness' of *Tout entière* is of a different order: not that of retrospection, but of a generality which studiedly disclaims all detail or preciseness of description. Ingeniously renewing a traditional amorous conceit,[1] Baudelaire here praises his lady's beauty by refusing, paradoxically, to describe it – on the grounds that to particularize in any way would be to disrupt the perfect harmony of the whole:

> *Le Démon, dans ma chambre haute,*
> *Ce matin est venu me voir,*
> *Et, tâchant à me prendre en faute,*
> *Me dit: 'Je voudrais bien savoir,*
>
> *Parmi toutes les belles choses*
> *Dont est fait son enchantement,*
> *Parmi les objets noirs ou roses*
> *Qui composent son corps charmant,*
>
> *Quel est le plus doux.' – O mon âme!*
> *Tu répondis à l'Abhorré:*
> *'Puisqu'en Elle tout est dictame,*
> *Rien ne peut être préféré.*
>
> *Lorsque tout me ravit, j'ignore*
> *Si quelque chose me séduit.*
> *Elle éblouit comme l'Aurore*
> *Et console comme la Nuit;*

[1] Cf. the examples from Petrarch, Malherbe, etc., cit. *FMCB*, p. 366.

> *Et l'harmonie est trop exquise,*
> *Qui gouverne tout son beau corps,*
> *Pour que l'impuissante analyse*
> *En note les nombreux accords.*
>
> *O métamorphose mystique*
> *De tous mes sens fondus en un!*
> *Son haleine fait la musique,*
> *Comme sa voix fait le parfum!'*

Baudelaire's enrolment of the Devil, as the tempter who incites him to the 'sin' of particularization, lends to the poem a special Platonic (or quasi-Platonic) refinement. We must not, of course, be misled into regarding this Devil as the agent of a real temptation: the poet is not really holding Satan at bay, he is using him as a pretext for amorous hyperbole. What raises the poem above the conventions of this genre, is the singular felicity of the concluding image, whereby the poet first synthesizes the lady's physical charms into a 'harmony' so exquisite as to resist analysis into its component 'chords', and then goes on to relate this harmony to the mysterious fusion into one of all the poet's senses: sound (the music of her voice) apprehended as perfume, perfume (the fragrance of her breath) transmuted into sound. Since this poem was ultimately dedicated to Mme Sabatier (which is not to say that it was originally conceived for her), it is piquant to set beside it the one 'Sabatier poem', *A Celle qui est trop gaie*, which furnishes some detailed description of her person, and thus effectively contravenes the prohibitions of *Tout entière*. In *A Celle qui est trop gaie*, the poet's initial enchantment with Mme Sabatier's charms quickly turns to a perverse anger: her radiant gaiety now seems an insult or humiliation, inviting in retaliation brutal fantasies of 'punishment'. Here, if anywhere, is the true Satanic impulse: the urge to destroy or mar physically (even if only in imagination) a beauty so intolerably exuberant that it seems to *compel* some act of crude violation.[1]

---

[1] I have chosen in this article to leave altogether out of account two poems of Baudelaire's final period, *Les Promesses d'un visage* and *Le Monstre ou le Paranymphe d'une nymphe*

Tout entière is, of course, exceptional in its refusal to particularize; the temptation to do so is after all one to which the love poet, almost by definition, constantly yields. He is not, however, obliged to see these particulars solely in their relation to the whole (as might a painter doing a full-length portrait); he may choose, instead, to focus his gaze upon particular features, or even upon a single feature (and here the analogy is rather with the portrait 'head' or 'bust', or with the 'detail' reproduced from a larger painting).[1] Thus the three quatrains of *Les Yeux de Berthe* are entirely given up to the evocation of the spell cast on the poet by the wide, dark eyes of his 'child':

> *Vous pouvez mépriser les yeux les plus célèbres,*
> *Beaux yeux de mon enfant, par où filtre et s'enfuit*
> *Je ne sais quoi de bon, de doux comme la Nuit!*
> *Beaux yeux, versez sur moi vos charmantes ténèbres!*

> *Grands yeux de mon enfant, arcanes adorés,*
> *Vous ressemblez beaucoup à ces grottes magiques*
> *Où, derrière l'amas des ombres léthargiques,*
> *Scintillent vaguement des trésors ignorés!*

> *Mon enfant a des yeux obscurs, profonds et vastes,*
> *Comme toi, Nuit immense, éclairés comme toi!*
> *Leurs feux sont ces pensers d'Amour, mêlés de Foi,*
> *Qui pétillent au fond, voluptueux ou chastes.*

The tone, it will be noted, is one of humble yet 'paternal' devotion. (The original title seems to have been 'Les Yeux de mon enfant',[2] and the poet's recurrent references to his 'child' here

---

macabre, in which the tribute, though similarly comprehensive, goes back to a rather different tradition, sufficiently indicated by the title of the anthology in which the first of the two appeared: *Le Nouveau Parnasse satyrique du XIXᵉ siècle* (1866); see *FMCB*, pp. 599–600.

[1] Cf., in this respect, the *blasons anatomiques* aforementioned.

[2] See Prarond, letter to Eug. Crépet, in: Baudelaire, *Œuvres complètes*, Paris, Le Club du meilleur livre (1955), vol. II, p. 1155 and n. 1, and cf., in the Pléiade edition of the *Œuvres complètes*, Paris, Gallimard (1966), pp. 1567–8, the excellent discussion by C. Pichois of the whole question of the poem's dedication.

imply something more than the purely amorous endearment – 'mon enfant, ma sœur' – of *L'Invitation au voyage*.) The poem as a whole is scarcely one of Baudelaire's happier inspirations: the sentiments are conventional and insipid, the phrasing at times perfunctory ('les yeux les plus célèbres', 'vous ressemblez beaucoup'); however, the sense of mysterious expansiveness is conveyed effectively enough through the 'strategic' placing of such favoured epithets as 'profonds', 'vastes', 'vaguement', as also through the elemental, almost primitive appeal of images of dark caverns and hidden treasure.

A sonnet dedicated to Jeanne, *Avec ses vêtements ondoyants et nacrés*, singles out with rather more felicity two beauties of her person. In the first quatrain her extraordinary grace of carriage is once again conveyed through the simile of the 'dancing' snake; but here the image is given a new dimension, and the 'cadenced', serpentine movement becomes the outward translation of an inner disposition, the symptom of an indifference and insensibility likened to those of certain forces of nature – the desert sand and sky, the long surge of the sea – that similarly unfold into the distance without heed of human suffering:

> *Avec ses vêtements ondoyants et nacrés,*
> *Même quand elle marche on croirait qu'elle danse,*
> *Comme ces longs serpents que les jongleurs sacrés*
> *Au bout de leurs bâtons agitent en cadence.*
>
> *Comme le sable morne et l'azur des déserts,*
> *Insensibles tous deux à l'humaine souffrance,*
> *Comme les longs réseaux de la houle des mers,*
> *Elle se développe avec indifférence.*

The tercets pursue a stage further this moral interpretation of Jeanne's physical attributes: what the poet has discerned already in the measured rhythms of her stride, he next reads into the cold, unrevealing eyes that equally stared out at us from a verse of *Le Serpent qui danse*. As in that poem, the image they suggest, with their hard, polished glitter and changing glints, is that of jewels or metals: there, iron and gold; here, steel, diamonds, 'charming' minerals of all kinds – these in turn becoming the perfect and symbolic expression of Jeanne's whole strange nature, with its blend of cold aloofness, calm inscrutability and 'sterile' majesty:

> *Ses yeux polis sont faits de minéraux charmants,*
> *Et dans cette nature étrange et symbolique*
> *Où l'ange inviolé se mêle au sphinx antique,*
>
> *Où tout n'est qu'or, acier, lumière et diamants,*
> *Resplendit à jamais, comme un astre inutile,*
> *La froide majesté de la femme stérile.*

The poet's tribute, in this sonnet, has a certain, entirely modern 'ambiguity'. He does not condemn Jeanne's cold remoteness; on the contrary, inasmuch as it is the psychological extension of certain physical qualities he admires, it constitutes even a potent ingredient of her charm. Yet the final line of the poem, and the final word especially, with its due emphasis: 'La froide majesté de la femme *stérile*', hold more than a hint of moral judgement, too – as if in recognition of the essential perversity of an admiration compelled by the very qualities that resist and frustrate it. A similar but stronger sense of compulsion, informs *Le Poison*:

> *Le vin sait revêtir le plus sordide bouge*
>   *D'un luxe miraculeux,*
> *Et fait surgir plus d'un portique fabuleux*
>   *Dans l'or de sa vapeur rouge,*
> *Comme un soleil couchant dans un ciel nébuleux.*
>
> *L'opium agrandit ce qui n'a pas de bornes,*
>   *Allonge l'illimité,*
> *Approfondit le temps, creuse la volupté,*
>   *Et de plaisirs noirs et mornes*
> *Remplit l'âme au delà de sa capacité.*
>
> *Tout cela ne vaut pas le poison qui découle*
>   *De tes yeux, de tes yeux verts,*
> *Lacs où mon âme tremble et se voit à l'envers . . .*
>   *Mes songes viennent en foule*
> *Pour se désaltérer à ces gouffres amers.*

> *Tout cela ne vaut pas le terrible prodige*
> *De ta salive qui mord,*
> *Qui plonge dans l'oubli mon âme sans remord,*
> *Et, charriant le vertige,*
> *La roule défaillante aux rives de la mort!*

The structure here follows a conventional Petrarchan pattern of hyperbole, and one that Baudelaire himself repeats in *Le Vin du solitaire:* the twofold eulogy of some beautiful object or keen pleasure, followed by the assertion of the still stronger claims of the real subject of eulogy – usually (as here) the poet's loved one.[1] What is more original is, firstly, the verse-form: three alexandrines broken by two intermediate seven-syllabled lines, giving a certain fitfulness, almost irregularity, of cadence; secondly, the actual terms of the hyperbole, with its successive invocation of the effects of wine, then opium, and finally, surpassing them both, of Marie's eyes as he looks into their bitter-green depths, of her saliva as he tastes the annihilating 'prodigy' of her kisses. (As with most hyperboles, the tribute is conveniently interchangeable from one mistress to another: 'Quand l'eau de ta bouche remonte/Au bord de tes dents,/Je crois boire un vin de Bohême,/Amer et vainqueur,' he had said of Jeanne in *Le Serpent qui danse*, while in *Sed non satiata* her mouth is declared to be an 'elixir' surpassing opium or the choicest of wines: 'Je préfère au constance, à l'opium, au nuits/L'elixir de ta bouche où l'amour se pavane . . .')[2] But the whole poem *Le Poison* seems to me particularly characteristic of Baudelaire, both in its amorous psychology, and its insight into the differing imaginative properties of certain intoxicants: wine, with its benign transmutation of reality (visionary porticoes, dreams of magnificence and luxury rising up within the most sordid hovel);

---

[1] Cf., among earlier examples, those cited in *FMCB*, p. 381: Ronsard, Voltaire, the Psalmist, as well as Petrarch.
[2] 'Nuits', of course, is a burgundy wine; 'constance' hails from the Cape – still more exotic than the 'Bohemian' vintage of *Le Serpent qui danse* . . . See J. Mouquet, 'Baudelaire, le Constance et l'Invitation au voyage', *Mercure de France*, CCL, no. 857 (1 March 1934), pp. 305–6.

opium, with its deep amplification of space and time, its expansion beyond what seem the 'possible' limits of ordinary experience. Yet all such 'charms' dwindle (he goes on to claim) beside the spell cast on him by Marie's eyes – those solacing lakes of green 'poison' in which he sees the inverted mirror-image not only of his face but of his mind, as if glimpsing the visual counterpart of his own bitterness and despair. It must be said that Baudelaire, as he bends in fascinated recollection towards these eyes and in retrospect seeks images that will convey the intensity of his feeling, trembles perilously on the brink of absurdity – if indeed he does not topple over into its 'gouffres amers' . . . (The forger of poetic conceits engages equally, in his fashion, in a kind of hazardous 'brinkmanship'.)

The ambiguity of attitude latent in *Le Poison* and *Avec ses vêtements ondoyants et nacrés* becomes explicit in the poem which, in both the 1857 and 1861 editions of *Les Fleurs du Mal*, follows immediately upon *Le Poison*. To convey the strangeness of Jeanne's nature in *Avec ses vêtements . . .*, Baudelaire had drawn on the image of the 'sphinx antique'; in *Ciel brouillé* he confronts the no less baffling enigma presented to him by Marie, as from the elusive, protean quality of her eyes he turns to speculate, half-fearfully, about the future of their relationship:

> *On dirait ton regard d'une vapeur couvert;*
> *Ton œil mystérieux (est-il bleu, gris ou vert?)*
> *Alternativement tendre, rêveur, cruel,*
> *Réfléchit l'indolence et la pâleur du ciel.*
>
> *Tu rappelles ces jours blancs, tièdes et voilés,*
> *Qui font se fondre en pleurs les cœurs ensorcelés,*
> *Quand, agités d'un mal inconnu qui les tord,*
> *Les nerfs trop éveillés raillent l'esprit qui dort.*
>
> *Tu ressembles parfois à ces beaux horizons*
> *Qu'allument les soleils des brumeuses saisons . . .*
> *Comme tu resplendis, paysage mouillé*
> *Qu'enflamment les rayons tombant d'un ciel brouillé!*

O femme dangereuse, ô séduisants climats!
Adorerai-je aussi ta neige et vos frimas,
Et saurai-je tirer de l'implacable hiver
Des plaisirs plus aigus que la glace et le fer?

The progression of ideas and images in these two quatrains is subtle and repays careful analysis. Into the shifting tints of Marie's eyes Baudelaire reads (in the one clumsy line of the poem, with its laboured 'alternativement' – a whole hemistich to one adverb!) an exactly corresponding symbolism of changing moods: blue for tenderness, grey for reverie, green for cruelty. But these alternations of colour, together with the curious, 'misted' quality of Marie's glance, suggest also some pallid sky with its lazy, slow-moving clouds. This analogy leads, in turn, into the metaphoric landscape which is the crux of the poem: an 'âme-paysage' whereby – reversing, as elsewhere in Baudelaire, the *paysage d'âme* of Romantic tradition – scene and climate are evoked as the equivalent of a temperament or mood. The mood, in the second verse, is in truth that of Baudelaire himself rather than of Marie: this mysterious 'illness', this autumnal neurosis which on days of warm, veiled whiteness mocks with its tensions the apathy of the mind and dissolves vulnerable sensibilities into tears, is none other than the endemic 'spleen' diagnosed in certain other, more purely self-descriptive poems.[1] But the next verse brings us back to Marie, and to the autumn vistas she suggests: misted suns glancing down through blurred skies and lighting up the humid distances below. Although Baudelaire may here speak of 'resemblance', there is, in fact, no exact comparison such as he makes in *L'Invitation au voyage*, where these same blurred skies and suns are directly related to Marie's 'treacherous eyes', as they shine through her tears; here, in this autumn landscape, what we are offered, rather, is a parallel image of beauty – though one first evoked in Baudelaire's mind, it is true, by these same eyes with their strange, veiled glitter. The last verse of all, if it is not to be

[1] e.g. *De Profundis clamavi, La Cloche fêlée, Spleen* [II] (*J'ai plus de souvenirs que si j'avais mille ans . . .*), *Spleen* [III] (*Je suis comme le roi d'un pays pluvieux . . .*), *Spleen* [IV] (*Quand le ciel bas et lourd pèse comme un couvercle . . .*).

misunderstood, must be seen as a prolongation of the preceding
'seasonal' imagery. The charms of Marie hold the same ambiguity
as those of autumn: they are at once seductive and threatening –
seductive in themselves, threatening because of the doubts, fears
even, as to what is still to come. To surrender to autumn is to
accept also the winter it implacably heralds: to surrender to
Marie's autumnal beauty is to accept – what? It may be, as he
passes on to this further, and ultimate, season of their love, that
from her 'snows' (the word is chosen to match exactly the transformation into frost of the real 'climates' of autumn: '*ta* neige et
vos frimas') he will draw pleasures keener even than ice or cold
steel. Yet these, significantly, are images less of pleasure than of
pain; and the poem ends, broodingly, on its still unanswered
question. . . .

With the exception of *Les Bijoux* – which draws for its rapt contemplation of the 'très-chère' on the recollection of a privileged
moment of deep intimacy – the poems discussed thus far have
held a certain timeless quality: the beauty they pay tribute to is
seen as if in its essential permanency. A final poem, *Le Possédé*,
affords a less intimate and at the same time more immediate and
circumstantial portrait. The woman (Jeanne?) is here seen,
through Baudelaire's eyes, at two contrasted moments and in two
contrasted (but for him equally irresistible) attitudes. The tone,
indeed, is of wholly indulgent, almost abject homage: whether her
mood be remote and taciturn, closed 'morbidly' in upon itself as
she drowses or smokes, or whether it be of petulant release as she
flaunts herself amid the hectic gaiety of some dance-hall – in
either guise, she still has power to command the admiration,
submission and adoration of her infatuated, her utterly 'possessed'
lover:

> Le soleil s'est couvert d'un crêpe. Comme lui
> O Lune de ma vie! emmitoufle-toi d'ombre;
> Dors ou fume à ton gré; sois muette, sois sombre,
> Et plonge tout entière au gouffre de l'Ennui;
>
> Je t'aime ainsi! Pourtant, si tu veux aujourd'hui,

112

Comme un astre éclipsé qui sort de la pénombre,
Te pavaner, aux lieux que la Folie encombre,
C'est bien! Charmant poignard, jaillis de ton étui!

Allume ta prunelle à la flamme des lustres!
Allume le désir dans le regard des rustres!
Tout de toi m'est plaisir, morbide ou pétulant;

Sois ce que tu voudras, nuit noire, rouge aurore;
Il n'est pas une fibre en tout mon corps tremblant
Qui ne crie: O mon cher Belzébuth, je t'adore!

This sonnet owes its interest and appeal less to the melodramatic Satanism of the final tercet, or to the somewhat contrived antitheses that precede it (Sun and Moon veiled in darkness, planet passing out of eclipse, dagger flashing from its sheath[1]), than to the intriguing glimpses it offers of the day-to-day framework of Jeanne's and Baudelaire's lives, the actual background against which they moved, quarrelled and loved. As Alan Boase himself has excellently shown,[2] we gain a similar feeling of sudden intimacy and insight across the centuries, from certain of Ronsard's *Sonnets pour Hélène* – as indeed again (to return to Baudelaire) in that other evocation of a Parisian dance-hall, in the opening lines of *L'Amour du mensonge*:[3]

Quand je te vois passer, ô ma chère indolente,
Au chant des instruments qui se brise au plafond
Suspendant ton allure harmonieuse et lente,
Et promenant l'ennui de ton regard profond;

[1] This line may have earned the unfortunate Baudelaire, from his publisher Poulet-Malassis, what would then be the first in that long line of esoteric-cum-Freudian interpretations to which he has been subjected: in rejecting this poem for his own *Journal d'Alençon*, Poulet-Malassis had ludicrously discerned in Baudelaire's 'dagger' (or so the poet suspected) an overtly phallic image . . . See *Corresp. gén.*, vol. II, p. 234, letter of 11th November 1858.

[2] *The Poetry of France*, London, Methuen (1964), vol. I, pp. lxxv–lxxvi.

[3] Cf. A. Feuillerat, 'L'Architecture des *Fleurs du Mal*', in: *Studies by Members of the French Department of Yale University*, New Haven (Conn.), Yale University Press, 1941, p. 309.

Quand je contemple, aux feux du gaz qui le colore,
Ton front pâle, embelli par un morbide attrait,
Où les torches du soir allument une aurore,
Et tes yeux attirants comme ceux d'un portrait,

Je me dis: Qu'elle est belle! et bizarrement fraîche!

Looking back in conclusion over this long series of tributes paid by Baudelaire to the women he loved, it is interesting to note the particular aspects of feminine beauty that most strongly compelled his homage, and the particular images through which this homage is conveyed. Baudelaire's descriptions are rarely static, or 'two-dimensional'; as he says of his youthful alter ego, Samuel Cramer, in the novella *La Fanfarlo*: 'Il aimait un corps humain comme une harmonie matérielle, comme une belle architecture, plus le mouvement',[1] and we have seen that in many of his love poems he evokes his mistress precisely in characteristic movement of some kind: walking, reclining, arching or curving her body, essaying different 'poses'. The most favoured posture is one of casual, leisurely grace: the apostrophe 'chère indolente' recurs, for instance, in two widely separated poems (*Le Serpent qui danse*, *L'Amour du mensonge*) addressed, at a distance of perhaps twelve years or more, to two different women who had this one characteristic at least in common. A sinuous litheness and softness of movement is conveyed through analogies with certain animals: the snake (*Le Serpent qui danse*, *Avec ses vêtements*), the swan (*Les Bijoux*), the monkey (*Le Cadre*), the elephant (*Le Serpent qui danse*), or by the notion of an 'amorous' interplay of limbs, a subtle 'marriage' with the 'properties' that surround them (*Chanson d'après-midi*, *Le Cadre*). But the image which best renders the elegant and complex harmoniousness of carriage that so delighted Baudelaire is that of the sailing-ship riding the waves (*Le Beau navire*, *Le Serpent qui danse*) – an image that always held for him a mysterious and potent charm which he was to analyse in an eloquent passage of his 'intimate journal', *Fusées*:

[1] Ed. C. Pichois, Monaco, Éditions du Rocher (1957), p. 89.

Je crois que le charme infini et mystérieux qui gît dans la contemplation d'un navire, et surtout d'un navire en mouvement, tient, dans le premier cas, à la régularité et à la symétrie qui sont un des besoins primordiaux de l'esprit humain, au même degré que la complication et l'harmonie, – et, dans le second cas, à la multiplication successive et à la génération de toutes les courbes et figures imaginaires opérées dans l'espace par les éléments réels de l'objet.[1]

The eyes are the other feature on which, in these love poems, Baudelaire's gaze rests with a particular and rapt fascination – a fascination that is as much moral and psychological as aesthetic: the eyes are seen not merely as objects beautiful in themselves, but as holding in some way the key to their owner's personality. Their very complexity of colouring (*Le Serpent qui danse*, *Avec ses vêtements* . . .) may thus suggest or promise hidden depths of feeling (*Ciel brouillé*). Not that Baudelaire falls victim to the illusion that a person's inmost thoughts can be read from (or into!) their eyes; he is aware that even the most 'speaking' eye can deceive as thoroughly as can a gesture or a tone of voice – that the most limpid may reveal no more than the literal surface of its retina, the most melting and 'profound' conceal only stupidity or indifference. And yet . . . knowing all this, he is still content to delight in the beautiful appearance, to ignore the disheartening reality that may lie behind:

> *Je sais qu'il est des yeux, des plus mélancoliques,*
> *Qui ne recèlent point de secrets précieux;*
> *Beaux écrins sans joyaux, médaillons sans reliques,*
> *Plus vides, plus profonds que vous-mêmes, ô Cieux!*
>
> *Mais ne suffit-il pas que tu sois l'apparence,*
> *Pour réjouir un cœur qui fuit la vérité?*
> *Qu'importe ta bêtise ou ton indifférence?*
> *Masque ou décor, salut! J'adore ta beauté.*
>
> (*L'Amour du mensonge*, L. 17–24)

[1] *Fusées*, XV (*Journaux intimes*, ed. J. Crépet and G. Blin, Paris, Corti, [1949], p. 32). Cf., in this whole connection, H. Peyre, 'L'Image du navire chez Baudelaire', *Mod. Lang. Notes*, vol. XLIV (1929), pp. 447–50.

At a more superficial level, the poetic contemplation of a woman's eyes seems particularly to invite the fashioning of audacious conceits – involving frequently, in Baudelaire's case, a curious amplification or exaggeration of scale. Thus in *Le Poison*, as we have seen, Marie's green eyes become a *lake* to which her lover's dreams throng to assuage their thirst; the dark eyes (Jeanne's?) which cast their spell in *Sed non satiata* are similarly imagined as the desert fountain, or 'reservoir', at which the winding caravan of Baudelaire's 'ennuis' can find refreshment (albeit not for long: in the next verse, these same eyes are transformed into the outlets or 'vents' through which the 'Mégère libertine' channels the flame of her passion!); whilst in a third, and later, poem, *Semper eadem*, the image is applied (with true poetic impartiality) to a third pair of 'beaux yeux' – those of Mme Sabatier, within which, in the *shade* of their lashes, her poet aspires to dream. . . . But these extravagances, when replaced within their contexts, are less obtrusive than their separate enumeration might suggest.

There remains one feminine attribute of which I have made almost no mention: perfume, the whole subtle fragrance of clothes, skin, hair. This element is of the greatest importance in Baudelaire's love poetry, and indeed constitutes for him almost the determining characteristic of the feminine universe, of what he was wont to call the *mundus muliebris*.[1] But its appeal for him, in such poems as *Parfum exotique* and *La Chevelure*, is above all imaginative rather than erotic or aesthetic; under its sway, as if forgetful almost of the woman's physical presence, the poet turns his gaze inwards into himself, inwards into his own personal past.[2]

F. W. Leakey

[1] Cf. *Un Mangeur d'opium* ('Chagrins d'enfance'), *Les Paradis artificiels*, p. 166; *Le Peintre de la vie moderne* ('La Femme'), *L'Art romantique*, p. 94. For the source of the phrase in question, see C. Pichois, *Baudelaire. Études et témoignages*, Neuchâtel, La Baconnière (1967), pp. 156–62.

[2] Cf., in this connection, my analysis of the two poems cited, in my book *Baudelaire and Nature*, Manchester University Press (1968), Chap. III.

Montaigne and the Concept of
the Imagination

‑››› ‑››› ‑››› ‑››› ‑››› ‑››› ‑››› ‑››› ‑››› ‑››› ‑››› ‑‹‹‹ ‑‹‹‹ ‑‹‹‹ ‑‹‹‹ ‑‹‹‹ ‑‹‹‹ ‑‹‹‹ ‑‹‹‹ ‑‹‹‹ ‑‹‹‹ ‑‹‹‹ ‑‹‹‹

IT HAS LONG been recognized that the imagination, far from
being the 'reine des facultés' of Baudelaire's aesthetic, was until
the later decades of the eighteenth century the 'folle du logis', and
that tradition viewed it with varying degrees of suspicion in the
fields of both psychology and aesthetics. I do not propose therefore to examine the historical position or consider its origins in
any detail;[1] suffice it to say that this suspicion had its roots in two
basic assumptions. On the one hand, in so far as the imagination
'invented', it strayed from the path of truth into the byways of
fiction and falsehood, and this indeed has been one of the major
obstacles facing poets who wished to raise the status of imaginative activity in their theories of poetry; and on the other, whatever variations might be found among the traditional attitudes, it
was generally agreed that the imagination was related to the body
or at best the lower realms of self, and was therefore likely to
come into conflict with essential being or the spiritual aspects of
the mind.

---

[1] Useful aperçus will be found in the following works: M. W. Bundy, The Theory of
Imagination in classical and mediæval Thought, University of Illinois Studies in Language
and Literature, XII (1927), fasc. 2–3; Grahame Castor, Pléiade Poetics, Cambridge
(1964); Anthony Levi, French Moralists: the Theory of the Passions 1585 to 1649,
Oxford (1964); M. H. Abrams, The Mirror and the Lamp, London (1953); Dudley
Wilson, 'Contraries in Sixteenth Century Scientific Writing', in Essays presented to
C. M. Girdlestone, University of Durham (1960), pp. 349–68.

In sixteenth-century France, no doubt, the traditional attitudes were still well entrenched, and indeed, inasmuch as some philosophers pressed the claims of reason and intelligence, the imagination was threatened with further demotion. Nevertheless, it would be misleading to think that there was a single, homogeneous view of the imagination accepted by one and all; not only can one detect important distinctions in the views handed down from antiquity, but some new ground is being broken here and there by sixteenth-century humanists. It is therefore a matter for regret that the ways in which the term 'imagination' is used by Renaissance writers have not been scrutinized as thoroughly as certain other key-words, such as 'experience' or 'intelligence'.[1] If one consults the Huguet or the Glossary of the Bordeaux edition, one will be disappointed;[2] a more rewarding exploration may be made in a seventeenth-century French-Latin dictionary by Philibert Monier,[3] but, outside treatises on the passions and the faculties, systematic analysis is hard to come by. Here I shall try to bring together some random soundings into Montaigne's concern with the topic; the material is too rich to be properly treated within the compass of a short article.

[1]

'Je suis de ceux qui sentent tres-grand effort de l'imagination', writes Montaigne;[4] and throughout the *Essais* we meet references to, and indeed discussions of, this interior sense of the mind.

---

[1] W. G. Moore, 'Montaigne's Notion of Experience', in *The French Mind Studies in honour of Gustave Rudler*, Oxford (1952); Dr S. J. Holyoake has written a Cambridge doctoral dissertation on the idea of intelligence in the *Essais*.

[2] Huguet's Dictionary, in fact, gives nothing on the imagination; the Bordeaux glossary defines imagination as: (i) 'faculté non seulement d'imaginer, mais de concevoir; pensée; esprit'; (ii) 'produit de cette faculté; pensée; idée; opinion', and adds some idioms.

[3] Philibert Monier, S.J., *Invantaire des deus langues françoise, et latine . . .* Lyon (1636).

[4] Montaigne, *Essais*, Paris, Bibliothèque de la Pléiade (1946), I, xxi, p. 110 (*a*). For the rest of the article, references will be inserted after the quotations in the text, with an indication of the early edition in question according to the customary use of (*a*), (*b*), (*c*).

What is interesting is the manner in which Montaigne appears gradually to move away from the traditional views, without, of course, completely rejecting them. Many factors may be involved in this shift of attitude: the blurring of psychological categories, the changing value he may attach to the different parts of the mind, more generally the relativism of his outlook.[1]

It may, however, help if we first clear the ground by summarizing the points at which Montaigne's view is in broad agreement with tradition. The imagination is seen as occupying an intermediate position between the senses which receive their data from the outside world and the allegedly higher 'faculties' of the mind, such as the intelligence, which are not affected like the imagination by physical factors. The latter is not in immediate contact with reality and this distance affords by definition yet another opportunity for the introduction of error and falsehood. From the outset the imagination is associated with *paraître* and held to be incompatible with *être*. This is evident at epistemological level, where Montaigne has already shown an extensive scepticism about our ability to acquire knowledge. He has said much on the unreliability of our sense data: our own senses, far from transmitting faithfully messages from outside, are seen to warp our apprehension of the world around us:

> Or, nostre estat accommodant les choses à soy et les transformant selon soy, nous ne sçavons plus quelles sont les choses en vérité: car rien ne vient à nous que falsifié et altéré par nos sens . . . L'incertitude de nos sens rend incertain tout ce qu'ils produisent (II, xii, p. 588 (*a*)).

[1] I shall confine myself to imagination as a 'faculty' of the mind, though, of course, the term *imagination* and its synonym *fantasie* are frequently used to denote not only the faculty but also the process and the product. Montaigne, like his contemporaries, may use the term in a very broad sense, so that it becomes hard to distinguish it from *âme*:

> D'autres, ayant leur imagination logée au-dessus de la fortune et du monde, trouveront les sieges de la justice et les throsnes mesmes des Roys, bas et viles (I, xxv, p. 147 (*a*)).

For the purposes of the argument, we shall try, as far as possible, to leave this broader connotation on one side at this stage.

We do not need to labour this point unduly, as it is a common-place of Montaignian commentary; but the role of the imagination must appear suspect, since its operation will inevitably increase the gap which our faulty senses have already opened up between ourselves and reality. More especially, the imagination is seen as an agent creating 'false objects'; now it is true that these products may be 'corrected' by the proper use of memory – and there is, of course, in traditional thinking, a normal connection between memory and the imagination:

> . . . la chose, comme elle est, s'estant logée la première dans la mémoire, et s'y estant empreincte, par la voye de la connoissance, et de la science, il est malaysé qu'elle ne se represente à l'imagination, délogeant la fauceté, qui n'y peut avoir le pied si ferme, ny si rassis . . . (I, ix, pp. 51–2 (*a*)),

so that its functioning reminds us of the explanation Taine gives us of the manner in which our 'hallucinations' turn out to be either true or false, according to the confirmation they may or may not receive from the recognitory memory. However that may be, the imagination appears to be a positive impediment to the finding of truth, and perhaps on two main counts. On the one hand, the very fact that it introduces a gap between *paraître* and *être* facilitates a certain intellectual irresponsibility on its part, so that it is capable, for instance, of conjuring up a whole host of interpretations to be put on reality, sufficient to drive one to despair:

> Son (sc. Simonides') imagination luy presentoit . . . diverses considerations aiguës et subtiles, doubtant laquelle estoit la plus vray-semblable, il desespera du tout de la vérité (II, xx, p. 660 (*c*)).

And on the other hand its position in the structure of the mind which holds it at one remove at least from reality means that its usefulness as a means to knowledge is negligible. When Montaigne writes:

> L'homme ne peut estre que ce qu'il est, ny imaginer que selon sa pensée (II, xii, p. 504 (*a*)),

he is, of course, thinking of human nature as a whole, but within the context the imagination is seen as something that does nothing to narrow the gap between man and reality, and may indeed widen it. As an epistemological tool, the imagination stands condemned.

But the indictment goes further; as a result of the imagination being traditionally associated with the body and the passions, it comes about that the gap between the imaginative self and reality is filled by the pressure of emotions or 'appetites'. In the Ficinian canon, the four affections linked with the imagination are *appetitus*, *voluptas*, *metus* and *dolor*;[1] in the *Essais* Montaigne dwells more especially on desire and fear. Much is written about fear and its distortion of the object, the paralysis of the self, the possible effects fear may have even upon the body; in short the interval between *paraître* and *être* is substantially increased by the presence of the passions. Montaigne, in tune with his contemporaries here, resents the unruly character of the imagination and is indeed disturbed and scared by the potential violence of its effects both on our behaviour and on our modes of thought; but he introduces a further, characteristic refinement, in that he sees the imagination as an intrusion upon his own liberty, bringing disorder and the unexpected into his house of consciousness. Sometimes this objection is voiced in vigorous terms; on other occasions, a more ambivalent attitude is discernible in which the wildest thoughts are not themselves condemned, but are rapped over the knuckles for entering unbidden:

> Mais mon âme me desplait de ce qu'elle produict ordinairement ses plus profondes resveries, plus folles et qui me plaisent le mieux, à l'improuveu et lors que je les cerche moins; lesquelles s'esvanouissent soudain, n'ayant sur le champ où les attacher; à cheval, à la table, au lit, mais plus à cheval, où sont mes plus larges entretiens (III, v, pp. 849–50 (*b*)).

Incidentally this is not the only passage where the case against the imagination is extended to cover the mind as a whole.[2] Elsewhere Montaigne complains that 'l'homme est l'esclave de ses fictions',

[1] Anthony Levi, op. cit., p. 24.
[2] See, for instance, *Essais*, II, xii, p. 544.

and that we are possessed by what we desire. And this is no doubt the more serious charge, that the imagination, by its links with the passions, dominates man and not the other way round; in other words, the case is strengthened by arguments of an ethical nature. Indeed, this moral distrust of the imagination may range very far, for Montaigne deplores in man the presence of an activity which may impel him to rival the gods and make him the victim of hubris:

> La presomption est nostre maladie naturelle et originelle . . . C'est par la vanité de cette mesme imagination qu'il (sc. l'homme) s'esgale à Dieu, qu'il s'attribue les conditions divines, qu'il se trie soy mesme et separe de la presse des autres creatures, taille les parts aux animaux ses confreres et compaignons, et leur distribue telle portion de facultez et de forces que bon luy semble (II, xii, p. 432 (*a*)).

The indictment of the imagination seems therefore to be damagingly comprehensive. At epistemological level, it adulterates our perception of the outer world and weakens our contact with reality; it may interfere with our intellectual and reasoning powers and it cannot take us beyond the confines of our self. In the moral field, it also introduces an element of turbulence and waywardness which Montaigne sees as a threat to the order of the mind and also as a sign of man's unwillingness to put himself in the second place. And so it is that one of the essential characteristics that distinguish man from the beasts is shown to carry more disadvantages than benefits: 'la folle du logis' is a source of error at both epistemological and ethical levels.

[II]

To leave the matter at that would, however, not be justified; Montaigne's attitudes do not lend themselves readily to convenient and tidy pigeon-holing, and one would hardly expect a writer who saw man as 'double' (II, xvi, p. 606 (*a*)) and was so conscious of the contraries in all things to dismiss without further ado this vital part of the mind. In three main ways, I suggest, Montaigne has taken a broader and more positive view of the imagination: in the problem of knowledge, in the relations between imagination and action, and more generally in its connection with experience. First of all, the epistemological problem.

In this field, our findings may prove to be rather more meagre than in the others, but even here I think that the imagination comes to acquire more prestige in the long run than it enjoyed in the traditional hierarchy. It benefits, in a negative manner, from the fact that Montaigne's scepticism about the efficiency of various branches of the mind succeeds in narrowing the distance between the imagination and the rest, and indeed reinforces a marked tendency in him to make the several categories overlap; in a situation where all mental faculties or activities come under suspicion, imagination may not be at any rate more open to criticism than the others. Reason itself, linked in some currents of thought with the Divine spirit, is fallible: 'l'humaine raison est un instrument libre et vague' (III, xi, p. 996 (*b*)); 'nostre raison est flexible à toute sorte d'image' (II, xxx, p. 690 (*c*)); or 'je trouve . . . ma concupiscence moins desbauchée que ma raison' (II, xi, p. 409 (*b*)). *Discours* is also capable of welcoming any *fantasie* that may come its way:

> J'estime qu'il ne tombe en l'imagination humaine aucune fantasie si forcenée, qui ne rencontre l'exemple de quelque usage public, et par conséquent que nostre discours n'estaie et ne fonde. (I, xxiii, p. 124 (*b*).)

Jugement, so often cherished, joins the ranks: it may be 'pipé par les sens', and it is as liable to be affected by illness as any other aspect of our mental activity:

> Si nostre jugement est en main à la maladie mesmes et à la perturbation . . . (II, xii, p. 554 (*a*)).

And a quotation from *De l'art de conferer* sums up the question succinctly:

> Je dis plus, que nostre sagesse mesme et consultation suit pour la plus part la conduicte du hazard. Ma volonté et mon discours se remue tantost d'un air, tantost d'un autre, et y a plusieurs de ces

123

mouvemens qui se gouvernent sans moy. Ma raison a des impulsions et agitations journallieres et casuelles . . . (III, viii, p. 906 (*b*)).

One could quote many further examples, were one not to resist the temptation that besets all writers on Montaigne to convert their articles into miniature anthologies; but several points emerge from what I have quoted. Our various faculties have lost any hierarchical privileges they may once have enjoyed, because Montaigne's relativism sees them all prone to similar weaknesses. On the one hand, they are all characterized by inconsistency, by discontinuity even, and on the other they undermine man's proper relationship with Nature (another concept in Montaigne which would repay close scrutiny). On more than one occasion Montaigne has opposed the overclever operations of the mind to the robust common sense and instinct of the 'homme grossier' who manages to see things in the round and behave accordingly. Intelligence can indeed be conceived as a sort of anti-Nature:

> L'intelligence nous a esté donnée pour nostre plus grand bien, l'employerons-nous a nostre ruine, combatans le dessein de nature, et l'universel ordre des choses, qui porte que chacun use de ses utils et moyens pour sa commodité? (I, xiv, p. 69 (*a*))

Here, Montaigne implies that the intelligence is capable of maintaining its integrity; but it can go wrong, and when this happens the reason seems to be that its activities are almost indistinguishable from those of the imagination. Indeed, a consequence of Montaigne's relativism is that the identities of these divers 'faculties' tend to merge into one another, and the terms which he uses to refer to mental processes and area lose firm meaning. This is particularly true of the intelligence and the imagination, whose operations are often compared and contrasted by Montaigne in such a way that their similarities are more evident than their differences. And chief among these similarities is their anti-natural quality:

> Je me deffie des inventions de nostre esprit, de nostre science et art, en faveur duquel nous l'avons abandonnée (sc. Nature) et ses regles,

et auquel nous ne sçavons tenir moderation ny limite (II, xxxvii, p. 743 (*b*)).

In these circumstances there seems little point in classifying faculties into 'good' or 'bad', and to that extent one may say that the imagination has acquired a relative parity of status. But to this one must add the point that Montaigne's mind has moved away from a preoccupation with the search for metaphysical Truth – in this domain man's very weaknesses lead him to accept a framework of belief and doctrine which are given – and our human faculties must be viewed in a very much more modest context, where, as we shall see, the need to live and the desire to know oneself will restore the imagination to a more significant role. So far as knowledge is concerned, the imagination can serve a proper purpose by its dynamic character. Montaigne makes the important point that it can produce *fantasies*, of variable quality and value no doubt, but which help us not so much to establish truth as to find it:

> Je propose des fantasies informes et irresolues, comme font ceux qui publient des questions doubteuses, à debattre aux escholes: non pour establir la verité, mais pour la chercher (I, lvi, p. 308 (*a*)).

And he goes on to say that these *fantasies* will be submitted to the judgement of those he consults for the governance of his thoughts and actions. As we know, the judgement maintains a privileged position for Montaigne, but imagination has its valuable role in that it provides material on which the judgement can work; it is an active principle within ourselves, able to set in motion processes which may lead to something of importance. The variables that may arise in art from the play of the imagination (which could include the *Essais*!) may be put to good use and not automatically to bad ends. The very fact that the imagination, with its capacity for throwing up contraries, may induce us to move either towards falsehood or to 'pensées solides et de toute vérité' should raise it above its traditional reputation. In all this it is clear that Truth itself is being removed from its pedestal; and one of the things which is borne in on Montaigne more and more is that our behaviour must be conditioned by the need to live in this world. So pragmatic an attitude will naturally affect the importance one may attach to question of truth and error.

[III]

This point is made very clear in a quotation from the *Apologie*:

> C'est la misere de nostre condition, que souvent ce qui se presente à nostre imagination pour le plus vray, ne s'y presente pas pour le plus utile à nostre vie (II, xii, p. 495 (*c*)).

And elsewhere, Montaigne affirms a pragmatic view of life:

> Nous sommes nés pour agir (I, xx, p. 102 (*a*)).

He sees man in a context where he has to come to terms with everyday conditions, where he has to choose and to act if he is to hold his own at all; and if a choice has to be made, action may be more important than truth. In this situation, the imagination will inevitably come into play: it introduces a gap between ourselves and present reality, and by that very fact becomes involved in an awareness of the future, that which is not yet. Our consciousness never coincides completely with our being at any given point, and this is one reason why our imagination will have some part in our establishing contact with reality absent either in place or in time, in creating the right relationships between art and nature. Of course, Montaigne is also aware of the *revers de la médaille*; we have already noted briefly that the imagination is closely connected with an awareness of the void and of the passions which seek to fill that void. It is striking how often the term *imagination* occurs in company with *désir* or cognate words:

> N'est-ce pas un singulier tesmoignage d'imperfection, ne pouvoir r'assoir nostre contentement en aucune chose, et que, par desir mesme et imagination, il soit hors de nostre puissance de choisir ce qu'il nous faut? (I, liii, pp. 301–2 (*a*))

Particular consideration is also given to the association of imagination with fear, frequently with death or rather the thought of death, and here Montaigne treads traditional paths. A fearful imagination may paralyse our will to act and inhibit our whole being. But Montaigne may ring changes on this theme; our imagination is capable of conjuring up *songes* which will put a more favourable complexion on the objects of our thoughts,[1] and therefore of helping us to face the future with greater composure. On occasion, it is true, Montaigne will reject the specious comfort which our *songes* may offer:

> Mais certes il y faudroit autre remede qu'en songe: foible luicte de l'art contre la nature (III, v, p. 815 (*b*)),

but so far as reality is concerned, the imagination seems to be condemned by Montaigne only when it impedes a proper relation to life; what is important is that we should live and act, and it is in this light that we may interpret the following statement:

> Ma philosophie est en action, en usage naturel et present: peu en fantasie (ibid.).

Montaigne would eschew a way of existence which rejected action in favour of day-dreaming or living in Wonderland; but that is not to say that he dismisses the imagination as a means of coming to grips with reality.

In so far as the imagination makes us aware of the future, it will also colour our attitude to that future, and more than once Montaigne has suggested that Nature uses not only intelligence but appetite and imagination to further her ends:

> Nature a maternellement observé cela, que les actions qu'elle nous a enjoinctes pour nostre besoing nous fussent aussi voluptueuses, et nous y convie non seulement par la raison mais aussi par l'appétit: c'est injustice de corrompre ses regles (III, xiii, p. 1079 (*b*)).

And with specific reference to the imagination he writes:

> Ceux qui accusent les hommes d'aller tousjours béant après les choses futures, et nous apprennent à nous saisir des biens présents, et nous rassoir en ceux-là, comme n'ayant aucune prise sur ce qui est à venir,

[1] *Essais*, III, v, p. 815.

voire assez moins que nous n'avons sur ce qui est passé, touchent la plus commune des humaines erreurs, s'ils osent appeler erreur chose à quoy nature mesmes nous achemine, pour le service de la continuation de son ouvrage, nous imprimant, comme assez d'autres, cette imagination fausse, plus jalouse de nostre action que de nostre science (I, iii, pp. 33–4 (*b*)).

Nature, on whom Montaigne lays so much stress, is thus seen as being more interested in living than in thought or the search for knowledge; and therefore what the intelligence or the judgement might deem error can still have a pragmatic value in an imperfect world:

Car il n'est deffendu de faire nostre profit de la mensonge mesme, s'il est besoing (II, xii, p. 494 (*a*)).

The important requirement is an impetus to action, and if this can be supplied by error or falsehood, why should we object? In any case the mind needs to develop a certain propelling force of its own, otherwise it may sink into vegetative torpor, and one might see in Montaigne's ideas the adumbration of a theory of action-myths. One significant statement is to be found in the *Apologie*:

Les secousses et esbranlemens que nostre ame reçoit par les passions corporelles, peuvent beaucoup en elle, mais encore plus les siennes propres, ausquelles elle est si fort en prinse qu'il est à l'adventure soustenable qu'elle n'a aucune autre alleure et mouvement que du souffle de ses vents, et que, sans leur agitation, elle resteroit sans action, comme un navire en pleine mer, que les vents abandonnent de leur secours (II, xii, p. 553 (*a*));

and, given the recognized link between the imagination and the passions, one can understand the active element which the imagination may inject into our existence. On a later occasion Montaigne suggests that the imagination can revitalize jejune emotions:

. . . il est excusable de le (sc. le corps) rechauffer et soustenir par art, et, par l'entremise de la fantasie, luy faire revenir l'appetit et l'allegresse, puis que de soy il l'a perdue? (III, v, p. 866 (*b*)).

The imagination, therefore, cannot only restore vitality to the inner life, but also give the self something of the impetus which it requires to perform its proper work in the framework of existence. Mind, if not action itself, is inextricably involved in action, and action is more important than the mind's attitude to the truth or otherwise of the spurs to action. In this context the imagination must be seen, not as a *trouble-fête* or a *remue-ménage*, but as a frequent collaborator and indeed indispensable agent in the efficient operation of the self *en situation*. If on occasion it appears to work like a pair of blinkers, for the most part it serves as a generator of energy, propelling the self into the paths of action.

[IV]

The imagination is, however, not concerned exclusively with the question of the future; it must also be seen in its relation to our apprehension of experience in general, which includes both the present and the past or the absent. This is a daunting topic, and only a few threads can be taken up here; but it seems to me that Montaigne shows interest more particularly in two aspects of the matter. On the one hand, he appears to suggest the need for us to establish a proper distance in our relationships with reality, and on the other, he sees the mind as creating the element of continuity in our experience which, for various reasons, can only be fragmentary and often discontinuous. On the first point, he recognizes, of course, that in any case we are at one remove from reality, by the very nature of our consciousness:

> Les choses presentes, nous ne les tenons que par la fantasie (III, ix, p. 968 (*b*));

but there are dangers, he thinks, in a too close or myopic involvement in reality. Here we are bordering on matters that concern the well-being of the mind. For instance, Montaigne, confessing to a certain hypersensitivity to events, thinks that a too immediate contact with reality may disturb or disrupt that well-being:

> Absent, je me despouille de tous telz pensemens; et sentirois moins lors la ruyne d'une tour que je ne faicts present la cheute d'une ardoise. Mon asme se demesle bien ayséement à part, mais en presence elle souffre comme celle d'un vigneron (III, ix, p. 924 (*b*)).

Elsewhere he notes that experience at second hand or at one remove is less likely to ruffle his sensibility than if he were himself involved:

> Je trouve plus de volupté à seulement voir le juste et doux meslange de deux jeunes beautés ou à le seulement considerer par fantasie, qu'à faire moy mesmes le second d'un meslange triste et informe (III, v, p. 868 (c)).

This does not, of course, mean that he wishes the imagination to provide simply an escape-mechanism from life, a comforting substitute for the buffeting of existence – and we have already touched on this point – but he may allow himself such consolation from time to time:

> Je ne m'esgaye qu'en fantasie et en songe, pour destourner par ruse le chagrin de la vieillesse (III, v, p. 815 (b)).

What he is seeking in the last analysis is some sort of *via media* between total immersion in the event and a deliberate shunning of it; his experience has taught him that enrichment of the mind may derive in part from the proper and timely refusal to be too involved in the real event.

In any case the experience which we value cannot always be immediately present in the literal sense; and the mind must of a necessity reduce the discontinuity of meaningful experience and fill in the gaps created by absence. This is one of the reasons why Montaigne values the mind in its imaginative capacity, making the absent present and the discontinuous continuous:

> La jouyssance et la possession appartiennent principalement à l'imagination (III, ix, p. 946 (b)).

Moreover, this point is developed with special reference to a subject very close to Montaigne's heart: friendship:

> En la vraye amitié, de laquelle je suis expert, je me donne à mon amy plus que je ne le tire à moy . . . Et si l'absence luy est ou plaisante ou utile, elle m'est bien plus douce que sa presence; et ce n'est pas proprement absence, quand il y a moyen de s'entr'advertir. J'ay tiré autrefois usage de nostre esloignement et commodité. Nous remplis-

sions mieux et estendions la possession de la vie en nous separant; il vivoit, il jouissoit, il voyoit pour moy, et moy pour luy, autant plainement que s'il y eust esté . . . La separation du lieu rendoit la conjonction de nos volontez plus riche. Cette faim insatiable de la presence corporelle accuse un peu la foiblesse en la jouyssance des ames (III, ix, p. 947 (*b*)).

It may be that the imagination is incapable of attaining Truth, but in an interesting aside, all too tantalizingly brief, Montaigne seems to suggest that only the empathetic activity of the mind, something that is by definition heavily dependent on the imagination, is really capable of understanding 'l'autre en tant que l'autre', of apprehending *l'altérité*:

Je n'ay point cette erreur commune de juger d'un autre selon que je suys. J'en croy aysément des choses diverses à moy . . . Je descharge tant qu'on veut un autre estre de mes conditions et principes, et le considere simplement en luy-mesme, sans relation, l'estoffant sur son propre modelle. Pour n'estre continent, je ne laisse d'advouer sincerement la continence des Feuillans et des Capuchins, et de bien trouver la continence l'air de leur train; je m'insinue, par imagination, fort bien en leur place (I, xxxvii, p. 233 (*a*)).

Thus it seems that the imagination not only maintains continuity in our relations with *autrui* (and things), but is also the sole means by which we can apprehend the nature and identity of *autrui*.

Imagination, then, is no substitute for immediate contact with reality, but it plays an indispensable role. In so far as experience – and there is no need to stress here the importance of that concept in Montaigne – is something more than the apprehension of immediate reality and involves the dimensions of continuity and value; in so far as the very circumstances of existence make it impossible for certain aspects of reality to be permanently present before us; and in so far as Montaigne emphasizes the need for us to respect the *quant à soy* of our mind, it is clear that our inner life can be assured of a genuine plenitude only if a satisfactory balance is achieved between immediate contact with and proper distance from reality. And in this operation the imagination may act as a legitimate buffer between the mind and reality, but also provides part of the continuum on which experience must rely if it is to acquire validity, and this in spite of its own tendency to waywardness or distortion.

This acceptance and indeed positive appreciation of the imagination is linked, as I have already hinted, with Montaigne's shift away from an undue concern with general truth or insights into the outside world towards the exploration of the inner self and a growing awareness of the nature of that self. If we are to 'jouyr loiallement de nostre estre' and 'composer nos meurs . . . & vivre à propos', this must surely mean, within an acceptable framework, the development of the self and the proper means of expression for its various elements. 'Contentement' would appear to be more important than truth, in that it implies truth to oneself, and in that sense we may interpret a (*c*) addition in Book I:

> Elle (sc. l'âme) fait son profit de tout indifferemment. L'erreur, les songes, luy servent utilement, comme une loyale matiere à nous mettre à garant et en contentement (I, xiv, p. 72).

Instead of subjecting ourselves to truths outside us, we make all elements of experience become grist for our own personal mill; and a certain plenitude will result from fidelity to oneself in action, and this is surely more satisfactory than a search for ultimate truths where we shall be best advised to rely on faith and consecrated tradition. We must therefore come to terms with the various constituents of our make-up; no more than that we should discount the body, is it right that we leave on one side any part so prominent as the imagination. We may wonder sometimes at its products which seem akin to folly, but who are we to judge correctly what is folly and what is wisdom?

> Nostre vie est partie en folie, partie en prudence (III, v, pp. 861–2 (*c*));

and, in any case, a little indulgence in fancy may save us from silliness:

> Il faut avoir un peu de folie qui ne veut pas avoir plus de sottise . . . (III, ix, p. 966 (*b*)).

In a *vision du monde* where reason may be folly and sometimes 'noz songes vallent mieux que noz discours' (II, xii, p. 554 (*c*), the wisdom of repressing the fertile principle of the imagination must be doubted:

> Il n'est si frivole et si extravagante fantasie qui ne semble bien sortable à la production de l'esprit humain (III, viii, p. 895 (*b*)).

Man is 'ondoyant et divers'; made up of contraries and full of a natural curiosity, he does not seem to settle to any one point of view. He is a form of movement, of *branle*; and the imagination, itself movement, must be an essential component of his structure. If our business is to come to know ourselves at least, how can we ignore the imagination which may often tell us a good deal about the peculiar complexion of the self?

It is not only a part of the self which Montaigne wishes to describe; more than once he has asked himself whether our thoughts are not a more reliable guide to our nature than are our actions:

> Je ne puis tenir registre de ma vie par mes actions; fortune les met trop bas; je le tiens par mes fantasies (III, ix, p. 915 (*b*)).

This is something that was already clear in the first edition:

> Ce sont icy mes fantasies, par lesquelles je ne tasche point à donner à connoistre les choses, mais moy (II, x, p. 388 (*a*)).

In other words, his *songes*, whatever their connection with truth beyond the self, remain important as an expression of the self, and the imagination is one of the keys to self-knowledge.

Two further points should be made about the imagination. In the first place, though Montaigne shares the traditional suspicion of the links between the imagination and the passions, he makes an interesting counter-point that the imagination has a therapeutic effect in the catharsis of the passions. The passions demand outlet, action, and if circumstances do not favour their working-out, the imagination may step in and offer an effective surrogate:

Et nous voyons que l'âme en ses passions se pipe plustost elle-mesme, se dressant un faux subject et fantastique, voire contre sa propre creance, que de n'agir contre quelque chose (I, iv, pp. 40–1 (*a*)).[1]

This cathartic action not only helps to maintain a proper balance in the functioning of the mind, since repressed emotions will introduce turbulence, but it contributes to the maintenance of the right distance between the self and reality.

The other matter is the problem of the imagination's alleged irresponsibility, a criticism that often arises in traditional treatment of the topic. Now, though in Montaigne's eyes the imagination may have its moments of gay abandon and may even sometimes impinge on the essayist's own freedom of action, he is far from always condemning it on this score, and what is more important, it would seem that Montaigne's psychology does recognize that it has certain built-in controls. One must point to the moderating effect which he believes custom, tradition and usage exert upon one's being and thought processes. Furthermore, with the passage of time, the essayist became increasingly aware of the *forme maîtresse* which resists the attempts of education to shape us and also the development of passions that do not harmonize with our being:

Regardez un peu comment s'en porte nostre experience: il n'est personne, s'il escoute, qui ne descouvre en soy une forme sienne, une forme maistresse, qui luicte contre l'institution, et contre la tempête des passions qui luy sont contraires (III, ii, p. 785 (*c*)).

I do not see that Montaigne had come to view the imagination as a threat to one's essential being. Either the *forme maîtresse* is perfectly capable of holding its own against any opposition offered by the imagination – in which case the traditional distrust of the imagination loses some of its force – or, what is more likely, the imagination will harmonize, as part of the mind, and in so far as

---

[1] The title of the Essay is equally explicit: *Comme l'âme descharge ses passions sur des objects faux quand les vrays luy defaillent.* For lack of space, I have left aside the whole question of the role of the imagination in literary, artistic expression, but the importance of the cathartic action in this context will be obvious.

it can deal with the passions, with the *forme maîtresse*. Since Montaigne has taken care to note down the stream of thoughts which have emerged from his imagination, and has deduced from this stream a certain pattern in time relevant to self-knowledge, the imagination has undergone promotion in the hierarchy, precisely because it reveals itself as pattern after all in its products.

Over and above this, it would seem that the imagination is, in fact, capable of accepting intellectual control. On one occasion Montaigne talks of pressing his *esprit* into this service, even if some *piperie* is involved (III, xiii, p. 1060 (*b*)); elsewhere, he finds a means of control by the very act of noting down the ideas which occur to him:

> Aus fins de renger ma fantasie à resver mesme par quelque ordre et projet, et la garder de se perdre et extravaguer au vent, il n'est que donner corps et mettre en registre tant de menues pensées qui se présentent à elle. J'escoute à mes resveries parce que j'ay à les enroller (II, xviii, p. 651 (*c*)).

The imagination may never rid itself of its inclination to play truant, but it forms too much of a pattern with the rest of the mind to cause serious concern.

[v]

In this discussion we have been hampered by an initial difficulty of principle. We have seen how in Montaigne mental categories tend here and there to become blurred, and this is equally true of the imagination. In so far as the *âme* is the principle of consciousness which not only distinguishes us from the animals, but makes us aware of the distinction between the self and the world, and in so far as that consciousness must also depend upon memory[1] and the awareness of time, it is virtually impossible to dissociate it from the imagination. We have seen that consciousness means the

---

[1] In traditional thinking there is a close connection between imagination and memory. Though no doubt Montaigne accepts this association, he does not appear to stress it in his remarks on the imagination.

awareness of a gap between ourselves and reality, at different levels, with the result that on the temporal plane this gap becomes an incentive to action. But in all this it is increasingly difficult to know where one can draw the dividing line between consciousness and imagination, especially when there has emerged an ethical attitude connected with the knowledge of the self.

To sum up. At one time Montaigne may have resented in the imagination its relative independence, and what he is anxious to enjoy is some measure of control upon his inner life. He may for a spell have seen in the imagination an outsider:

> . . . c'estoyent des pensemens vains, en nuë, qui estoyent esmeuz par les sens des yeux et des oreilles; ils ne venoyent pas de chez moy (II, vi, p. 359 (*a*)).

But by the time he had come to write *De l'experience*, he had surely reached a *modus vivendi* with this part of his mind which was a familiar rather than an outsider, which did not, after all, disrupt his inner existence, and which had a further, special function in that it shed much light upon the nature of the self:

> Je n'ay poinct à me plaindre de mon imagination: j'ay eu peu de pensées en ma vie qui m'ayent seulement interrompu le cours de mon sommeil, si elles n'ont esté du désir, qui m'esmerveillent sans m'affliger. Je songe peu souvent; et lors c'est des choses fantastiques et des chimeres, plustost ridicules que tristes. Et tiens qu'il est vray que les songes sont loyaux interprètes de nos inclinations, mais il y a de l'art à les assortir et entendre (III, xiii, p. 1069 (*b*)).

Above all, in so far as the imagination provides the stimulus for other parts of the mind to work on, it is performing an indispensable service, indeed perhaps its great value lies in its powers of instigation at the level of both thought and action. And if we cannot go so far as Montaigne himself did in describing some historical figure: 'Ce qu'il fantasioit, il l'estoit' (III, xi, p. 1003 (*c*)), we may claim that for him the imagination was an incentive to thought and action, an instrument of inner balance and catharsis, a collaborator of experience in our relations with the outside world, and finally an aspect of identity. And what indeed are the *Essais* but the imagination in action?[1]

I. D. McFarlane

[1] I am grateful to my friends Alan Steele and Dudley Wilson for valuable help with the first draft of this essay.

Prose Inspiration for Poetry:
J. B. Chassignet

⫸ ⫸ ⫸ ⫸ ⫸ ⫸ ⫸ ⫸ ⫸ ⫸ ⫸ ⫷ ⫷ ⫷ ⫷ ⫷ ⫷ ⫷ ⫷ ⫷ ⫷ ⫷ ⫷

THERE HAVE been many attempts to describe, define and categorize the styles of French prose and poetry in the period which stretches from about 1570 to 1630. The discussion has ranged from arguments based on specific and recurring themes such as metamorphosis or inconstancy,[1] to the study of the influence of a single author such as Seneca.[2] Nearly all the critics who have worked on this period have noted the importance for literature of the spirit of that time, disturbed by scientific discoveries and Wars of Religion, and stimulated by the erudite productions of the late Renaissance. And yet, only very recently have they started to explore these problems in some detail.[3] The greater part of the literature published in the years 1570–1630 is principally concerned with moral, philosophical or spiritual matters, and it seems that before a satisfactory stylistic assessment of the period

[1] Jean Rousset, *La Littérature de l' âge baroque en France*, Paris (1953).

[2] George Williamson, *The Senecan Amble*, London (1951).

[3] Professor Boase's searching introduction to the *Méditations* of Sponde, Paris (1954), outlines the scope of these problems. The articles of M. W. Croll, 'Juste Lipse et le mouvement anticicéronien à la fin du XVIe siècle', *Revue du XVIe siècle* (1914), pp. 200 ff., '*Attic* Prose in the seventeenth century', *Studies in Philology* (1921), pp. 79 ff., 'Muret and the History of *Attic* Prose', PMLA (1924), pp. 254 ff., 'The Baroque Style in Prose', *Studies in honour of Frédéric Klaeber*, Minnesota (1929), pp. 427 ff., and the work of Louis Martz, *The Poetry of Meditation*, Yale (1954), are also invaluable, but they have by no means exhausted the field, particularly as far as France is concerned. Mario Richter's recent articles show the rich sources which need to be explored: 'Il Processo Spirituale e Stilistico nella poesia di Jean de Sponde',

can be made a much more precise examination of these sources is needed. For by 1570 poets had turned for inspiration not so much to the Italian or Classical poetic examples as advocated in the manifestos of the Pléiade, not to the poetic practice of their French predecessors, but rather to prose sources in Latin or newly translated into French. In the works of the ancient Stoics made available by scholars like Lipsius, in the French versions of the Bible whose number increased almost daily, and in the moral and spiritual handbooks which proliferated throughout the sixteenth century, one finds both the themes listed by Rousset: 'instabilité, vicissitude, le monde à l'envers, fragilité, inconstance', and the detailed stylistic devices whose novelty has often puzzled literary historians. In this essay I wish to discuss some specific examples drawn from this vast corpus of moral and devotional works.[1] I hope to show how close they are, both thematically and stylistically, to poems of the period. My discussion will be illustrated throughout from the work of Chassignet.

Müller in his short biography of Chassignet states: 'Il est inutile de faire observer combien la pensée chrétienne, l'inspiration biblique, le souvenir des psaumes de la pénitence, des textes de la liturgie pénètrent toute cette poésie'.[2] Such a general statement suggests the extent of Chassignet's debt to biblical sources; it does not, however, reveal the nature of the debt. Nor does it show how the Bible provided both a general source of inspiration (especially the poetical books: Job, the Psalms and the Song of Solomon), and offered a rich fund of aphorisms and images, of ideas waiting to be explored and expanded. The

---

Ævum (1962), pp. 284 ff., 'La Poetica di Théodore de Bèze e le *Chrestiennes Méditations*, '*Ævum* (1964), pp. 479 ff., and 'Una fonta calvinista di J. C. Chassignet', *BHR* (1964), pp. 341 ff., and Terence Cave has examined the treatment of death in devotional literature in 'The Protestant Devotional Tradition', *French Studies*, XXI (1967), pp. 1 ff.

[1] I have chosen examples which seem to be typical expressions of the themes of life and death. Obviously, one can only be highly selective when dealing with a tradition of devotional literature which stretches back at least to St Augustine and Gregory the Great.

[2] Armand Müller, *J. B. Chassignet*, Paris (1951), p. 25.

striking centre-piece of Chassignet's Sonnet 423 for example:

> *Treuvant iniquité en les anges parfais,*
> *Le ciel croule et fremit sous ta main redoutable* . . . (vv. 5–6)

– lines which mark out the poet's sense of the despairing littleness of man – are, in fact, a fairly faithful expansion of Job IV, 18 'et a trouvé malice en ses anges'. In the French sonnet they provide the extreme of despair against which Chassignet can give extra resonant and persuasive power to the conviction of his final line:

> *En toy regeneré, j'ay domté le peché.*

Man presented as a tree, ears of corn, a worm, a leaf driven by the wind, a flower which fades, a fleeting shadow, a moth, a broken vessel, a cloud or the breeze; life seen as a fragile spider's web; man's days represented as clouds or a shadow in flight, as withered grass; all ultimately find their source in the Book of Job.[1]

Moral and philosophical traditions had long ago developed the themes of the instability, the inconstancy and vanity of the world which lay behind such images. Most of the exploration of these themes in the vernacular (in sermons, etc.) have been lost. There survive, however, multiple examples of Sebastian Brandt's popular *Ships of Fools* (first French edition 1497), which had been concerned to show the topsy-turvy nature of the world, and the equality of all men who live in it despite apparent social discrimination: 'nous semblons l'eaue qui sans demeure par la riviere passe et court', or 'le monde va tout au rebours'.[2] His preoccupations had already been explored and expanded with more specific biblical borrowings by Jean Gerson in his popular *Mirouer de la vie de l'homme et de la femme*, where life is described as 'umbre . . . muable comme est la banniere pleine de vanité/et de

---

[1] The popularity of the Book of Job in the sixteenth century is no doubt to be explained, in part, by the influence of the Calvinist insistence on man's miserable state. Chassignet translated the Book of Job about 1592 to console himself in the face of 'le trouble et misérable calamité de nostre tems' (preface); he also translated the Psalms.

[2] Edition used Paris (1579), pp. 170, 255.

misere'; man is 'ung peu de'herbe/qui tost s'en va'; his days disappear like a 'vapeur qui chiet devant la face du soleil/ou comme la flammesche qui monte en vollant . . . comme ung passant passage ou songe/dont on ne trouve rien quand on se resveille'.[1] As in Sponde's sonnet 'Mais si faut-il mourir', Gerson accumulates one image after another and lets their very number speak. Such uncommented accumulation is, in fact, his principal means of expression and persuasion; the images are presented as examples, as proofs even, he needs only to draw conclusions. Such love of enumeration extends beyond his use of image. He spares no details in his description of the effects of death on man's body 'fresle et tenue comme la toille de une araigne'; with great care and deliberation he notes the physical disintegration of 'les pieds froissez/les iambes roides/le ventre vuyde de la pointrine seiche et les bras ployez/la bouche serree/les levres pallies/le nez estouffe les oreilles sourdes/la teste enclinee/les yeulx renversez . . .'[2] Thus the reader is battered into accepting his point of view.[3]

Realistic detail was also one of the main elements of the Emblem, where the graphic representation of a heart on a plate, a crown being beset by worms, or a helmet housing honey bees, helped to rivet the attention of readers.[4] The fact that the image was given clearly defined form in the woodcuts or engravings of the hundreds of emblem books produced in the sixteenth century

[1] Quoted from ch. 3, 'De la mort'; this work is not paginated. Gerson's work was known throughout France in the sixteenth century; his *Opusculum*, for example, was given official status by the French episcopate 'obliging the clergy to read a division of it to their congregations every Sunday and to put it into their rituals' (Sister M. O'Connor, *The Art of Dying Well*, Columbia University Press, 1942, p. 22).

[2] In the *Ars moriendi* tradition, Gerson is but one writer among many to stress the detail of physical decrepitude. For the extent of this tradition see O'Connor, op. cit., *passim*. Cave quotes a similar description from St Peter Damian, art. cit., p. 5.

[3] Enumeration and similar themes are used widely in sixteenth-century prose and poetry. An outstanding prose example would be Louis Le Roy's *De la Vicissitude et variété des choses humaines*, Paris (1576). Poetic parallels are discussed in note 3, p. 149.

[4] This particular moral tradition has aroused much interest; for a brief bibliographical history of the Emblem see my article 'Moral Intention in the Fables of La Fontaine', *Journal of the Warburg and Courtauld Institutes*, 23 (1966), p. 268, note 17.

allowed their inventors to concentrate their efforts on explaining the meaning of the image, on exploring the possible interpretations. An arresting picture, an enigmatic aphorism (often a play on words in Latin or a startling paradox in French such as 'mort vivifiante'),[1] plus a poem of explanation constitute the three essential parts of the Emblem. All three elements reveal significant stylistic assumptions on the part of the moralist; first, the primary importance given to the image as a means of persuasion, then (implicit in the form of the aphorism) the appeal to ingenuity and its ability to arouse interest, and finally the conviction that poetry with its greater power of concentration strikes the imagination more forcibly than prose.[2]

The vision of life and of man which emerges from these innumerable emblem books is largely the same as the miserable version provided in the Book of Job. Man is vacillating, uncertain and weak; he is a puff of smoke, a candle or a flower which lasts only a few hours; his joys and achievements are as soap bubbles blown through a pipe; his life hangs on a frail thread ever threatening to break. 'Instabilité, fragilité, imbécillité, vicissitude, la brièveté de la vie, la toute présence de la mort': these are the themes which dominate, the preoccupations to which writers ever return:

> *Nous n'avons point un quint d'heure asseurance,*
> *Pour demeurer en estat permanent;*
> *D'estre certains n'avons point d'apparence,*
> *Que de cela que nous voyons maintenant.*[3]

---

[1] The title of no. 30 of Boissard's *Emblemes*, Metis (1588). Chassignet might well have known Boissard, since the latter was tutor to the brother of Baron de Rye, one-time Governor of Besançon.

[2] A conviction held by Montaigne and echoed by Chassignet. I have included Emblems in this survey of moral and devotional prose sources for poetry, since by the end of the sixteenth century they carried for the most part a prose commentary which analysed the significance of the Emblem poem, picture and motto.

[3] Gilles Corrozet, *Hecatongraphie*, Lyons (1543). Emblem entitled,
> *Mal dessus mal croist la douleur sans faincte,*
> *Ainsi l'estat de ce monde varie.*

Similar statements on instability were expressed by La Roche Chandieu in the many editions of his *Octonaires sur la vanité et inconstances du monde.*

Two elements are common to all the sources I have so far indicated: the themes which they develop, and the stylistic details they employ. These elements are equally present in the last two sources I wish to discuss; in the sixteenth-century editions and especially French translations of the ancient Stoic thinkers[1] – in particular Seneca – and in the devotional literature of the century, principally that written in the vernacular.[2] Unremittingly in his *Treatise on Constancy*, in his *Consolations on Death* and in his *Letters*, Seneca stressed the inconstancy and fluidity of life, its brevity, its ills and its uncertainty, and from this basis tried to promote intelligent attitudes towards death. His discussion of these age-old themes, however, seems more *nuancé* and more particularized than the expositions of the same themes found elsewhere. This impression might well come about from the fact that Seneca relies not so much on enumeration and abundance of images to make his points, but rather on a judicious use of paradox: 'ignoriez-vous que le vivre n'est qu'une fuitte?' or 'dès l'heure qu'il [l'homme] a premierement veu la lumière, il est entré en chemin de la mort', or 'nos acroissemens sont autant de diminutions', or 'chaque moment de nostre vie est la mort d'un autre'.[3] Such statements inevitably give an air of considerable powers of argumentation to Seneca's writings. One senses that while he is actually writing he is feeling his way through his thoughts. This impression is enhanced by the abruptness of his questions and exclamations – they seem more a means of thought than a way of communicating. The answers, too, are abrupt and expressed with startling concision – the kind of condensed phrases one might expect in poetry.[4] When he does use an image

---

[1] See the work of Williamson and Croll quoted above, and L. Zanta, *La renaissance du Stoïcisme au XVIe siècle*, Paris (1898).

[2] J. Dagens, *Bibliographie chronologique de la littérature de spiritualité et de ses sources 1501–1610*, Paris (1953), gives comprehensive information on titles and editions.

[3] *De la consolation de la mort* (edn. Paris, 1593), pp. 78v, 96, 96v, and *Epistres*, p. 30v, published at the end of Duplessis-Mornay's 1581 Paris edition of *Excellent Discours de la vie et de la mort*.

[4] Abruptness of question and answer was, of course, a traditional technique in devotional works which set out to teach and explain doctrine, and to analyse spiritual

it is made to carry a weight of implications; his description of man, for instance, is of 'un corps imbecille . . . nud et naturellement sans armes', and this is given sharp emphasis in the image 'un vaisseau de nulle force et fragile'.[1] On another occasion man is presented traditionally as 'un ombre et un songe'. Sometimes the image is given extra directness of impact by its verbal form; such is the abrupt statement which opens his *Consolations on Death*, 'Il faut se haster, la mort nous talonne'.[2]

The abrupt questions used by Seneca which receive equally striking and concentrated response are also the main method of argument employed in the extremely popular *Manual* of Epictetus; this work had at least three separate French translators in the sixteenth century.[3] All the questions have the simple directness and colloquial appeal of 'Qu'est ce que l'homme?' – 'semblable à une pomme . . . à un petit bouillon . . . aux fueilles de l'arbre qui non seulement voltigent, et tremblent en l'air, mais encor chient, et tombent en terre, au moindre vent qui souffle . . . aussi . . . à une fleur'.[4] Thus, in Coras's adaptation of Epictetus, it is thought that the way to provoke reflection in the reader is to combine a conversational starting-point with a traditional accumulation of images, which are then expanded into a complete description of the fragile nature of man. On this occasion abundance of image replaces the necessity to explain.

For centuries the Fathers of the Church had been accumulating their wisdom in vast Latin tomes of sermons, commentaries on the Bible and so on. These had been available only to a privileged minority of priests, monks and scholars; the sixteenth century, however, saw the vulgarization of such works, their dissemination

states. The extent to which this technique impinged on style will be discussed in the case of Granada below.

[1] *De la consolation* . . ., p. 79v.
[2] ibid., p. 78v.
[3] The *Manual* was translated into French by Du Moulin in 1544, by Coras in 1558 and by A. Rivaudeau in 1567. L. Zanta published an edition of this last work in 1914.
[4] Coras's translation, pp. 163 ff. A similar technique of colloquial questions and images provided as answers can be found in the *Cantiques* of le sieur de Maisonfleur, Paris (1586).

in French to laymen in the form of useful handbooks teaching how to 'bien vivre à fin de bien mourir'. It is difficult to exaggerate the number, popularity and importance of these works. They provide not only the richest source of imagery, and the most complete treatment of the themes of worldly inconstancy and the certitude of death, but also set out their discussion in a way which was to influence the habits of composition of several generations of poets. Out of the great number of such works I have selected two authors for relatively detailed comment; first, the many French versions of the work of Luis of Granada, the very bulk of which demands the consideration of scholars,[1] and secondly, the *Spiritual Exercises* of St Ignatius, whose importance has never been seriously questioned, but whose influence on French poets in particular has been curiously neglected.[2]

Granada's self is presented as the portrait of man in general: 'Quel nom est-ce-qu'on me donnera? Ver, mouschillon, fourmy?'[3] and later, 'moy miserable, que suis-ie, sinon un vase plein de fiente et de corruption, un ver puant et espouvantable . . . de qui les jours passent comme l'ombre, la vie croist et descroist comme la Lune, et comme la fueille qui croist en l'arbre, et en peu de temps devient seiche'.[4] Self-identification and eager

---

[1] I have found ten editions of Granada's work in French before the publication of Chassignet's poems. There are also innumerable Spanish, Italian and Latin versions. The works and editions I have used most frequently are *L'Arbre de vie*, Paris (1575), *Le vray chemin*, Paris (1579), *Le mémorial*, Paris (1602), *La* (sic) *guide des pescheurs*, Paris (1663), *Le miroir de la vie*, Paris (1602). Cave, art. cit., p. 3, notes the importance of Granada as a source. Other devotional writers whose work deserves more study are: Louis Le Blois, *Institutions spirituelles*, Paris (1553), and Jean de L'Espine, *Excellent discours . . . touchant le repos et contentement de l'esprit*, La Rochelle (1588). The style of these writers has been discussed by Martz, but their subsequent influence has been examined only as far as English poetry is concerned (see E. M. Wilson, 'Spanish and English religious poetry of the 17th century', *Journal of Ecclesiastical History* (1958), pp. 38 ff., and in this article Wilson is mainly concerned with the importance of Ledesma).

[2] I have used the Paris 1620 edition. The influence and popularity of the writings of St Ignatius have been assessed by A. Brou, *Les Exercices spirituels de S. Ignace*, Paris (1922), pp. 81 ff., and discussed by Martz, op. cit.

[3] *Dévotes contemplations*, Paris (1583), p. 208.

[4] *Le miroir de la vie*, pp. 7v–8.

participation in the sense and feelings of what he is describing distinguish the writings of Granada from the work of his contemporary moralists who stand back at a greater distance from their words. 'Clouez-moi,' he shouts impulsively as he contemplates Christ on the Cross.[1] He is both spiritually and emotionally involved in what he has to say. Such involvement is reflected in the large-scale enumeration in which he often indulges, as though only more and more data can finally turn his mind from the miseries of the world: 'un magasin de travaux, une école de vanitez, un marché de tromperies, un labyrinthe d'erreur, une prison de tenebres, un chemin de voleurs, un lac sale et bourbeux, une mer agitée de continuels orages, une terre stérile, un champ pierreux, un bois rempli d'épines, un pré verd mais plain des serpens';[2] and so he goes on interminably, juxtaposing pleasant places with their natural opposites, carried away by his own power of eloquence, never once doubting the accuracy of his imaginative inventions. He says himself that he uses his imagination to give clear visible form to abstract ideas, to place his arguments *'devant les yeux'* of his readers.[3] The latter are not allowed to be lulled into dull or sleepy receptivity by uninterrupted lists of images; their minds are kept ever alert by sudden intrusions such as 'Considère donc, ô homme, ce que tu estois avant que tu nasquisses',[4] by strange colloquialisms and exclamations, now addressed to man: 'O cendre de quoy loues-tu?'[5] or 'Plaignez-vous, miserables, plus variables que le vent',[6] now to God: 'O clarté et splendeur de lumiere éternelle, vie qui donne vie à toutes chose qui vit, lumiere illuminant tout ce qui reluit.'[7] The language is self-creative. Sentences are built up through playing on the words and their sense. Dramatic changes of narrative occur. The narrator speaks familiarly no longer to himself or

---

[1] *Dévotes contemplations*, p. 260.

[2] *La Guide des pescheurs*, pp. 495 ff.

[3] *Le vray chemin*, p. 90; the italics are mine throughout.

[4] *Le miroir de la vie*, p. 6.

[5] ibid., p. 8v.

[6] ibid., p. 34.

[7] *Dévotes contemplations*, p. 263.

to God, but to Death depicted as a powerful personnage: 'tu vas par tout, tu circuis tout, et te trouve en toute place: tu ronges les herbes, humes les vents, corrompts l'air'; the repetitive active verbs increase the impression of dominance, which is crowned by the images 'tu est un marteau qui frappe toujours, espée non jamais engainée'.[1] And finally, as though this picture of Death were incomplete, Granada urges the reader: 'tu dois prier Dieu qu'il *te face sentir* quelque peu ce qui se passe en ceste bataille dernière'.[2] There follows the grim, realistic details of a body suffering in the throes of a death agony. If we were to add antithesis, comparisons and prayer, then we would have run the whole gamut of Granada's stylistic devices, all used to explain, to point out, to demonstrate, to persuade and finally to encourage the faithful not only to be better people and to make themselves worthy of God, but also to know themselves more intimately. The overflowing exuberance of the language often hides searching analyses, woven into a clear framework of prayers and preludes, which stress the vivid, concrete context of the often invisible, and colloquies spoken direct to God which never allow the reader to forget that the end and purpose of life is a spiritual one.

Much more deliberate and specific is the use of, and appeal to, the senses in the *Spiritual Exercises* of St Ignatius. To present any abstract ideas for the consideration of his readers he felt it essential, in his first prelude on Death for example, 'que *je m'imagine vivement*, de me voir couché dans un lict abandonné des Medecins, sans aucun espoir de vivre plus longtemps',[3] and secondly (2e Prelude) 'que je demande grace à Dieu de *ressentir maintenant* les ennuys, regrets et fascheries qui ordinairement nous assaillent à l'heure de la mort'.[4] Only if readers can be made to share in the *imagining* and *feeling* of such thoughts and experiences can they understand and overcome the fear of death. In order to urge his readers to greater spirituality, he methodically displays before

[1] *Le vray chemin*, p. 106v.
[2] *Le vray chemin*, p. 108v.
[3] 1620 edition, p. 74.
[4] ibid., p. 74.

them the horrors of Hell, spelling out the impact made on the five senses, and using to the full their various powers of sensation. 'Le premier Poinct, de *voir par imagination* les grands feux de l'Enfer . . . Le 2e *ouyr aussi par l'imagination* le grand dueil, les plaintes et regrets . . . contre Jesus Christ, . . . Le 3e de *sentir par un flair imaginaire* la fumée, le souphre, l'infection qui sort de là . . . Le 4e de *gouster semblablement* des choses très amères comme larmes, rancoeur et le vers de conscience . . . Le 5e de *toucher en certaine façon* ces flammes.'[1] After such a clear demonstration of the persuasive power of method combined with the action of the senses, it is hardly surprising that poets like Jean de La Ceppède seem to be following St Ignatius's instructions to the letter when they fix their attention on a particular moment of the Passion of Christ, then conscientiously apply their senses to this moment, and finally explain and interpret their poetic effusions in the cold rationalizations of a prose commentary.

This exploration of a variety of source materials serves to demonstrate that there is a noteworthy similarity between the themes which are thoroughly examined and analysed by the French prose writers and moralists of the sixteenth century and those explored by religious poets of late sixteenth- and early seventeenth-century France. The closeness of such themes of inconstancy, change, metamorphosis, brevity of life and pre-occupation with death in poetry and prose might not at first seem particularly significant until it is seen that there is similar correlation in the manner in which they are expressed. The very nature of these themes seems to demand that they are given the most vivid form possible, then the image becomes the primary means of expression; the central paradox of life and death is most strikingly stated through aphorism and antithesis, which stress the latent contradictions, the alternatives and co-existing opposites in the theme. Throughout the discussion of these themes it has been apparent that the intention of the authors seems to be equally divided between Meditation and Persuasion: Meditation, which

[1] ibid., pp. 84 ff.

calls for considerable analytical powers, for clear definitions, lucid exposition and an awareness of the limits of the meaning of a word; Persuasion, which necessitates argument and which might indulge in complicated, syntactical distortions and witty word play for the learned – 'Qui apprend à mourir, desapprend de servir'[1] – and which assumes a directness of approach, producing exclamations, questions, friendly colloquialisms, references to harsh reality and a great quantity of examples and images to aid demonstrations for the unsophisticated layman.

J. B. Chassignet published his *Mespris de la Vie et Consolation contre la mort* in 1594.[2] On his own admission the composition of these 434 sonnets employed his undivided attention for six months, and it is natural that in order to accomplish such a feat he had recourse to specific sources of inspiration which he used freely. It is precisely the speed with which this work was composed, and the consequent closeness of many of the poems to their sources (some of them are virtually translations, very like simple scholastic exercises, or certainly very close adaptations of the original texts), which make Chassignet's work valuable to the literary historian. His borrowings echo his sources so faithfully that one is able to judge in detail the nature of the influence of prose writers on this poet whose work falls right in the middle of the period 1570–1630.[3] He says himself that he used extensively the Bible and the work of Lipsius,[4] and scholars have found that

---

[1] Seneca, *Epistres* (1582), p. 86.

[2] I quote for the most part from Müller's edition of the *Mespris*, Paris (1953), supplemented by sonnets from A. M. Schmidt's *Poètes du XVIe siècle*, Pléiade (1959), and in some instances I have used the first edition 1594 (B. N. Rés, Ye 2003 bis).

[3] There are other poets employing similar techniques and themes at this time, whose work would also illustrate my points: Jean d'Avila, *Epîtres spirituelles*, n.p. (1586), Jacques de Billy, *Sonnets spirituels*, Paris (1575), Y. Rouspeau, *Quatrains spirituels*, n.p. (1586), and the work of Sponde. The popularity of such works can be gauged from the printer's remarks to the 1587 edition of Maisonfleur's *Cantiques*: they are works 'que les hommes d'entendement, dont la France ne manque point en ce siecle, leur ont raizonnablement adiugé le premier rang en l'ouvrage des Muzes', sig.a ij.

[4] 1594 edition, p. 241: 'A quiconque voudra diligemment esplucher ce discours tiré des œuvres de Lipsius . . .'

150

his preface is no more than a strange patchwork of sentences from Montaigne,[1] and that some of his poems are direct translations of passages from Duplessis-Mornay's *Excellent Discours*[2] and from Seneca's writings.[3] He must have been a voracious reader, making indiscriminate use of both Catholic and Protestant writings,[4] and anxious to devour all the latest products of erudition whether they were the learned editions of Justus Lipsius or, for his *Paraphrases sur les douze petis Prophetes* (completed in 1598), the learned commentaries of Arias Montanus in his *Bible d'Anvers* of 1583.[5]

The main theme of the book, preparing himself and others to face, even to welcome death, needed no apology. As we have seen, the miseries of life and the all-powerful domination of the fact of death had been one of the major preoccupations of all the prose writers of the sixteenth century.[6] In addition his theme was especially suited to that historical moment: 'ie choisis un suiet conforme au malheur de nostre siecle' (preface, p. 12).[7] His work, then, both from its title and its context, prepares an attitude, and possibly proposes a solution to the personal and general distress felt as a result of the Wars of Religion. Meditating upon

---

[1] R. E. Leake, jun., 'J. B. Chassignet et Montaigne', *BHR*, 23 (1961), pp. 282 ff., shows that although Chassignet's borrowings from Montaigne are particularly striking in the preface to the *Mespris*, he owes little to him in the body of his work.

[2] See Richter's article 'Una fonta calvinista', art. cit., *passim*.

[3] J. C. Arens, 'J. B. Chassignet of Seneca', *Neophilologus* (1963), pp. 73 ff. This problem has not been thoroughly explored in this article, whose author uses as a basis for his argument an edition of the *Letters* of Seneca published ten years after the *Mespris*.

[4] It was not unusual for Protestant and Catholic writers to borrow from each other's work. As Terence Cave has pointed out, it is virtually impossible to distinguish two separate traditions, since writers, whatever their creed, were working from the same devotional and stoic sources.

[5] See Müller's biography, p. 33.

[6] 'Death' had, of course, inspired great poetry in the sixteenth century, to name but Ronsard. Although the influence of poetry upon poets at this time was undoubtedly great, I prefer to limit myself here to prose sources.

[7] Chassignet also stresses in his *Sonnet au Lecteur* that he writes to relieve his conscience; his words are:

> *Enfans spirituels du remords langoureux*
> *Qui sans aucun respit me bourrelle et martire . . .* (vv. 3–4).

151

the swift passage of time, on the inadequacies of life and the re-
wards of life after death, Chassignet follows very closely both the
intentions and the method of devotional writers such as Granada.
Müller's edition of selected sonnets gives a misleading impression
of Chassignet's work. This consists of nine series of sonnets, each
preceded by a long prose introduction, interspersed with extended
prose sections addressed to immediate friends which explain his
intentions. The series of sonnets are separated by long lyrical
poems, prayers to God which often seem like litanies of hope,
expressed in the form of opposing ideas brought together in
matching rhythms and parallel constructions:

> *O clarté sans laquelle il n'est point de clarté*
> *Lumiere sans laquelle autre n'a point esté*
> *Clarté obscurcissant la clarté coustumière*
> *Lumière esblouissant toute estrange lumière . . .*[1]

Alternatively, they may take on the form of psalms of conviction
and thankfulness, using multiple images as proofs:

> *O Seigneur tout Puissant, maintenant je voy bien*
> *Que les fresles honneurs du monde ne sont rien*
> *Qu'une ombre passagere, une fumiere, un songe*
> *Une fable, un phantosme, un inconstant mensonge . . .*[2]

There are long acts of contrition, *syndarèzes*,[3] analyses of conscience, followed by more general poems designed to summarize
the main themes of each section. The layout of the work with its
personal moments of conscience and contrition, and the general
applicability of its theme, differs in no way from the divisions of a
prose work of meditation, except in the important respect that
the matter of meditation is here rendered in poetry. Chassignet
even feels the need to defend his use of poetry by quoting

[1] 1594 edition, p. 361.

[2] ibid. p. 391.

[3] *Syndarèze* is the normal term used in meditation to signify analysis and clarification
of conscience, and remorse; p. 140 of the 1594 edition reads, for example, 'Cette
syndarese fait voir à l'oeil en quelle confusion languit le pecheur, qui se deffiant de la
misericorde du pere celeste adresse sa plainte aus hommes.'

Montaigne's opinion that verse has a greater power of persuasion: 'ainsi me semble-il que la sentence passee aus pies nombreus de la poësie s'élance bien plus brusquement et nous siert d'une vive secousse';[1] the impact of poetry is more immediate, its effect more lasting.

The mingling of poetry and prose had become common in emblem and devotional literature. La Ceppède's *Théorèmes* have extended commentaries; de Billy announces in the title of his *Sonnets* that they are 'commentés en prose'. But Chassignet goes much further in matching his poems to prose works of meditation. In the section addressed to Pierre Bichet, 'L'Autheur s'émerveille que nous ne mourons plus librement, parce que la fin de toutes nos actions est le repos . . . comme l'Autheur te le propose icy sans l'assouvissement des cinq sens corporels ne pouvant autrement expliquer la grandeur et perfection des ioyes spirituelles que par la conference d'icelles avecques les choses que nous avons de plus exquises et délicieuses en ce monde'. Chassignet, a good student of Granada and Ignatius, then exploits the five senses literally and systematically:

> *De l'oreille et de l'oeil que ie t'ay recité*
> *Le goust y prendra part . . .*[2]

> *L'odeur que l'on y sent? c'est bien toute autre chose*
> *Que le lis que le thym, que l'oeillet et la rose . . .*[3]

Perhaps the first feature of Chassignet's style which strikes a reader of his poems is the abundance of the imagery – images of the same type which we have encountered in prose works of meditation. Through images, abstract ideas about life and death are given concrete and sometimes almost dramatic form. In Sonnet 98 for example, to answer the question 'Qu'est ce de vostre vie?' Chassignet supplies a series of images – 'une bouteille molle,/Qui s'enfle dessus l'eau', 'un mensonge frivole, un songe',

---

[1] 1594 edition, preface, p. 18.
[2] ibid., pp. 269 ff.
[3] ibid., pp. 281 ff.

and 'un tourbillon roüant/De fumiere a flos gris'. Each image is briskly described; each one contains or implies assumptions about the worthlessness of existence, assumptions which in the last three lines of the poem are presented as proofs of worthlessness:

> *Puis vous negligerez dorenavant le bien*
> *Durable, et permanent, pour un point qui n'est rien*
> *Qu'une confle, un mensonge, un songe, une fumiere.*

Thus, in a final line, Chassignet draws together his images as 'proofs', giving a sense of indisputable conclusion to his poem. He employs the same traditional technique in his following poem (Sonnet 99):

> *Desires-tu sçavoir à quoy je paragonne*
> *Le fuseau de tes ans? Au sa[v]on blanchissant*
> *Soufflé par un tuyau de paille jaunissant,*
> *Dont un fol enfançon ses compagnons estonne;*
>
> *En son lustre plus beau sa gloire l'abandonne,*
> *Au moindre choc de l'air, fragile, se froissant:*
> *Ainsi devers le soir va la fleur ternissant,*
> *Qui, sur le point du jour, vermeillement fleuronne.*
>
> *L'ombre est tantost icy, et puis soudainement*
> *Elle s'evanouit: ainsi legerement*
> *S'enfuit la vie humaine, inconstante et volage.*
>
> *Aveugle, cependant, sur tes jours passagers*
> *Tu fondes ton espoir, qui passent plus legers*
> *Que ne fait le sa[v]on, ny la fleur, ny l'ombrage.*

As he tells us in his opening question, Chassignet deliberately sets out to make a demonstration through image. The first, 'savon blanchissant', is given extended treatment into the second quatrain, its fragile beauty being broken not only by the movement of the breeze, but already undermined by the adjective 'fol' and the choice of the verb 'estonner'; there is exact correspondence with the author's view of worldly 'gloire'. The second image of the fading beauty of the flower is tersely and conventionally stated. In a quickening rhythm the fleeting presence of the shade is felt in the first tercet, leaving just room for the comparison with human life, and the important characterizing words 'soudaine-ment, inconstante, volage'. As a demonstration the poem could well have ended here. Chassignet, however, knew how to handle the sonnet form in such a way that the maximum degree of per-suasion is achieved. In the final tercet he makes an abrupt and direct appeal to the reader, then spells out the implications of his poem by drawing the three images together again in a final line as in the previous sonnet.

His definition of Hope which occurs in Sonnet 364 provides a particularly striking example of Chassignet's use of accumulation of image:

> *L'Esperance du monde est un glas à l'ardeur,*
> *Du Soleil chaleureus, son tourment et sa peine*
> *De L'Automne souillart, une fiebvre quartaine,*
> *Ses esbas sont d'Avril une caduque fleur;*
>
> *Ses ris du mois de Mars ressemblent la splendeur*
> *Qui tost s'esvanouit, ses chans sont de Syreine,*
> *Ses desirs esventez sont semence en l'areine,*
> *Ses pensers sont du vent evaporez en pleur.*
>
> *D'un ferme diamant, il compose sa guerre,*
> *La tresve qu'il impetre est un fragile verre,*
> *Ses dedains sont un feu en la paille attisé.*
>
> *L'hydre nait de sa peur; son amour desloyale*
> *Est celle de Phebus dans les chams [de] Thessale,*
> *Son service d'araigne un travail mesprisé.*

A continuous series of images flows on uninterruptedly. There is an overall impression of analysis, and yet the images are left un-explained, their significance being contained either in the very choice of images, such as 'ses chans sont de Syreine', or in a qualifying word or phrase, 'caducque' or 'Qui tost s'esvanouit'.

The final tercet opens out into images of greater scope and grandeur, but their force is cut off by the adjective 'desloyale', and Hope is moulded to appropriate insignificance through the deflationary effect and disillusionment of the final image.

Such accumulation is a favourite technique of persuasion in Chassignet's poetry; he strings together not only images, but nouns, verbs and adjectives. Nevertheless, he often chooses to explore the possibilities of a single image as in Sonnet 383, where the force of the wind is gradually, painfully built up:

> *Sur le commencement à grand peine respire*
> *Le vent debile et lent, puis venant escrouler*
> *Les fresnes et les pins, il fait au ciel voler*
> *Le sablon tournoyant au voiloir de son ire* . . .

At first the wind 'debile et lent', kept back until the second line of the poem, hardly seems to breathe, then gathering momentum through two enjambements it sends the sand whirling through the air. Then active verbs build up its strength:

> *De là plus furieus, il sappe, il heurte, il tire*
> *Le rocher contre val et fait en bas rouler*
> *Les arbres arrachez, tempester et bransler*
> *Des monstres mariniers le fluctueus empire* . . .

The rhythm has noticeably speeded up and the movement is now more violent as the most stable elements of nature, trees and rocks, are uprooted and thrown down; the raging of the seas completes the tempestuous tide. The acceleration and the rising noise and damage of the storm are matched to the gentle, insinuating charms of the world, whose skill disarms the powers of reason:

> *Ainsi le monde caut, par mille dous appas,*
> *Peu à peu nous tirant doucement au trespas*
> *N'use pour quelque tems de ses plus fieres armes.*
>
> *A il gaigné le fort de la foible raison,*
> *Il s'enfle, il frappe, il met le feu dans la maison* . . .

With triple verbs matching the pattern and rhythm of verse 5, worldly temptation destroys man. A final exclamatory line of general implication, 'Heureus qui clot l'oreille aus accens de ses charmes!' is the only necessary word of warning after the persuasive force given to the movement of the rest of the poem.

Sometimes the image is made arresting in itself, like the realism and associations of verses 10–11 (135):

> *Et le morceau glouton du dommageable fruit*
> *Nous pend encore à tous à la bouche rebelle . . .*

or the personalization of:

> *Las! je suis le courbeau qui s'arreste, et ne fait*
> *Comte de revenir en la Sainte nascelle* (vv. 5–6, 424),

so that further explanation seems superfluous. Self-condemnation is already contained in the identification of the author and the crow. The much more personal note which emerges from this poem occurs mainly in the final sonnets of Chassignet's work, and in the long lyrical prose and poetic passages which separate the nine series of sonnets. Much more frequent is the pointedly argumentative twist given to the image of 133. The sonnet begins with a general commonplace:

> *N'est-ce pas la raison que le profit redonde*
> *Au lieu duquel il sort?*

This is followed by the image describing the restricted and regulated movement of the waves:

> *. . . et que dedans la mer*
> *Les fleuves ondoyans se viennent renfermer,*
> *Puisque de la mer mesme ils derivent leur onde?*

The image is merely a stepping-stone in the main argument which moves from the conclusion Chassignet has arrived at on the sea to a similar conclusion made about the earth. The demonstration is then transferred through a repetition of the word 'earth' to the

157

sphere of the world: 'Tout ce qui vit au monde est de la terre fait'. This general maxim is the pivot of the poem. Its accuracy seems now unchallengeable and takes the poet naturally and uninterruptedly to the final commonplace statement of 'Une ville poussiere, en poussiere retourne'.

Throughout this discussion of Chassignet's use of the image, it will have been apparent that the material he chooses is very familiar. Life is 'un songe, une fleur, un fuseau'; it is also 'une vapeur' (2), 'un espais nuage' (246), 'un chemin tortueus' (15), 'une lampe enfumée' (40), 'un filet incertain' (145, 250, 291), 'une prison' (352), 'une toile d'araigne' (257). Similarly man is an 'esquif' (69, 250), 'escorce, cocque fragile' (97), 'ver' (114), 'couleuvre' (122), 'glaive fragile' (285), 'chandelle' (290), 'ombre ou fleur' (395) and so on. Death is 'un masque' (49, 149), 'un havre' (52, 53, 59), 'logis' (283), 'horloge' (336) and 'un monstre' (150). We have encountered all these images before, echoed from the prose works of sixteenth-century moralists; Chassignet clearly points to his spiritual fathers both in the choice of image he makes and in the persuasive power he attributes to it. It is, of course, in the recognition of this last point that Chassignet is able to demonstrate his own individuality and originality as a poet. Since he is able to assume a certain familiarity on the part of his reader with most of the images he uses, he can readily assume a quick understanding of, and even agreement on, the general points he makes. He can also afford to use our knowledge, and, by puncturing our normal expectations, teach us – through surprise as it were. Sonnet 283 begins conventionally enough with the presentation of practical facts of spring and early summer:

> *Quand les arbres fruitiers au Primte[m]s fleurissans,*
> *Mettent hors de leurs trons mille jetons fertiles,*
> *C'est un signe evident que les courbes faucilles*
> *Doivent tost retrancher les rameaus surcroissans . . .*

Then, without any word of explanation, comes the unexpected parallel, which is almost brutal in its simplicity, and even spine-chilling in the vague evocation of verse 8:

> *Voir naistre en la maison les enfans innocens,*
> *C'est un ajournement aus peres de familles*
> *D'aller pourrir en bref comme plantes steriles*
> *Sous la muette horreur des tombeaus pallissans.*

Deliberately disturbing the normal syntax of the phrase, Chassignet matches the rhythm of the opening lines of 404 to the content of the image he has chosen:

> *Parmi les vers herbis, la brebis esgaree*
> *Seulette entre les rocs, les mons et les destrois,*
> *Ne sçait de quel chemin elle doit faire chois,*
> *S'estant de l'air voilé la clarté separee.*

The sheep picks its way through a complex syntax which holds up both the main verb and the explanation of why it is lost. Physical isolation makes the obstacles which pile up in front of it – 'les rocs, les mons et les destrois' – seem innumerable and insurmountable; even 'les vers herbis' loom up to hide the way. After underlining the hesitant, panicky steps of the sheep in the first words, the next four lines seem at first to linger on the mental distress of the animal:

> *De ça de là courant, triste et desesperee,*
> *Pensant au cris piteux de sa dolente vois*
> *Attirer son pasteur . . .*

This slow long phrase, lengthened by description and explanation, suddenly accelerates, and within seconds the wolf has arrived and greedily eaten the sheep:

> *. . . fait sortir hors du bois*
> *Le loup qui de sa chair prend sa gloute curee.*

The poem continues with Chassignet's personal identification with the sheep, already so sympathetically painted; he sees himself already in the clutches of the wolf – 'Mes cris desesperez de ce monstre testu' (v. 10) – when he recalls the power of God, His strength and ability to save the life of the sheep that was lost. Perhaps the emotional content of this particular sonnet is its most powerful element of persuasion; but however one defines it, it is evident that persuasion, argument, as well as meditation, have been present in all the examples we have analysed from Chassignet.

His determination to persuade himself and others of certain attitudes towards life and death was by no means limited to his handling of imagery. He resorts to strange inversions, which do not always seem to be simple clumsinesses or archaic use of language; he uses long periphrases (336), intellectual demonstrations by multiple examples (193). His work is littered with argumentative terms, with 'donc, mais, tant que, telle, ainsi, afin de, alors', and with demonstrative words which point out, clarify and explain. Most consistent, however, throughout his poems is Chassignet's addiction to aphorisms and paradox, often accompanied by a sustained playing with words and sounds.

Writing on the subject of death in his *Letters*, Seneca comments 'Celuy qui presche de penser à la mort, presche de penser à la liberté. Qui apprend à mourir, desapprend de servir.'[1] The first two quatrains of Chassignet's second sonnet read:

> *Celuy quiconque apprend à mourir constamment*
> *Des-aprent à servir, et n'y a violence,*
> *Torture, ny prison dont l'extreme souffrance*
> *Rompe de ses desseins le stable fondement.*

> *Mediter à la mort, c'est le commencement*
> *De vivre en liberté; douteusement balance*
> *Sans resolution, jouet de l'inconstance,*
> *Celuy qui du trespas redoute le torment.*

The poet has simply changed the order of Seneca's aphorism, introducing more detailed examples to draw out the meaning of the maxim. There is no doubt that Chassignet found many of his most dramatic phrases in the works of Seneca and others;[2] the

---

[1] *Epistres* (1582), p. 86.

[2] Principally in Duplessis-Mornay's *Excellent Discours* (1581 edition), p. 2, for example, 'Nous appellons vie, une mort continuelle: et mort, l'issue d'une mort vivante', or p. 16, 'Nous cerchons la solitude pour fuir la solicitude', or p. 19 v, 'en toute la vie n'y a rien de certain, rien d'asseuré, que la certitude et incertitude de la mort'.

important fact to consider, however, is not so much where he found such lines, but why he felt the need to look for them and use them in so great a quantity. Reference has already been made to the provoking power of paradox, and to the fact that such a contradictory way of saying things conveniently expresses the nature of the themes which interest Chassignet most. These are natural opposites – permanence and impermanence, certainty of death and uncertainty of life, the pull of the world measured against the possible disasters of after-life, and so forth. To show how close death is to life, to bring out the dangers always present in living in the world, what better way of doing this than by stating categorically, 'Nostre vivre n'est rien qu'une éternelle mort' (44, v. 3). Chassignet places such challenging statements at the most dramatic points of his poems – either the first or last lines of a sonnet, where they can arouse the greatest interest from his reader, and carry the most conviction: 'On ne vit point quant l'ame à la mort est sujette' (14, v. 14); either they are proved true by the elaboration of the poem, or they appear as natural conclusions to a demonstration already made clear. Occasionally they serve as stepping-stones in an argument used to bridge an awkward jump, as in Sonnet 133 above; yet always, it seems, they are assumed to be statements of truth, of general application, of a universality such that they admit of no serious challenge. We all become familiar with them because they stay so easily in the memory, we repeat and accept them like proverbs; they are, in the final analysis, totally convincing.

Such statements receive extra power of communication and retention if they are underlined by the sound of the words. The paradox 'Nostre vie n'est rien qu'une éternelle mort' (44, v. 3) acquires extra force at the end of 245 by the simple repetition of the idea 'death' in two senses, 'Et mourant par la mort nous retournons en vie'. This same idea is contained in the final line of 429, 'Je serois ja perdu si je ne me perdoy', but this time with a play on the meaning of 'perdre'. Words which sound alike are irresistible for Chassignet and his contemporaries; 'mort' and 'mord' are constantly brought clashing together to provoke the mind of the reader, as in 'Tant sa mort a le mord de la mort sur-montée' (81, v. 4). In all probability this would not have been considered an unfortunate pun by sixteenth-century readers, but rather as a legitimate means of arousing interest.[1] The complex play on the word 'monde' with double meanings, contrasted with its natural opposite 'immonde', provides Chassignet with one of his favourite themes. While developing an idea suggested already by the word play of Duplessis-Mornay's 'Nous ne pouvons faire mourir le monde en nous: et pour se separer du monde, se faut sesparer de soy-mesme',[2] he theoretically poses the problem whether it is possible to combat 'En nous mesmes le monde pour le monde' (62, v. 5). The sonnet had begun with a dramatic and forceful statement:

> *Toujours contre le ciel la terre estrive et gronde,*
> *La chair contre l'esprit . . .*[3]

exposing the difficulties which continuously beset man in the world. The poem ends on six lines which depend for their impact exclusively on a relentless repetition of the words 'monde/immonde':

> *Tasche-tu d'eschapper du monde desastreus?*
> *Le monde te poursuit au cercueil tenebreus,*
> *Et le monde trompeur, par le monde t'offence.*
>
> *Par tout le monde est monde, et l'immunde mondain*
> *Le treuve autant immunde au pays plus lointain,*
> *Que le monde est immunde au lieu de sa naissance.*

Such apparently tight argumentation, although dependent on the simple expedient of word play, constituted Chassignet's most

---

[1] See Professor Boase's discussion of this point in Sponde, *Poésies*, Paris (1949), pp. 110–11.

[2] *Excellent Discours*, p. 15.

[3] See Duplessis-Mornay for the source, ibid., p. 15: 'Mais le pis est, que lors que nous sommes hors de toutes ces guerres et travaux extremes, nous sentons d'autant plus une guerre intestine en nous-mêmes, la chair contre l'esprit, la passion contre la raison, la terre contre le ciel, le monde combattant en nous mêmes par le monde . . . ' Perhaps Sponde remembered this passage when he wrote his sonnet 'Tout s'enfle . . .'

effective way of showing his readers how the world clings to those who live in it, and how drastic must be the means to avoid its dangers and pitfalls.

It would be wrong to assume from these examples that Chassignet's approach to the reader was always an argument held at arm's length, presented to delight the intellect. Persistent throughout his writings is the desire to make direct contact, to shock his readers into thought, with an opening which pointedly dramatizes, 'Le voicy, je le voy', then once curiosity has been thoroughly aroused, he introduces 'ce faus prince du monde' – the subject of his Sonnet 418. On other occasions he imitates the questioning style of Epictetus's *Manual*, abruptly demanding 'Qu'est ce de vostre vie?' (98), or again he colloquially asks:

> *Que te chaut-il mortel, à quelle heure tu sorte*
> *Puis qu'il te faut sortir? (10)*

The abruptness with which the question is posed startles the reader into agreement, and the poet having posited the fact of death so convincingly can then set about his work of consolation. A similar kind of shoulder-nudging familiarity is present in 427 when he asks:

> *Quoy ma chair, jusqu'à quand feras tu peu d'estime*
> *De la droite raison?*

The straightforward question seems to take away the conventional covering from this age-old problem, giving this theme a fresh approach.

When not only the manner of procedure is straightforward and frank, but also the very matter of his considerations distinctly unusual, then Chassignet attains the maximum of impact. Such is the opening of 282 in the context of a series of poems which assert one after the other the inescapable certitude of death:

> *O mort, c'est fait de toy, il n'en est plus memoire;*
> *Ton aiguillon est mort.*

The shock of such an apparently contradictory statement can

163

only be absorbed when it is made clear that the poet is speaking for Jesus Christ, and adapting the words of the Apostles; and yet, even with this knowledge the effect of the astounding opening to the poem is lasting.

There remains one final way which Chassignet employs to ensure the full attention and participation of his readers. He attacks them, provoking them with names and warnings, 'Malheur à vous, mondains qui vivez en plaisirs' (325, v. 1), or again, 'Pauvre ver qui tracasse et travaille sans cesse' (373, v. 1); the insult is made stronger by the implied futility of the worm's exhausting activities. Chassignet deliberately arouses indignation in order to humble, in order to quieten the passions he provokes, by proofs of the miseries of life, and the constant upholding of Christian death as the only worthwhile goal for mortal man. Mortality with all the accompanying decrepitude rests at the forefront of the poet's mind; to arouse our disgust at ourselves, in particular at our bodies, he links a lyrical appeal with stark realism:

> Mortel, pense quel est dessous la couverture
> D'un charnier mortuaire un cors mangé de vers,
> Descharné, desnervé, où les os descouvers
> Depoulpez, desnouez, delaissant leur jointure (125, vv. 1–4).

One is not allowed to deny the nasty truth of this relentless reminder, which is sustained throughout the length of the sonnet. It recalls the crude descriptions of the oncoming of death imagined by Granada or brought into the conscious mind by the alert senses of St Ignatius.

Moral and devotional prose works were undoubtedly well known to Chassignet. He imitated their themes and their method, giving prime importance to the persuasive power of the image. The fact that his work is largely devoid of the musical qualities of earlier sixteenth-century lyric poetry might be explained by his theme, which stresses persuasion and consolation. It might also be explained by a style which had been modelled, consciously or unconsciously, both on the practice of Stoics – acknowledging their abruptness and power of argument – and on a close reading of works of meditative literature, recognizing the directness of their appeal and the cumulative effect of images and paradox. In any event, exploration of the detail of such sources and their confrontation with poems of this period are obviously needed before it is possible to give an adequate stylistic or historical account.

Margaret McGowan

Henri IV and James VI and I

⟫⟫ ⟫⟫ ⟫⟫ ⟫⟫ ⟫⟫ ⟫⟫ ⟫⟫ ⟫⟫ ⟫⟫ ⟫⟫ ⟫⟫ ⟪⟪ ⟪⟪ ⟪⟪ ⟪⟪ ⟪⟪ ⟪⟪ ⟪⟪ ⟪⟪ ⟪⟪ ⟪⟪ ⟪⟪

TO MENTION in collocation the names of these two monarchs may seem the prelude to an essay in antithesis.

Navarre appears always as a heroic figure. Bred to hardihood among the youth of Béarn, with whom he is said to have sometimes played barefooted, as well as bareheaded, throughout his life he displays a very high courage, promptness and resolution.

He has a pretty wit which sometimes leads him into injudicious jokes, as when he says that the three great mysteries of his age are – whether Maurice of Nassau was personally brave; of what religion he himself was; and whether Queen Elizabeth was a maid or not?[1]

Yet, in the main, his speech is pithy and he can say the decisive word – *le Roi de Navarre disait toujours ce qu'il fallait dire*, and his speech is matched by his deeds. He is *un Roi à la Française, un roi à cheval, soldat et capitaine*,[2] always the man of action; yet always *homme de cœur*, not only in his love affairs, but also in his concern for the humblest of his subjects.

James VI on the other hand, educated in his feeble youth to pedantry, seems to shamble across the historic stage; weak-legged, loose-lipped, timorous, undecided, sly, a talkative theorist – the 'Dominie King'.

The popular images of these two personalities need some adjustment.

The generosity of Henri was tempered by a shrewd self-interest

[1] *Secret History* I, p .75.
[2] Mariéjol I, pp. 297, 307.

167

which he identified – not without justice – with the interest of France. He was ambitious, and drove always to his end.

His changes of religion can be justified by the pressure of necessity in a changing age; but they were sometimes a little kaleidoscopic. Bred in strict Calvinism by his mother, he abjured to save his life in the St Bartholemew; when he escaped from court in 1576, he at once became the champion of the Protestant *résistance*. When division appeared in the Roman Catholic ranks he made a '*politique*' alliance with the French king, and when he mounted the throne himself he 'received instruction' in 1593 and became a Roman Catholic. 'Paris was well worth a Mass!' – though he did his best for his Protestant subjects by the Edict of Nantes in 1598.

In that year he made a 'separate peace' with Spain at Vervins, abandoning Elizabeth (who had constantly supported him with men and money – £377,000 in 1591–3 – but was demanding guarantees) with the remark 'J'ayme autant estre mordu d'ung chien come gratigne d'ung chat'.[1] While he pled poverty to explain his action, and also his inability to aid the old ally Scotland, he managed to conduct the successful war against Savoy which acquired for France the useful little duchies of Bress and Bugey on her south-eastern flank (1601).

He has been deemed inconstant in his loves and in his friendships, one who forgot services as well as injuries; and the thirty-two wounds that Biron had taken for France did not save him when he conspired against his king.

For all his gallantry Henri was a realist.

James, for his part, was not altogether the grotesque figure of the *Fortunes of Nigel*.[2] The picture has been willingly received by English writers, who attributed the contrast between his reign

---

[1] S. P. Dom, 1595–97, October 5-15, John Petit to Peter Halins (who was really Thomas Philipps, the decipherer).

[2] Scott's picture, which in any case showed an ageing king, was founded upon the *Character of King James* written by Sir Anthony Weldon, an Englishman, who had lost his post in the royal household for writing a lampoon upon the Scots. *Secret History* II, p. 1.

and that of Elizabeth to the shortcomings of an outlandish king;
though, in fact, the last years of the great queen were beset by
difficulties – financial, constitutional, religious, and political –
which would have confronted any successor.

He was feeble of foot, but a very good horseman;[1] he was not
ill-looking – an Italian observer, who saw him when he went south
in 1603, was favourably impressed: 'e di facci bella, nobile e
giovale'.[2] He lacked personal dignity; but he could use the good
Scots tongue, and had a real sense of humour. His erudition and
eloquence were generally noted by his contemporaries.

He was naturally timorous. Perhaps owing to his mother's
experiences during the murder of Rizzio some months before his
birth, with him, as with Thomas Hobbes, 'fear was born with
him'; but he did his best to conquer his fears.

A French observer wrote in 1584: 'Pour avoir esté nourry en
crainte il a encore ce manque . . . et néantmoins, il ayme
extremement d'estre estimé hardy et redouteux.'[3] Yet he went
over a rough sea in an inclement season to get a wife, to whom in
the course of his married life he gave seven children.

Though he abhorred war, he took arms against his rebellious
subjects – without any great distinction – on more than one
occasion. His 'kingcraft', described by smug Mrs Hutchinson as a
'wicked and ungodly cunning'[4] and derided by many, was not
ineffective; it enabled him to outmanoeuvre the Kirk and placate
his turbulent nobles at home, while he staved off interference
from without; and it brought him to the throne of England. Behind his *grotesquerie* James was a realist, too.

Opinions of Henri about James

Whatever adjustments must be made to the popular pictures, the
fact remains that the personalities of the two princes were very

---

[1] Cecil III, 60. Cf. Evidence of C.S.P. XIII and his Household Book on the Milne
Home MSS. (*Hist. MSS. Comm.* 1902).
[2] S. R. Gardiner, *History of England* (ed. 1883) I, p. 87, n[2].
[3] Cecil III, p. 60 (Report of Fontenay).
[4] *Life of Colonel Hutchinson.*

different indeed; and it is not surprising that the valiant Henri gave vent to disparaging opinions about pacific James in his outspoken way.

The oft-repeated story that he called James 'the wisest fool in Christendom'[1] may not be true; and it is not certain that he said 'to one that called our James a second Solomon' that he hoped he was "not David the fiddler's son" '.[2] Yet we have Sully's evidence that he had dubbed James *Capitaine ès arts et clerc aux armes*.[3]

When, in 1602, the English ambassador in France, Winwood, asserted that James was 'a Prince, wise, moderate, and discreet, and so well founded in the Religion he professeth that ther was no fear that he wold suffer himselfe to be seduced',[4] Sully replied that 'Ambition did know no other Religion, than that which did make way for the Advancement of her Desseigns'; and from Henri's correspondence with his ambassadors in England, Boississe and Beaumont,[5] it is plain that Henri, though he might flatter upon occasion, continued to hold James in suspicion as regards both competence and reliability.

The careers of the two princes compared

Yet the careers of these two princes, so different one from another in personality, had very much in common; and to the eyes of watching Europe their cases must have seemed much the same.

They were, by birth, roughly contemporaries. Henri was born in December 1563, and James in June 1566. Each was, by descent, ruler of a land which was geographically attached to a powerful kingdom; and to the crown of that kingdom each had, or came to

---

[1] *Passim.*

[2] *Secret History* I, p. 231.

[3] *Mémoires de Sully* (ed. 1814), III, p. 218.

[4] Winwood, I, 388; cf. the opinion of Father Alexander MacQuhirrie, S. J., 'that to all appearance James would take the crown of England from the hand of the Devil himself'. Forbes Leith, p. 270.

[5] Jean de Thumery, Sieur de Boissise (1598–1602), and Christophe de Harlay, Comte Beaumont (1602–5), were successive ambassadors of Henri in England.

have, a title which would be legitimate if the ordinary rules of succession were observed. Each made it the supreme aim of his life to make the title good. Each, being born a Protestant, encountered as his main opposition the force of the Counter-Reformation backed by the fleets and armies of Spain. Each found that the religious issue intensified antipathies of a quarrelsome aristocracy. Each fell, for a time, into the hands of his opponents. Each made, for his own end, some compromise about religion.

Within this general pattern of resemblances of career there were great differences of circumstances.

The career of Henri

Henri's father was Antoine de Bourbon of the princely house of Vendôme; his mother, Jeanne d'Albret, was heiress of the princedom of Béarn and of the kingdom of Navarre (though the kingdom had been lost to Spain in 1512–13), and she was, through her mother, a niece of Francis I, King of France. Jeanne was a resolute Calvinist, and when her husband (1562) and her brother-in-law (1569) were killed in the Wars of Religion, her influence prevailed to have her son Henri, not yet sixteen years of age, recognized as leader of the powerful Huguenot party. Henri's importance, as a prince of the blood and as head of the Huguenots, was recognized when in 1572 he was married to Margaret, the sister of the reigning King, Charles IX, who, under the influence of Coligny, was then trying to unite all France against the Spaniards.

In the violent reaction which produced the Massacre of St Bartholemew, Henri saved his life by abjuration, but it is significant that, when in the years which followed he was detained at Court, he was recognized as a royal prince. His Gascon accent, and some disregard of the *convenances*, may have raised some polite eyebrows in a sophisticated Court, but he became the *gai compagnon* of Henri III, whom he sometimes accompanied on the penitential processions by which 'les plaisirs'[1] were punctuated. Henri was a

[1] Mariéjol I, p. 215.

Frenchman – and the grandson of Margaret the author of both *The Heptaméron* and the *Mirror of a Sinful Soul*.

Yet when he escaped in 1576 he became at once a Protestant combatant in wars which brought him reputation both for courage and military skill; and when in 1584 the death of Anjou (formerly Alençon), the King's only surviving brother, brought him into direct succession to the crown, the Roman Catholics felt him to be so dangerous that they determined to exclude him by every possible means.

Headed by the powerful house of Guise, they found a rival candidate in his uncle, the Cardinal de Bourbon – old but ambitious; they made a 'Ligue' in 1584–5; gained the patronage of Spain, and in September 1585 obtained from the Pope Sixtus V a Bull which not only deprived Henri of his position of heir-presumptive of the crown, but absolved his subjects of Béarn and Navarre of their allegiance.

'The most Christian King' must needs oppose a heretic, and Henri III rather reluctantly gave his adhesion to the *Ligue* (Treaty of Nemours: July 1585).

The case of Navarre seemed desperate, but he had certain assets. He was supported by Elizabeth and some German princes; his good arms won him a victory at Coutras in October 1587; moreover his opponents were soon at odds one with another. There was in France a general dislike of Spain, and her Gallican sympathies resented the interference of the Pope.

The aristocratic Ligue fell out with a revolutionary Ligue of Paris, and the arrogance of the Guises led the King to compass the murder of the Duc de Guise at Blois in December 1588.

Perforce Henri III joined hands with his cousin of Navarre; together the two kings made an advance on Paris which was stopped only when Henri III was murdered at St Cloud by a fanatical monk on 1 August 1589. He died recognizing Navarre as his heir, but warning him that unless he embraced the Catholic religion he would never be a real king of France.

The event proved his words to be true. Despite his good victories at Arques (1589) and Ivry (1590), and the death of his uncle the pretender, his attempts to enter Paris were foiled – largely by the intervention of Parma from the Netherlands – and in 1593 he felt that the only way to bring unity and prosperity to France was to 'receive instruction' in the Catholic faith, which he did in July 1593. Next year he entered Paris amid acclamations. By 1595 the last of the Ligueurs were quelled; the Pope gave absolution. Henri was King of France indeed, and before long was busied in beginning to restore the economy of France, in guaranteeing the welfare of Protestant subjects, in making peace with Spain while he settled with Savoy, and in pursuing his plan to reduce the power of the Habsburgs.

The career of James

Set upon the throne at the age of thirteen months by the nobles who had compelled his mother to abdicate, James was for years a puppet in the hands of four successive regents, who maintained the Protestant cause with the aid of England. His precocious talents were developed by able teachers, but he was kept in awe by his governess, Lady Mar, and, though his learning was shown off to visitors, he was bullied by George Buchanan, and the effect upon his character was twofold.[1]

In the first place he came to have an exaggerated belief in his own intellectual powers, and an exaggerated belief in the dignity of 'kingship' – the one asset left to the unhappy boy, who discovered too soon that one of his keepers said that he was 'nott the king's sunne but Davy's'.[2]

When in 1578 a quarrel amongst the lords gave him some semblance of power, he, not unnaturally, fell under the influence of his gay cousin, Esmé Stuart D'Aubigny, who was a papist; and of the adventurer, James Stewart, who believed in absolute

[1] Sir James Melville's *Memoirs*, pp. 261–2; James Melville's *Diary*, p. 48; C.S.P. (Foreign) p. 48, Killigrew to Walsingham 30 June 1577; cf. 'The Library of James VI (S.H.S. Misc. I). The Englishman Killigrew is most appreciative of the boy of eight years old – master of Latin, French and English. He was able to dance properly.
[2] *Papers of the Master of Gray*, p. 16. Said by the King, with tears in his eyes, to a not very distinguished messenger from England, Cuddy Armourer.

government. From their machinations he was removed by some Protestant nobles in the 'Raid of Ruthven', August 1582, and by them detained till June 1583. It is not surprising that, when he escaped from this durance, he not only substituted Episcopacy for the Presbyterian system, but even made an approach to the Pope in 1584.

If he had really meant to go to Rome, he found his path blocked there, too, and that by his own mother, Queen-Dowager of France, of the *haut sang* of Lorraine, legitimate Queen of Scots and, in the eyes of those who did not recognize the union of Henry VIII and Anne Boleyn, legitimate Queen of England, too; Mary refused to yield any of her prerogative to her son.

She would never give him the royal title, even in an 'Association' with herself, and until 1583 persuaded France not to recognize him by the sending of an ambassador.

In the megalomania which besets exiled sovereigns she still regarded herself as the ideal spearhead for the crusade of the Counter Reformation against England. Disappointed by France's *entente* with Elizabeth, she tried to unite France and Spain in the grand venture, and when that plan failed she (secretly) put herself under the protection of Philip II. In so doing she was foolish, for Philip had no intention of conquering England in order to set a French princess upon the throne, and her manoeuvres, not unknown to the English Government, had the effect of moving Elizabeth to make, in 1586, an important treaty with James.

Professedly its object was the defence of the 'True Religion'; but James was given an annual pension (which Elizabeth ceased to pay in full), and also vague hopes of the succession to the England crown. At least he had gained something; and when in 1587 his mother was executed for her alleged complicity in the Babington plot,[1] he, the King of Scots, stood forth as the strongest Protestant claimant to the English throne. When the invincible Armada

---

[1] Mary certainly knew of the plot to liberate her; but there is no clear evidence that she knew of a definite purpose to murder Elizabeth. An incriminatory passage in one of her letters may have been forged by Philipps the decipherer.

failed, and the chances of a Spanish nominee declined,[1] James, who, despite some secret dealings with the Catholics, had stood firm in the crisis, may well have thought that his own little ship might now glide easily into the desired haven.

If so, he was disappointed. Elizabeth would not declare him her heir; he was an alien, and there were other possible claimants in England including his first cousin Arabella, whose descent from Henry VII was unblemished by alien birth. There was also fear, too, that one of Elizabeth's favourites, perhaps Essex, might try for the crown. Moreover, there was frequent friction upon the Borders.

In his own land troubles abounded. The Kirk was claiming an almost independent sovereignty. The Isles were restless, the nobles were quarrelsome, and some of the greatest intrigued with Spain. Abroad, other Roman Catholics, hoping that James would, like Navarre, 'receive instruction', approached the Pope, who believed, like many others throughout Europe, that the old faith would be revived in England 'postquam ea mulier e vita decesserit, quae occulto dei iudicio tam diu vixit et valuit.'[2]

From these manifold difficulties James extracted himself by his kingcraft. If this seems at first to be a policy of being 'Mr Facing-Several-Ways', it must be remembered that James regarded monarchy as a divine institution, and that, believing the Christian Church to be one, he felt that between strident Calvinists and Papistical tyrannicides there must be a way which would commend itself to all moderate men once it was pointed out by a clear-thinking king – like himself.

What he did then was this. He remained officially Protestant, retaining his English alliance and his English pension, and maintaining relations with influential Englishmen. Moreover, he seized

---

[1] Philip persisted in his claim until his death. In 1594 Father Persons (writing as R. Doleman) produced a book to show that Philip (by a twofold descent from John of Gaunt) was the true king. After his death his son Philip III at first claimed the title, which afterwards he agreed to pass to his sister Isabella, the Great Infanta, who married her cousin the Archduke Albert, and the pair jointly ruled the Netherlands.
[2] Meyer, p. 1 n.

175

the opportunity provided by a ministerial affront to Elizabeth to outmanoeuvre the Kirk, and to establish a sort of 'synthetic Episcopacy' which could be approximated to the English system.

At the same time he declined to persecute his Roman Catholic subjects, shutting his eyes to the Spanish intrigue of some and the *démarches* towards Rome of the others, or circumventing their policies by his own obscure negotiations with the Catholic powers abroad. He even approached Spain itself after the death of Philip II, but his main hope lay in those Roman Catholic powers who dreaded the ascendancy of Spain – Venice, Tuscany, France, and even the Pope.[1]

So he staved off foreign intervention, and when, after the fall of Essex, he established a secret alliance with Robert Cecil, the most influential of the English ministers, his path to the throne was secure.

Relations between Henri and James

Although the two princes, each in his own way, pursued his path towards his own end, their careers inevitably impinged one upon the other.

This relationship took on different forms at different times according to the policy of each.

Proposed Protestant League

In the early eighties, when Catholic activities loomed large in western Europe, and the emergence of a grand league[2] against Protestantism was suspected, Henri of Navarre endeavoured to create a European League in the defence of Protestantism. In 1583 he sent Ségur Pardailhan[3] round the Protestant courts of Europe, but in a mission of twenty months he received only general approval from the sovereigns he visited. Among these was Elizabeth. He did not visit James at all, perhaps because James's

---

[1] *S.H.R.* XXI, 267–82.

[2] e.g. Calderwood III, p. 488 and S.H.R. XII, p. 2, for exaggerated Protestant fears.

[3] Warrender I, pp. 184, 186; II, pp. 69, 83, 98.

religious policy was then most uncertain.[1] When two years later Pardailhan returned to the attack he got little satisfaction from Elizabeth, who had her own plans for some Protestant League,[2] and this time, though he did not visit James, he sent him a letter, along with it a personal letter from Navarre.[3] In his own letter, after recording the progress of his mission, he warned the King of Scots of the danger of Roman Catholics, who had already got a Bull excluding his master from the French crown. Henri supported his plea that two kings of a common religion should unite in the face of a common danger by a reference to 'l'ancienne alliance et l'amitié très étroite de noz maisons'; and Ségur, after apologizing for his inability to come to Scotland, concluded by asserting that Henri had the greatest regard for the King of Scots, and hoping that 'vous ne lui dénierez aussi votre amitié et que doresnavant il y aura entre vous deux une meilleure correspondance que par le passé'.

At this stage it is Henri who is the suitor. The alliance between the French king and the Guises was menacing, and he was very anxious to have troops from Scotland.

Already Scots were serving in his armies,[4] among them Sir James Colville of Easter Wemyss, who had fought in his ranks at Coutras; and in 1588 and 1589 Wemyss was in Scotland endeavouring to raise men. He does not seem to have secured 'the thrie thousand waidged men' he is said to have wanted,[5] but Henri did obtain some reinforcements, including Highlanders, whose uncouth equipment caused some amusement, and in October 1589 'a thousand well-armed Scots' arrived at Dieppe.

Whilst this 'recruiting drive' pursued its way there emerged another proposal for strengthening the links between Scotland

[1] See *supra*, pp. 175–6.
[2] Warrender I, p. 187 n.
[3] Teulet III, pp. 331, 333.
[4] The levying of Scots troops for Navarre had been alleged by Henri III to be a breach of the Auld Alliance.
[5] Warrender II, p. 103 n. Cf. Francisque-Michel II, pp. 123–8.

and Navarre. This was a proposal for a marriage between the King of Scots and Henri's sister, Catherine de Bourbon.

The proposed marriage alliance

In the diplomacy of the sixteenth century the marriage of a monarch was an important thing. James was still unmarried, and it was believed that Elizabeth was doing her best to keep him unmarried.[1] None the less, for some years (since 1585) there had been proposals for a marriage alliance between James and a daughter of the King of Denmark, with whom he was connected by descent. The negotiations hung fire, partly because the Danes suggested as part of the contract that they should redeem the Isles of Orkney and Shetland, which had been pledged to Scotland in lieu of 58,000 florins, as part of the dowry of Margaret, who married James III.

The proposal for the Bourbon marriage came from France. In the summer of 1587 there arrived at the Court of James the Sieur du Bartas, a gentleman of Henri, distinguished alike in arms, diplomacy and letters. James had translated some of his poems and had invited him to Scotland for his literary eminence. According to Sir James Melville, it was he who first broached the suggestion of a marriage, representing that the overture was made on his own initiative at the suggestion of Henri's secretary; but as du Bartas had come through England it was thought that Elizabeth had not disapproved of his mission. Henri himself, in a letter accrediting a letter du Bartas, dealt mainly with the hope of joint action in defence of Protestantism;[2] and though in four subsequent letters he did not mention the marriage specifically, he became more and more cordial[3] as the months passed. By December 1588 he discloses that he has sent Mr Secretary Cecil a most important communication, adding that there was such an affinity between the two kingdoms and churches that each must suffer if

[1] Sir James Melville, *Memoirs*, pp. 363, 364, 368.
[2] Warrender II, p. 54. August 2nd, 1587.
[3] Warrender II, pp. 72, 75, 90.

the other were attacked, that Christendom looked for great things from James, and that, united as they were in friendship, religion and interest, everything would be possible to their courage.

In the following March his ill-spelt autograph[1] assured James that he valued his goodwill more than that of any prince in Christendom, and that 'Il ne reste que nos fortunes soyent unyes pour estre par vous soulage an mes labeurs'. Meanwhile du Bartas, who evidently tried to urge other agents of Henri to promote the match, had urged it on himself with the utmost eloquence.[2] If there was a question of marrying the princess to a Christian prince, there was no one so suitable as James, who followed the same religion in doctrine and in discipline. If a king were wanted, he will find in James a monarch who has already won a crown, and who is almost certain to secure two more. If you seek a potentate 'beau, brave, eloquent, actif, et accort, et bref qui soit vostre image et pourtraict, il faut accepter le roi d'Ecosse' – Henry has already given to the cause, his goods, his youth, his life, 'give to it now your sister for on this union is founded the happiness of Christendom'.

James for his part was not unresponsive. According to Sir James Melville, he had sent Melville's own brother to survey the situation and the lady, and had had a good report. In September 1588 he directed to the princess a letter of great admiration, written in the best style, instructing the Sieur de L'isle, who was returning to Navarre, to see on what terms the marriage could be made, and personally to assure Madame Catherine that he would send a special gentleman to explain the full meaning of his letter, which had in fact, ended – 'Je vous prye cependant, Madame, estimer de moy comme d'un qui espere vous faire scavoir l'amour qu'il vous porte, et vous demeurera'.

Vostre tres affectioné à jamais.[3]

---

[1] ibid., p. 102.
[2] ibid., pp. 7, 68; cf. pp. 95, 96.
[3] Warrender II, pp. 80, 81.

In December, Catherine sent a becomingly modest reply;[1] but in July 1589 James broke the whole thing off with a *gaucherie* which he probably considered extremely tactful. In writing to Navarre, he begged him 'd'offrir mes tres humbles and affectionnees recommendations a Madame vostre soeur la priant de m'appardonner que je ne luy ay sceu escrire a cette fois à raison de mon defaut de loisir comme peut suffisament tesmoigner le barbouillement de la presente, et vous scaves qu'il ne faut rien presenter que lexquis aux dames'.[2]

Less than three months later he was writing cordially to Anne of Denmark,[3] whom he married at Oslo on the 24th of November.

What was the reason for this *volte-face*? Some have thought that James discovered that Catherine was not so young or so beautiful as he had supposed,[4] some have thought that Henri was not really keen on the completion of the match – which he had used as a bait to draw Scots soldiers into his army. It may be argued that Navarre, having now come to terms with the King of France (April 1589), was less concerned about the recruitment of Scottish troops; what is certain is that the Danish alliance was more popular, especially among his merchants, than was the French. According to James Melville, Elizabeth then did not want James to marry at all and secretly obstructed the match.

Possibly Henri, aware of James's subterranean dealings with the Roman Catholics, may have reckoned James an uncertain ally. Yet it seems probable that he, who, like a good brother, wanted to see his sister well married, resented the part played by James; and when, after a lapse of several years, James tried to renew the friendship, he met with a poor response.

[1] ibid., p. 92.

[2] ibid., P. 108.

[3] ibid., p. 109. James had already married Anne by proxy (the Earl Marischal) on August 20.

[4] Sir Robert Cecil, who saw her when he visited France in the spring of 1598 to prevent Henri from making peace with Spain, reported her as of painted face, ill dressed and strangely jewelled. She was married in the spring of 1599 and became Duchesse de Bar, but died in February 1604. Boissise I, p. 342; Beaumont I, p. 185.

Attempts to renew the Auld Alliance

In 1594 James took the opportunity of inviting to the christening of his son, Henry, persons of consequence, among them the new King of France, to whom he sent a special messenger by the reliable Wemyss; but, although Henri replied by promising to send a special messenger of his own back with James, he sent neither an ambassador nor a present,[1] though he afterwards apologized for his inability to attend; and in September 1597 James was still awaiting the arrival of an ambassador in accordance with a promise given to Wemyss[2] three years before. The situation was altered now. Henri was King of France.

As King of France, Henri could renew the Auld Alliance, which as King of Navarre he had been unable to do, and for some years James pressed vigorously for its revival.

The instructions he gave to Wemyss[3] rest upon the assumption that the Alliance still existed, but that some of its terms had not been fulfilled of recent years. This non-fulfilment had been a grievance for some time,[4] and James had already mentioned it in the reign of Henri III.

Posts in the Archer Guard were no longer given exclusively to Scotsmen. The Guard was a *corps d'élite*; its ranks were filled by gentlemen, and the higher offices were in effect sinecures, which might be held by kinsmen of the King. The Scots company of Men-at-Arms had disappeared altogether; this formation was less distinguished than the Guard, but it was very honourable, being the senior of the fifteen companies – *Les Gens d'Ordonnance*, established in 1445 – and it had given employment to many Scots of martial instincts and good birth.

The Scots merchants had lost their trading privilege, and the whole nation no longer enjoyed what was almost a mutual naturalization established when Mary, Queen of Scots, was married to the Dauphin.

[1] *C.S.P.* XI, pp. 345, 383, 479; and Birch, *Life of Henry*, p. 2.
[2] *S.H.R.* XVI, p. 143.
[3] *C.S.P.* XI, pp. 479–82.
[4] *Analecta Scotica* II, p. 329; *S.H.R.* IX, p. 376.

These grievances were mainly matters of money, and might be easily remedied as France gained in prosperity. The renewal of the Old Treaty, however, for which Wemyss was also to ask, was a different matter. For although its fruits were to be seen in the literature, the architecture, the academic life, and the philosophy of Scotland, the Auld Alliance was primarily a military treaty, and primarily directed against England. Revived in its original form which had been repeated throughout the centuries, it could not now be renewed for it was specifically against the English, whom Henri valued as allies, and over whom James hoped to reign. None the less James wanted to renew the formal alliance, and in 1597 prepared a long memorandum which emphasized the services which Scotland had rendered to France.[1]

In September of that year he wrote to Henri that he had delayed sending an ambassador to Henri 'pour renouveller l'ancienne amitie alliance et confederation qui este entre les couronnes de France et d'Ecosse'.[2] In fact, he did not succeed in sending a special ambassador to France even in 1598, when there was to be a great sending out of ambassadors. Wemyss went to France again (to deliver *en route* a reproachful letter to Queen Elizabeth), but there is no definite evidence of a formal mission to Henri.[3] Henri, for his part, was willing to do something to gratify James, but he feared to offend Elizabeth. Early in 1599 he suggested a solution of the difficulty by making the Old Alliance the basis of a Triple Entente, as, in fact, it had been during the reign of Henry VII, and for a time, after the battle of Pavia, in the reign of Henry VIII: 'Au lieu de la bastir sur l'inimityé des Anglois, comme ont esté les precedentes nous la fonderons sur la conservation de nostre commune amityé et confederation avec la dite Royne'.[4]

Henri's scheme was in consonance with his *idée fixe*, namely 'le

---

[1] Warrender II, pp. 336–53.
[2] *S.H.R.* XVI, p. 143.
[3] *C.S.P.* XIII (i), pp. 140, 149, 155, 162.
[4] Some *démarche* was made by Bellenden, who was in close touch with Beaton the ambassador. In reply Henri suggested the triple entente. Boissise II, pp. 24, 30. Cf. Beaumont II, pp. 114–5.

groupement de toutes les forces protestantes de l'Europe, sous la direction de la France, contre la maison d'Autriche'.[1] This was the germ of the famous 'Grand Design' attributed to Henri by the ageing Sully which was, in its complete form, imaginary;[2] but even in this limited form it was unrealizable.

Almost at once Boissise wrote to his master that Elizabeth was dead against the plan, and Henri replied that he would postpone renewing the Auld Alliance with Scotland. Elizabeth expressed her gratification, and before long wrote to James, thanking him for informing her of the overture and cautioning him upon a too great reliance upon France.[3]

She wanted to keep her treaty of 1586 with Scotland apart from a treaty which she had made with France in 1596, and before long she was holding conversations with Spain and the Netherlands, from which both Scotland and France were excluded. Henri and James might resent her actions, but dared not oppose her openly – Henri lest she should come to terms with Spain, James lest he should be excluded from the succession.

Henri compromised by at last sending to Scotland an ambassador in the person of Sully's brother, Philippe de Béthune, charged with very cordial 'Instructions' (dated 13–23 May 1599)[4]. He was to explain that Henri was very short of money, but would try to redress the grievances about the Archer Guard and the Men-at-Arms; he had already (15 March 1599) confirmed most of the privileges of the Scots merchants; poverty had compelled him to make peace with Spain, but France had no intention of abandoning old friends. Yet the Auld Alliance could not be renewed in its traditional form, and James was counselled to maintain his friendship with Elizabeth.

James kept 'pegging away'. Lennox, who went on a self-sought mission to France in 1601, raised the questions of the Auld Alliance and the grievances, but Henri said that he 'n'a rien

---

[1] Beaumont I, p. 82.
[2] Sir Geoffrey Butler, *Studies in Statecraft*.
[3] Teulet IV, pp. 211, 215, 216. Cf. *Letters of Elizabeth and James*, pp. 143, 149, 155.
[4] C.S.P. XIII, pp. 467–74.

traitté de particulier avec moy'.[1] Various private persons may have raised the subject of the renewal of the Auld Alliance. When in July 1602, James sent Lord Hume to congratulate Henri on his escape from Biron's conspiracy, he again referred to the 'tresancienne confideration de noz deux couronnes'[2] as if it remained in being.

The Succession to the English crown

One reason, perhaps the most important, for James's strong desire to have the Auld Alliance renewed was that he wished to ensure that, on the death of Elizabeth, Henri would support his claim to the succession, or at least would not support any other candidate. Reference has already been made to potential rival candidates, and James was not quite certain about the position of France.

There had even been talk that Henri himself might marry Arbella and make a throw for the English crown.[3] This was probably a fantasy. Yet Henri had said, when his son César was borne by his Norman mistress Gabrielle d'Estrées in February 1601, 'it may be we find a bastard of Normandy to conquer those chalk hills shining in the eyes of France'.[4] Doubtless he was joking, but there had been talk of Condé, or another French prince, as husband to Arbella,[5] and James may have suspected that the newly converted King of France might support some Catholic (but not Spanish) successor to Elizabeth.

In fact, James Beaton, the exiled Archbishop of Glasgow, who had at one time been an ambassador to France from Queen Mary, and who had been reinstated to his title by James, continued, in the eyes of Catholics, to represent Scotland in Paris until his death in 1603, and had been active in encouraging Scotsmen in France to bestir themselves in reconciling James to the Pope.

[1] Boissise II, p. 252. For Lennox's supposed instructions and his mission. *C.S.P.* XIII (ii), pp. 769, 837, 903.
[2] *C.S.P. XIII* (ii), p. 1025. Cf. Teulet IV, p. 275.
[3] *C.S.P. XII*, p. 267.
[4] *C.S.P.* XIII (ii), p. 770.
[5] Handover, pp. 131–3.

His own Queen Anne, who was converted about 1600, did her best to hurry Scotland along the path to Rome, and was believed in France itself to be conspiring against her husband's life.[1]

While there was some doubt in France as to whether James would succeed Elizabeth, there was also doubt as to whether Henri wished him to do so. His dislike of a union of the British Crowns had long been common knowledge in diplomatic circles,[2] and that dislike was founded upon good reasons. By the Union of the Crowns his traditional ally might give added power to France's traditional enemy England, since England was far stronger than Scotland; and to the increased power of the new monarch would be added the old claim of the English sovereigns to the crown of France.[3] Elizabeth had never given Henri the title of 'King of France', but always referred to him as 'The Most Christian King'; and, in fact, when James was proclaimed at Whitehall in 1603, it was as 'King of England, Scotland, France, and Ireland'.

It was most improbable that James would try to make the title good, but even so the rise to power of a monarch so uncertain in his religion was fraught with hazards.

If he should play the Protestant champion, the Huguenots, with whom he had long entertained relations, might be stirred to demand fresh concessions and upset the balance hardly won by the Edict of Nantes.

If he declared himself Catholic – as Henri had done – he would not be supported by Spain, whose candidate, the Infanta, had already the support of some English Catholics; but he might gain help from the Pope, and from the moderate Catholics who feared Spain. Altogether, he might become too strong.

Would there be a chance, then, that papal influence might avail to secure the accession of a moderate prince more acceptable to moderate Catholics than the doubtful James?

[1] *C.S.P.* XIII (ii), pp. 1017, 1029, 1033, 1049; Winwood I, p. 326. Beaumont II, p. 103. There is no evidence of any murder plot, though Anne certainly negotiated with Rome and had some dealings with the Ruthvens [cf. Meyer, and Forbes Leith].
[2] *S.H.R. XXI*, p. 275, n. 6.
[3] The claim was not formally abandoned till 1800.

Towards the end of 1601 a likely candidate was found. This was Odoardo Farnese, brother of the Duke of Parma, who could claim a descent from John of Gaunt senior to that of the Infanta; he was a cardinal, but the Pope might release him from his vows that he might marry Arbella, and the joint claim would be formidable.

So thought the French ambassador at Rome, Cardinal d'Ossat, who wrote urging his master to support this candidature.[1] Henri's statesmanship, always realistic, appears in his reply.[2] He wished, like the Pope, that the kingdom of England would fall into the hands of a Catholic prince, and he knew well the reasons which made the union of the crowns undesirable; but 'le Roi d'Ecosse est le vrai heritier dudit Roiaume', and he was far better placed than any other to secure the succession. It would be *injustice* to oppose the legitimate successor, and it would be *imprudence* to engage in an enterprise so little likely to succeed as that proposed with the approval of his Holiness. It would be better to let James have the crown in the hope that he would return to the bosom of the Church.

Henri seemed to have taken his stand. As early as February 1599 he had told Boissise, his ambassador in England, that he must understand 'que je suiz sans jalousie de la reunion de ces deux royaulmes, a laquelle le roy d'Ecosse aspire, n'ignorant la consequense d'icelle';[3] but at that time he was anxious to soften his refusal to renew the Auld Alliance, and he may have indulged in some politic exaggeration. Certain it is that even after his firm declaration of 1601 he was in considerable doubt until the very end of Elizabeth's reign.

It seems that Beaumont, who succeeded Boissise as ambassador in 1602, moved more freely about the Court than his predecessors had done, and that many rumours[4] reached his ears. These he duly reported to his master.

[1] Ossat V, p. 66.
[2] ibid., app. 54.
[3] Boissise II, p. 39.
[4] Teulet IV, pp. 283–7.

The name of Arbella was much canvassed; some of the councillors were unreliable. There was fear that, if he succeeded, James would take his revenge upon the politicians who had compassed Mary's death. It was even rumoured that Henri supported Arbella's claim expressly to prevent the union of the English and Scottish crowns. Himself, he thought it would be a wise thing to induce the Scots to compel James to have his son crowned King of Scots as soon as he mounted the throne of England. Elizabeth was annoyed because Henri had sent an ambassador to Scotland. Spain was spending much money in Scotland. James had already promised to do something for the Catholics of England.

None the less, in October 1602 Beaumont felt sure that James would succeed; and by March 1603 he was sure that the succession would be without difficulty.[1]

Henri was less certain of James; only seven days before Elizabeth's death he wrote to Beaumont:

> Il se monstre aussy si legier et inconsideré en toute ses actions, qu'il est dificille de bastir sur ses paroles et ses actions ung solide fondement.[2]

He knew all about James's practices in Rome, Spain, and other places, but was sure that he would misfire in them all. If his wife had really sworn his death, he might well be overtaken; he went on to ask whether Arbella had embraced the Catholic religion.

Henri had been misinformed. Beaumont, with all his goings about, had not detected the essential factor in the situation, namely that James, soon after the fall of Essex, had succeeded in making a secret compact with Robert Cecil. All was prepared, and on March 24 James was duly proclaimed King in London, while Robert Carey was speeding north to salute the new king in Holyroodhouse.

Henri, though he had been disturbed by the rumours, had taken no action upon them, and could with justice write to Beaumont early in May:

[1] Teulet IV, p. 254.
[2] Teulet IV, p. 289. Where Henri recommends caution to Beaumont., Beaumont II, p. 103.

Comme vous sçavez que mon intention n'a jamais esté de traverser ny empescher la succession a la corone d'Angleterre du Roy qui est à present, mais au contraire la favoriser en tous lieux et par tous moyens possibles.[1]

Henri was a realist. James turned out to be more of a realist than Henri suspected.[2] Side by side, if not always hand in hand, each of the two princes came to his desired haven.

J. D. Mackie

[1] Beaumont II, p. 110.

[2] Henri discovered to his disappointment that his endeavour to persuade James to continue the war with Spain (from which he himself had retired) was quite unsuccessful, though it was promoted by the able Sully sent as ambassador to England soon after James's accession – *Mémoires de Sully*, Liv. IV and XV.

Authorities

Analecta Scotica, 2 vols (1842, 1827).

BEAUMONT (Ed. P. Laffleur de Kermaingant), *Mission de Christophe de Harlay, Comte de Beaumont, 1602–1605*, 2 vols (1895).

THOMAS BIRCH, *Life of Henry, Prince of Wales* (1760).

BOISSISE (Ed. P. Laffleur de Kermaingant), *Mission de Jean de Thumery, Sieur de Boissise 1598–1602*, 2 vols (1886).

D'OSSAT (Ed. Amelot de la Houssaie), *Lettres du Cardinal D'Ossat*, 5 vols (1714).

DAVID CALDERWOOD, *History of the Kirk of Scotland*, 8 vols (1842–9), Woodrow Society.

C.S.P., *Calendar of Scottish Papers*.

CECIL, *Calendar of the Manuscripts of the Marquis of Salisbury* 1883 – in progress – *His. MSS. Com.*

WILLIAM FORBES LEITH, *Narratives of Scottish Catholics* (1889).

FRANCISQUE-MICHEL, *Les Écossais en France, les Français en Écosse*, 2 vols (1862).

S. R. GARDINER, *History of England* (edition 1883).

GRAY, *Letters and Papers relating to Patrick, Master of Gray*, Bannatyne Club (1835).

LUCY HUTCHINSON, *Life of Colonel Hutchinson*.

P. M. HANDOVER, *Arbella Stuart* (1957).

JEAN H. MARIÉJOL, *Histoire de France*, vol. VI (in *Histoire de France*, Ernest Lavisse, not dated).

JAMES MELVILLE, *Autobiography and Diary of Mr. James Melville* (Woodrow Society edition, 1842).

SIR JAMES MELVILLE, *Memoirs of his own life*, Bannatyne Club (1827).

MILNE HUME, *Report on the Manuscripts of Colonel Milne Hume*, Hist. MSS. Com. (1902).

S.H.R., *Scottish Historical Review*.

S.H.S., *Scottish History Society*.

S. P. DOM, *Calendar of State Papers, Domestic*.

SIR GEOFFREY BUTLER, *Studies in Statecraft* (1920).

SECRET HISTORY, *Secret History of the Court of James I*, 2 vols (1811) [Anon: Contemporary Tracts (ed. Sir Walter Scott)].

SULLY, *Mémoires de Sully*, 6 vols (1814).

ALEXANDRE TEULET, *Relations Politiques de la France et de l'Espagne avec l'Écosse au XVIe siècle*, 5 vols (1862).

WARRENDER (Ed. A. I. Cameron and R. S. Rait), *The Warrender Papers*, 2 vols, S.H.S. (1931–2).

WINWOOD (Ed. Edmond Sawyer), *Memorials of Affairs of State in the Reign of Queen Elizabeth and King James I*, 3 vols (1725).

L'*Hippolyte* de Garnier *et l'*Hippolytus
de Sénèque

>>> >>> >>> >>> >>> >>> >>> >>> >>> >>> >>> ‹‹‹ ‹‹‹ ‹‹‹ ‹‹‹ ‹‹‹ ‹‹‹ ‹‹‹ ‹‹‹ ‹‹‹ ‹‹‹ ‹‹‹

Hippolyte peut sembler la pièce la moins originale qu'ait écrite Garnier. En effet dans le reste de son théâtre, même lorsque les sujets sont empruntés aux auteurs anciens et alors même que l'atmosphère demeure essentiellement sénéquéenne, certains thèmes se font jour qui ne doivent rien aux dramaturges grecs ni à Sénèque. Ce sont les thèmes que suggèrent à Garnier les problèmes et les événements de son époque : droits et devoirs des souverains, misères de la guerre et ivresse de la conquête, bien fondé du régicide ou de la révolte contre la loi. C'est ainsi que la sensibilité personnelle de Garnier lui fait poursuivre, sous une forme plus ou moins satisfaisante, la création d'une tragédie politique, et cela dès ses premières pièces.

Rien de tel pourtant dans *Hippolyte*. Aucun des problèmes que je viens de mentionner ne vient troubler les protagonistes ni donner au chœur l'occasion de s'indigner ou de se plaindre. En fait, comme l'ont noté tous les critiques, l'*Hippolyte* de Garnier suit de si près l'*Hippolytus* de Sénèque qu'on pourrait d'abord croire sinon à une traduction, du moins à une paraphrase du texte latin, ou tout au plus à une brillante adaptation lyrique du modèle choisi. Les quelques modifications qu'apporte Garnier au dessin général de la pièce paraissent au premier coup d'œil d'une portée assez limitée. Ne s'agirait-il donc que de changements très superficiels, destinés à embellir le sujet, soit en ajoutant de riches broderies, soit aussi en pastelisant des couleurs trop crues? Certes le long prologue d'Égée, qui ne se trouve pas chez Sénèque, permet à Garnier d'inclure une de ces belles tirades où se déploie un art de la rhétorique très prisé au seizième siècle. Et s'il nous épargne le passage assez déplaisant dans lequel, chez Sénèque, Thésée cherche à rassembler, avec quelque difficulté, les membres déchiquetés de son fils,[1] n'est-ce pas simplement là l'indication d'un goût plus fin? Déjà cependant dans cette omission, qui ne porte que sur un détail, se révèle l'attitude d'un écrivain très conscient de tout ce qui sépare l'imitation de la traduction.

L'imitation étant un principe d'art au seizième siècle, les ressemblances que présente forcément une œuvre avec celle qui lui sert de modèle, risquent souvent de nous dérober la valeur esthétique d'une savante alchimie, ou pour mieux dire de cette 'conversion en sang et nourriture', grâce à laquelle s'affirme le génie personnel de l'écrivain. Or ce qui m'intéresse dans le cas d'*Hippolyte*, ce n'est pas une recherche des sources – cela a déjà été fait et plus méthodiquement que je ne saurais le faire ici – mais de montrer brièvement que l'imitation implique ici une transformation profonde, une transformation 'structurale', ce qui dissipe la première impression que nous pourrions avoir d'un travail de surface. Cette recherche d'une structure d'ensemble est d'autant plus fascinante que l'on tend volontiers à admirer les dons poétiques de Garnier, et non ses qualités dramatiques.

Ne cherchons pas cependant l'unité et la cohérence dans la création des personnages. Ce serait d'ailleurs un anachronisme. Le seizième siècle ne s'applique pas à construire un caractère ni à donner aux sentiments qu'exprime le protagoniste une armature logique. Je dirai même que l'on trouve plus d'invraisemblance chez Garnier que chez Sénèque. Par exemple la violence du choc qu'éprouve Hippolyte devant la révélation de Phèdre est plus explicable chez Sénèque. En effet jusqu'à ce moment-là l'Hippolyte latin n'a dans l'esprit que ses joyeuses préoccupations de chasseur et vit dans la tranquille assurance d'avoir trouvé le secret

---

[1] *Quae pars tui sit dubito, sed pars est tui.*
   Hic, hic repone: non suo, at vacuo loco (vv. 1267–8).

du bonheur. Chez Garnier, au contraire, dès le début de la pièce, le héros est un être troublé et qui s'attend au pire : un rêve lui a présenté une effroyable chasse au cours de laquelle il était victime d'un lion monstrueux et, de plus, depuis cinq ou six jours la nature n'est plus un cadre riant et aimable, mais un ciel peuplé d'oiseaux de malheurs. Chez les deux dramaturges la nourrice est prête à soutenir, à grands renforts d'arguments, les opinions les plus opposées, mais Garnier ajoute encore au manque de cohérence du personnage en lui donnant la parole une dernière fois, au quatrième acte, après que Thésée a demandé à Neptune de frapper Hippolyte. C'est une étrange tirade au cours de laquelle l'individualité du personnage s'affirme d'abord, s'efface ensuite et se recompose finalement. Saisie de remords, la nourrice éclate en lamentations, puis, prenant pour ainsi dire du recul, se figeant dans le rôle d'un spectateur, à la façon du chœur, commente la fragilité du bonheur des rois ; après quoi, se rappelant son propre destin tragique, elle se tue, éprouvant déjà les tortures de l'enfer. Le seizième siècle nous a certes habitués à cette instabilité des caractères, et nous savons combien est flottante alors la ligne qui sépare le personnage du chœur. Phèdre également est plus complexe chez Garnier, moins consistante, car si d'un côté elle a le sentiment d'une déchéance morale, elle n'hésite pas à défendre avec conviction les droits amoraux de l'amour.

Ces modifications, ce désordre apparent que Garnier introduit ainsi dans la psychologie des personnages n'est pas enrichissement gratuit. Mais avant même d'en chercher la justification dans le dessin général de la pièce, notons quelques changements assez simples que Garnier fait subir à l'architecture formelle de la tragédie, et qui certainement révèlent un sens du mouvement dramatique qui n'existe pas au même degré chez Sénèque. L'action, chez Garnier, se déclenche avec plus de lenteur – les deux premiers actes correspondant au premier 'acte'[1] de Sénèque – car Garnier prend son temps pour établir une atmosphère sinistre de prédictions et de mauvais augures. Par contre il

---

[1] La pièce latine est divisée en cinq parties, chaque partie se terminant par un chœur.

accélère la marche des événements à la fin de la pièce : au cinquième acte, le récit du messager, le premier mouvement de remords chez Thésée sont immédiatement suivis par l'arrivée de Phèdre, sa confession et son suicide, les plaintes du chœur et le désespoir de Thésée. Sénèque au contraire consacre deux actes aux mêmes événements, introduisant une coupure après le récit du messager : le chœur disserte sur les dangers qui menacent les puissants de la terre. D'où un relâchement de la tension dramatique.

Il y a donc chez Garnier un effort pour régler de façon plus satisfaisante le 'tempo' de l'action. Un effort aussi, pourrait-on ajouter, pour concentrer davantage sur Phèdre les rayons des projecteurs. Car c'est Phèdre chez lui, et non le chœur comme dans Sénèque, qui s'extasie sur la beauté d'Hippolyte et de même c'est Phèdre et non la nourrice qui demande à Diane d'attendrir le cœur d'Hippolyte.

Ce ne sont là encore que des ajustements d'importance secondaire. La véritable unité et cohérence d'*Hippolyte* tient essentiellement à la structure symphonique de la pièce.

Le seizième siècle, on le sait, attachait une grande valeur aux discours bien composés, aux belles tirades, et Garnier, plus que tout autre dramaturge, trouve dans la tragédie l'occasion d'écrire de superbes passages lyriques. Mais *Hippolyte* ne se présente pas comme une succession de morceaux de bravoure, plaqués, avec plus ou moins de pertinence, sur l'intrigue. Le contenu poétique de la tragédie est organisé suivant un dessin compliqué mais harmonieux.

Deux grands thèmes poétiques s'opposent ou se combinent tout au long de la tragédie, thèmes qui sont l'un et l'autre intimement liés au destin tragique d'Hippolyte.

Le premier, le plus important, est un thème sombre : c'est celui des puissances du mal exerçant leur influence surnaturelle sur les hommes et dans la nature. Thème sénéquéen, qu'ont repris les élizabéthains, mais que Garnier accentue particulièrement dans *Hippolyte*. Pour cela d'abord il emprunte à une autre pièce de Sénèque le fantôme de son prologue. L'ombre d'Égée vient tout droit du noir séjour :

> *Je sors de l'Achéron, d'où les ombres des morts*
> *Ne ressortent jamais couvertes de leurs corps;*
> *Je sors des champs ombreux . . .* (Acte I)

Ce prologue qui nous annonce les catastrophes prêtes à fondre sur Thésée en ce monde et dans l'autre est suivi par le rêve prophétique d'Hippolyte, et par les présages sinistres qui s'accumulent autour du jeune homme. Il se crée ainsi une atmosphère qui nous rappelle les orfraies et les choucas de *Macbeth*:

> *Depuis quatre ou cinq nuicts le hibou n'a jamais*
> *Cessé de lamenter au haut de ce palais . . .* (Acte I)

Thésée lui aussi lorsqu'il apparaît au quatrième acte revient des Enfers, encore tremblant de son horrible voyage. Le monde infernal n'est d'ailleurs chez Garnier jamais très loin des protagonistes. Il semble être sous leurs pieds, toujours béant, toujours prêt non seulement à vomir des fantômes ou des monstres mais à engloutir les personnages. Cette rapidité avec laquelle l'Achéron vient s'emparer de sa proie explique le brusque changement de ton dans la dernière tirade de la nourrice: les furies surgissent avant même le dernier soupir:

> *Il me semble desjà que les flambeaux ardans*
> *Des filles de la Nuict me bruslent au dedans:*
> *Il me semble desjà sentir mille tenailles,*
> *Mille serpens retors morceler mes entrailles.*
> *Je porte, ains que je tombe en l'aveugle noirceur*
> *Du rivage infernal, mon tourment punisseur.* (Acte IV)

De la même façon les lamentations passionnées de Phèdre devant le cadavre d'Hippolyte sont brutalement interrompues. A peine a-t-elle plongé l'épée dans son sein que le monde des enfers se renferme sur elle, perçu d'abord comme une sensation physique de terreur à l'état pur, puis comme une série d'épouvantables visions:

> *Mon coeur, que trembles-tu? quelle soudaine horreur,*
> *Quelle horreur frissonnant allentist ta fureur?*
> *Quelle affreuse Mégère à mes yeux se présente?*
> *Quels serpens encordez, quelle torche flambante?* (Acte V)

La pièce s'achève par l'évocation d'un paysage lugubre, celui que Thésée va chercher comme étant le seul en accord avec son morne désespoir:

> *Je veux choisir un lieu commode à mon tourment,*
> *Où le mortel hibou lamente incessamment,*
> *Où n'arrive personne, où tousjours l'hiver dure,*
> *Où jamais le printemps ne sème sa verdure* . . . (Acte V)

Paysage état d'âme, très semblable au paysage funèbre de d'Aubigné: champs déserts, jonchés de feuilles mortes, vols de noirs corbeaux.

A ce monde de cauchemar (dans lequel s'inscrit si bien la description du monstre marin), à cette intrusion constante des messagers de la mort s'oppose la beauté de l'univers vivant: bondissement des chevreuils et des biches, forêts verdoyantes, sources claires, lumière dorée du soleil, doux rayonnement de la lune.

Le thème de la forêt se trouvait déjà chez Sénèque et sa tragédie commence par le grand discours d'Hippolyte à ses compagnons:

> *Ite, umbrosas cingite silvas*
> *Summaque montis juga Cecropii!* (vv. 1–2)

magnifique épopée de la chasse qu'anime un remarquable réalisme lyrique. Mais chez Garnier la beauté de la nature sauvage est évoquée avec plus de force, plus de fréquence, et parfois plus de pittoresque (pensons à ces 'phoques vagabondes' dont nous parle Phèdre au deuxième acte) et surtout donne lieu à toutes sortes de variations de ton:

Rythme allègre du chant joyeux des chasseurs au premier acte:

> *Ô montagneuse, ô bocagère,*
> *Aime-fonteines, porte-rets,*
> *Guide nos pas en tes forests,*
> *Après quelque biche légère* . . .

évocation mélancolique d'un paysage qui s'estompe dans les harmonies langoureuses de la plainte de Phèdre:

196

O vous creuses forests qui recélez ma vie,
Que bien jalousement je vous porte d'envie!
O vous coustaux pierreux, . . .
        . . . O vous aussi, fontaines,
Qui allez ondelant par les herbeuses plaines,
Et par tortis cavez roulez tousjours à val,
Que je vous veux, hélas! que je vous veux de mal! (Acte III)

cri de désespoir d'Hippolyte se sentant souillé par la déclaration de Phèdre:

      . . . O rochers esgarez!
O coûtaux! ô vallons! ô bestes! ô forests! (Acte III)

De plus Garnier a modifié le personnage de Phèdre pour l'intégrer à ce second thème de sa pièce. Sous le fragile vernis de la moralité conventionnelle apparaît la force sauvage de l'amour tel qu'il est dans la nature, instinctif et amoral. D'où ce côté 'païen' de Phèdre, son adoration de la beauté physique d'Hippolyte. D'où son amoralité, ou plutôt la révolte contre les lois de la société d'une femme qui n'accepte que les lois de la nature:

Les hommes, nos tyrans, violant la Nature,
Nous contraignent porter cette ordonnance dure . . . (Acte II)

nous dit-elle, alors que tout ce qui peuple la terre, l'air et la mer est libre de ces entraves:

Là l'innocente amour s'exerce volontaire,
Sans pallir sous les noms d'inceste et d'adultère . . . (ibid.)

Ainsi nous avons d'un côté l'affirmation de la liberté, le frémissement de la vie, la beauté du monde sensible, la clarté et de l'autre les menaces du destin, la présence de la mort, l'apparition des monstres, le paysage noir.

Mais ces deux thèmes sont aussi traités sur un mode mineur, et les deux atmosphères qui se contrastent peuvent parfois s'interpénétrer car la pertinence de lyrisme n'exclut pas les nuances. La nuit, par exemple, n'est pas toujours une nuit infernale. Elle est aussi promesse de calme et de repos sauf dans le cœur de Phèdre où veille, sentinelle solitaire, sa malheureuse passion:

Quand la nuict tend son voile et qu'elle embrunist l'aer,
Tout sent l'oublieux somme en ses membres couler;
Le silence est par tout, tout est coy par le monde,
Fors qu'en ton âme seule, où l'amour fait la ronde. (Acte III)

Ces vers de la nourrice, avec leur délicatesse de ton et la subtile image qu'ils contiennent, sont caractéristiques de ces demi-teintes, de ces 'fondus' que nous trouvons chez Garnier. Aussi n'est-il pas surprenant qu'un moment d'incertitude, signe avant-coureur du cauchemar qui va suivre, soit pour Hippolyte un moment crépusculaire, où il ne fait *'ny jour ny nuict, mais tous les deux ensemble'* (Acte I).

La mort elle-même peut prendre ces couleurs adoucies et n'être pas toujours un gouffre plein de supplices qu'éclairent violemment les flambeaux des furies. Elle est aussi ce néant qu'apporte aux morts l'eau grise du Léthé, et que refuse Thésée:

Boire en l'oublieux fleuve une longue oubliance. (Acte V)

Parce que, des deux thèmes, celui qui exprime le malheur et l'horreur est le plus important, il tendra à se superposer sur l'autre, car la lumière doit être vaincue par l'ombre, le foisonne-ment de la végétation remplacé par la stérilité d'un éternel hiver, la beauté détruite. C'est pourquoi la nature sera équivoque. La forêt si verte et si fraîche qu'aime tant Hippolyte est aussi le décor sinistre de son rêve. Les animaux sont tour à tour la proie et le chasseur, des êtres familiers, gracieux et légers, ou des lions dangereux, des monstres d'une espèce inconnue. Ils sont invoqués par Phèdre, nous l'avons vu, pour justifier l'amour libre mais ils sont également mentionnés par Thésée comme portant respect *'aux degrés du lignage'* (Acte IV).

Ces quelques illustrations (il y en aurait bien d'autres) mon-trent le genre d'orchestration, à la fois vigoureuse et nuancée, que Garnier compose sur les deux thèmes. Il est rare qu'il sacrifie l'unité de cette structure symphonique à la tentation de placer une de ces dissertations moralisantes sur des lieux communs que Sénèque et les dramaturges du seizième siècle se font un devoir et un plaisir d'intercaler dans leurs pièces. Et ce souci de perti-nence est évident dans les passages du chœur.

Chez Sénèque les quatre tirades du chœur, qui forment les divisions entre les 'actes', (à part de brèves allusions aux protagonistes), sont consacrées à des considérations générales sur (1) l'amour, (2) la beauté, (3) la Fortune, (4) les dangers de la grandeur. Garnier s'écarte de Sénèque et donne au chœur un rôle particulier. A la fin de chacun des quatre premiers actes le chœur exprime sa confiance en les dieux, confiance dramatiquement démentie par les événements. Il s'adresse d'abord à Diane quand nous savons déjà qu'Hippolyte est condamné par le destin. La prière à Vénus suit la scène entre Phèdre et la nourrice alors que les dangers de la passion effrénée ne sont que trop évidents. Au troisième acte, la catastrophe devient inévitable mais après la déclaration de Phèdre, la violente indignation d'Hippolyte et le projet criminel de la nourrice, le chœur invoque Pallas, déesse de la sagesse et de la mesure. Au quatrième acte, Thésée demande à Neptune de frapper Hippolyte et le chœur, toujours optimiste, espère que le 'juste Neptune' ne se croira pas tenu par sa promesse à Thésée. Ainsi jusqu'au cinquième acte, le chœur prend-il une valeur d'ironie dramatique, et forme une sorte de contre-point dans le dessin poétique de la pièce. Le dernier chant du chœur, au cinquième acte, est placé entre le suicide de Phèdre et les adieux de Thésée. Le rythme est empreint d'une grâce particulière :

> *Faisons, ô mes compagnes,*
> *Retentir les montagnes*
> *Et les rochers secrets*
>   *De nos regrets.*
> *Que la mer, qui arrive*
> *Vagueuse à nostre rive,*
> *Face rider les flots*
>   *De nos sanglots.*
> *Que les larmes roulantes* . . . (Acte V)

Ici encore effet de contraste ; une note de tendresse claire entre deux grandes tirades violentes, entre deux évocations des Enfers. Le retour périodique du petit vers de quatre syllabes et les nombreux enjambements donnent l'impression d'une danse mélancolique sous un ciel dont le chœur reconnaît enfin qu'il est 'contraire' aux humains.

Il me semble donc que dans *Hippolyte* Garnier est très proche de cet idéal du drame poétique qui consiste à fondre en un tout harmonieux l'élément dramatique et l'élément poétique. Il arrive à cela suivant une technique qui lui est personnelle et que l'on retrouve d'ailleurs dans d'autres de ses tragédies (les trois premiers actes des *Juives* ont aussi cette structure symphonique) mais nulle part, à mon avis, de façon aussi complète que dans *Hippolyte*.

Est-ce à dire que la pièce de Garnier est supérieure à celle de Sénèque? Je me garderai de l'affirmer.

Il nous est difficile d'apprécier l'effet musical d'une œuvre écrite dans une langue morte, et de toute façon je ne suis pas une spécialiste de littérature latine. Mais je me risquerai à dire que les qualités les plus évidentes de l'*Hippolytus* sont des qualités de style. Qualités d'imagination auxquelles Garnier a été si sensible que dans certains cas il est resté très près du texte latin, comme par exemple dans l'exclamation d'Hippolyte:

> *Quis eluet me Tanais? aut quae barbaris*
> *Mœotis undis Pontico incumbens mari?*
> *Non ipse toto magnus Oceano pater*
> *Tantum expiarit sceleris: o silvae! o ferae!* (vv. 715–18)

que reprend Garnier:

> *En quel Tigre, en quel Gange, en quel gouffre aboyant,*
> *En quelle ondeuse mer m'iray-je nettoyant?*
> *Non, le grand Océan, avecques toute l'onde*
> *Dont il lave en flottant ceste grand' masse ronde,*
> *Ne me sçauroit laver* . . . (Acte III)[1]

Mais comment convertir en sang et nourriture l'admirable dialogue sénéquéen?

---

[1] Même inspiration d'origine sénéquéenne dans Shakespeare:
> *Will all great Neptune's ocean wash this blood*
> *Clean from my hand?* . . .

PHAEDRA :	*Precibus haud vinci potest?*
NUTRIX : *Ferus est.*	
PHAEDRA :	*Amore didicimus vinci feros.*
NUTRIX : *Fugiet.*	
PHAEDRA :	*Per ipsa maria, si fugiat, sequar.*
NUTRIX : *Patris memento.*	
PHAEDRA :	*Meminimus matris simul.*
NUTRIX : *Genus omne profugit.*	
PHAEDRA :	*Paelicis careo metu.*
NUTRIX : *Aderit maritus.*	
PHAEDRA :	*Nempe Pirithoi comes.*
NUTRIX : *Aderitque genitor.*	
PHAEDRA :	*Mitis Ariadnae pater.* (vv. 239–45)

Combien nous apparaît lent et pâteux le passage correspondant chez Garnier, et pourtant, en un point, il s'efforce, avec les ressources qu'offre la rhétorique française, d'imiter la vigueur nerveuse de Sénèque :

> NOURRICE : *Que vous dira Thésée, s'il retourne une fois?*
> PHÈDRE : *Mais moy, que luy diray-je, et à son Pirithois?*
> NOURRICE : *Et encor que dira vostre rigoureux père?*
> PHÈDRE : *Qu'a-t-il dict à ma soeur? qu'a-t-il dict à ma mère?* (Acte II)

Devant la concision qu'autorise le latin et la force dramatique qu'elle apporte, on comprend pourquoi les dramaturges français poursuivront la création d'un 'style coupé' que seuls Corneille et surtout Racine arriveront à manier parfaitement dans leurs tragédies.

Garnier, lui, ne peut atteindre cette énergie brutale que par l'audace de ses notations concrètes :

> PHÈDRE : *Je porte dans les os mon cruel adversaire;* (Acte II).

Mais dans l'ensemble la force de son lyrisme est dans l'étendue alors que celle de Sénèque est dans la retenue.

Comparons la façon différente dont les deux dramaturges finissent le discours dans lequel Thésée demande à Neptune de punir Hippolyte. Chez Garnier la tirade s'achève sur un grand mouvement ample et un dernier vers splendide qui semble tracer d'immenses cercles à la surface de l'océan:

> *Souvienne toy, grand dieu, de ta saincte promesse;*
> *Trouble toute la mer; un seul vent ne relaisse*
> *Au creux éolien; mutine avec les flots*
> *Tes grans troupeaux monstreux que la mer tient enclos* (Acte IV).

Le réussite de Sénèque est d'avoir interrompu le mouvement solennel de la malédiction par une brusque interrogation:

> *Inter profunda Tartara, et Ditem horridum,*
> *Et imminentes regis inferni minas,*
> *Voto perperci. Redde nunc pactam fidem,*
> *Genitor. Moraris? cur adhuc undae silent?*
> *Nunc atra ventis nubila impellentibus*
> *Subtexe noctem; sidera et caelum eripe;*
> *Effunde pontum . . .* (v. 950–7)

Je trouve extrêmement beau ce calme étrange et soudain dans la nature, ce moment d'hésitation, de 'suspense', avant le déchaînement des éléments et l'injuste destruction d'Hippolyte.

L'objet principal de cette brève comparaison était d'essayer de saisir, dans l'imitation même, ce qui est chez Garnier création individuelle. Mais l'imitation n'est pas uniquement un enrichissement pour celui qui imite. Non seulement la tragédie de Garnier laisse transparaître, ce qui est une beauté de plus, le modèle dont elle s'inspire, mais, dépouillé de tout ce qu'un imitateur savant et artiste pouvait lui prendre, l'*Hippolytus* s'éclaire, montrant ce qu'a de très précieux et d'irréductible le génie d'un écrivain et le génie d'une langue.

Odette de Mourgues

Le texte des citations est emprunté aux éditions suivantes:
SÉNÈQUE, *Tragédies*, Tome I, Classiques Garnier, Paris s.d.
ROBERT GARNIER, *Œuvres Complètes*, Edition L. Pinvert, Tome I, Paris (1923).

Les recueils de sonnets sont-ils composés?

⟫-⟫-⟫-⟫-⟫-⟫-⟫-⟫-⟫-⟫-⟫-⟪-⟪-⟪-⟪-⟪-⟪-⟪-⟪-⟪-⟪-⟪-⟪

QUE LES SONNETS d'un canzonière ne soient disposés ni au hasard, ni dans la succession chronologique de leur composition, c'est l'évidence même; ils ont été soumis à un modelage, ils s'organisent selon un plan; le modèle pétrarquien se profile impérieusement à l'horizon. Mais quel est ce plan? nous est-il encore perceptible? Et s'il est perceptible, quel sens désigne-t-il?

Si le recueil est plus qu'une poussière de poèmes dont les meilleurs peuvent se détacher sans dommage pour revivre dans les anthologies, il en résulte que nous avons à lire chaque sonnet dans sa solidarité avec tous les autres; c'est l'ordonnance d'ensemble qui sera porteuse de sens. Cette question, je vais la poser à quelques-uns des canzonières de la seconde moitié du XVIe siècle.

Du Bellay: l'Olive

La priorité chronologique reviendrait à la *Délie* de Scève, mais la *Délie* est un canzonière de dizains. Puisque j'ai décidé de m'en tenir aux seuls recueils de *sonnets* amoureux, c'est Du Bellay qui se présente le premier avec son *Olive* de 1549–50.[1] J'examine l'ouvrage complet, les 115 sonnets de l'édition de 1550, en forte augmentation sur la première, et dont le dessein apparaît plus franchement, pour peu que l'on rapproche l'ouverture et le finale: une ample trajectoire, qui suggère une théophanie; une divinité apparaît, séjourne sur terre, puis s'éloigne, désignant le

[1] On consultera V. L. Saulnier, *Du Bellay, L'homme et l'œuvre*, Paris (1951), pp. 56–8: 'l'œuvre se ferme comme un reliquaire'.

ciel; entre deux, les déchirements, les épreuves de l'amant terrestre. La 'grand' déité' mise au centre de cet exercice d'adoration, c'est l'Amour, c'est la femme louée sous le nom d'Olive, mais elle n'est pas seule et voici le trait qui va renforcer le dessin de l'itinéraire: derrière la divinité féminine s'en profile une autre, qui n'est rien moins que le Christ. Discrètement, par touches furtives au début et à la fin de son recueil, Du Bellay suggère un parallélisme entre l'Homme Dieu et la Femme déifiée, tous deux images et reflets sur terre du monde supra-sensible, l'un et l'autre s'offrant à l'amour de l'adorateur pour l'entraîner, par la puissance de cet amour, vers l'au-delà.

Le sonnet V, sonnet de la rencontre instauratrice, est à cet égard d'une parfaite netteté:

> *C'etoit la nuyt que la Divinité*
> *Du plus hault ciel en terre se rendit,*
> *Quand dessus moy Amour son arc tendit*
> *Et me fist serf de sa grand' déité.*

La nuit de Noël a été choisie, en ce début de l'aventure, pour mieux déclarer le caractère épiphanique de cette double descente du ciel sur la terre. Mais on doit noter aussitôt que le parallélisme ne va pas sans une disjonction, déjà sensible dans ce premier quatrain, plus encore dans le second:

> *Ny le sainct lieu de telle cruauté*
> *Ny le tens mesme assez me deffendit:*
> *Le coup au cœur par les yeux descendit,*
> *Trop ententifz à ceste grand' beauté.*

La 'Déité' profane à laquelle l'amant est désormais asservi va le détourner de la 'Divinité' chrétienne, dont il ne sera plus question si ce n'est à la fin, dans une série de pièces conclusives (CVII ss), qui soudain, en ce lieu privilégié qu'est un finale, réintroduisent la transcendance religieuse en mêlant au thème chrétien le thème platonicien. Les sonnets CVII et CVIII rappellent l'incarnation et la nuit de Noël du sonnet V, mais s'achèvent en une prière qui paraît en prendre le contre-pied:

> . . . *D'un nouveau feu brusle moy jusq' à l'ame,*
> *Tant que l'ardeur de ta celeste flamme*
> *Face oublier de l'autre le tourment.*

On pourrait croire que le 'nouveau feu' va se substituer au feu de l'amour terrestre; mais non, l'*Olive* ne débouche pas sur une conversion qui tournerait le dos à la passion analysée au long d'une centaine de sonnets antérieurs; la conjonction du Christianisme et du Platonisme est là pour assurer la fusion des deux amours, le glissement de la passion profane au feu céleste. Après deux sonnets sur la mort du Christ – renvoyant ainsi à la fin de son recueil le vendredi saint qui chez Pétrarque coïncidait avec la première rencontre – Du Bellay dispose une pièce de transition: le sonnet CXII, poème de la prédestination chrétienne en langage platonicien,

> *Dedans le clos des occultes Idées* . . .

Il suffit de le comparer à son modèle italien récemment retrouvé[1] pour voir combien il a été platonisé par le poète français qui renforce particulièrement le système des images aériennes de l'envol et de l'aile.

Ce sonnet mixte prépare au suivant, le CXIII et dernier de la série, purement platonicien celui-ci, qui ramène au premier plan la Dame apparemment oubliée dans les pièces chrétiennes, c'est le beau sonnet:

> *Si nostre vie est moins qu'une journée/En l'eternel* . . .

Poème de l'ascension de l'âme volant, de degrés en degrés, du temps vers l'éternité et de l'obscurité vers la lumière, jusqu'à la Cause de son épuisante passion:

> *La, ô mon ame au plus hault ciel guidée!*
> *Tu y pouras recongnoistre l'Idée*
> *De la beauté, qu'en ce monde j'adore.*

A la fin de son voyage, l'amant voit le ciel s'ouvrir. Il lui est révélé que l'objet réel de sa poursuite transcende la femme aimée;

---

[1] E. Caldarini, 'Nuove fonti italiane dell ''*Olive*'' ', *Bibliothèque d'Humanisme et Renaissance*, t. XXXVII (1965), pp. 21–3. Il s'agit d'un sonnet de Veronica Gambara, dans le recueil Giolito *Rime di diversi* . . . II, p. 112 v.

celle-ci n'est qu'un reflet, mais sans ce reflet il n'eût pas été conduit à la source de toute beauté terrestre.

Cette conclusion religieuse d'un canzonière profane lui donne rétrospectivement une unité et un sens; ce sens est celui d'une montée douloureuse qui s'achève en un brusque envol.

Il faut convenir toutefois que cette organisation se dessine tardivement et que la projection platonico-chrétienne, si elle nous vaut un admirable finale, n'est pas consubstantielle au recueil. Il n'en sera pas de même avec un platonicien rigoureux, Peletier du Mans.[1]

Jacques Peletier: L'Amour des Amours

'Amores . . ., ut soleo dicere, Platonis imitatione scriptos', c'est ainsi que Peletier, dans sa leçon d'ouverture à l'Université de Poitiers, définit ses *Amours* de 1555. Nous devons à cette obédience le plus cohérent, le plus construit des canzonières du XVIe siècle. Un néo-platonisme médité agit ici comme principe d'organisation, articulant étroitement l'amour et la connaissance en sa 'longue et hautaine entreprise': un diptyque, dont la composition binaire est soulignée par l'emploi successif de deux formes poétiques nettement différenciées, d'abord une suite homogène de 96 sonnets amoureux, puis une série de pièces strophiques à sujets 'scientifiques': pluie, grêle, neige, corps célestes; après la forme close et arrêtée du sonnet, la forme libre et ouverte des strophes. L'amour se dit en sonnets; aux 'secrets de la nature' convient l'ode, non seulement parce qu'elle est plus noble, de plus haut style, mais surtout parce qu'elle correspond au mouvement d'ouverture à l'espace céleste qui est celui de cette seconde partie; ainsi que l'a bien montré Hans Staub,[2] la connaissance chez Peletier a le caractère d'une expansion infinie.

---

[1] Pour ce qui concerne les *Regrets*, on se reportera à H. Weber, *La création poétique au XVIe siècle en France*, Paris (1956), t. I, pp. 419–22; l'auteur y reconnaît des séquences, des 'chapitres' s'ordonnant en conformité avec le sujet du recueil, pièces liminaires, sonnets sur le voyage, satires de la vie romaine, etc. . . .

[2] H. Staub, 'L'aspiration infinie de Jacques Peletier du Mans', *Saggi e Ricerche di Letteratura francese*, vol. VI (1963), Università di Pisa, pp. 39–80.

Entre ces deux volets du diptyque que distinguent si bien leur sujet et leur forme, il peut sembler qu'il n'y ait aucun rapport. Or c'est le contraire qui est vrai. Le lien existe, étroit et organique. Et c'est même l'existence et la nature de cette relation qui mettent hors de pair l'*Amour des Amours*. A travers une expérience amoureuse qui, loin de l'enfermer dans les liens corporels, l'en dégage, l'amant s'allège de son poids matériel et se trouve finalement capable de s'élever au-dessus du sensible, guidé d'abord, porté ensuite par la Dame qui l'entraîne dans son vol; elle le dépose sur le Parnasse pour le confier à un nouveau guide, la Muse céleste Uranie,[1] détentrice de la science du ciel et des phénomènes atmosphériques qu'elle va lui exposer méthodiquement.

Mais pour que cette contemplation du ciel fût possible, il fallait l'étape préalable de l'expérience amoureuse. Pas d'élan strophique sans une longue chaîne de sonnets antécédents. Epreuve et 'cage', la traversée de l'étroit couloir des sonnets était la condition nécessaire d'une mutation qu'exprime l'essor des odes; le lecteur éprouve le changement de forme comme une brusque libération. Pour Peletier, 'le même élan qui anime l'amour porte aussi la connaissance . . ., à la différence de Ficin qui exalte la suprématie de l'amour, Peletier soumet l'amour au désir de connaître.'[2]

Les derniers sonnets, précédant immédiatement le passage à la nouvelle forme et au nouvel horizon, préparent déjà l'esprit à cet envol par une purification de la vision; comparée au soleil, symbole de beauté éternelle, la Dame, d'abord voilée par l'écran corporel qui l'enveloppait comme une nuée, surgit maintenant à découvert, 'd'éternité vêtue', dans sa pure transparence:

> *Apprêtez-vous, mes yeux, pour recevoir*
> *L'ouvert rayon sortant hors de la Nue;*
> *Mon beau Soleil montrant sa face nue*
> *Après l'obscur sa splendeur vous fait voir* (Sonnet 94).

[1] réincarnation de la Béatrice de Dante, cf. A. M. Schmidt, *La Poésie scientifique en France au XVIe siècle*, Paris (1938), ch. I.
[2] H. Staub, art. cit., pp. 62–3.

Nouvel Icare, mais sûr de ne pas périr dans son 'vol audacieux', l'amant va s'élever au savoir le plus haut; il le doit à l'*aile* qu' Amour lui a entée:

> *Ravi en l'amour de ma Dame,*
> *Je sens dedans moi s'émouvoir*
> *Un ne sais quel nouveau pouvoir (L'Amour volant).*

Ce que Ronsard séparera, distribuant les *Amours* et les *Hymnes* dans des recueils distincts que rien ne relie entre eux, Peletier l'a uni dans un recueil homogène dont la composition bipartite reflète un itinéraire étagé mais continu, modelé sur la poussée du désir ascendant, jusqu'au 'coup d'aile' vers ce ciel où le contemplateur pourra prendre possession à la fois de l'univers et de lui-même:

> *Il est besoin être hors de soi-même*
> *Pour contempler ce qu'on a dedans soi* (Sonnet 93).

Ronsard: Le Second Livre des Amours

Je choisis d'examiner ce canzonière dans son èdition de 1578, parce qu'avec sa seconde partie *Sur la mort de Marie* il représente dans l'œuvre de Ronsard un cas privilégié: le recueil s'ordonne très visiblement sur un schéma romanesque, d'origine pétrarquienne, qui conduit une passion de sa naissance à son dénouement, de la présence à l'assomption de l'aimée. L'insertion tardive d'un chapitre pour Marie morte modifie la résonance de l'ensemble, lui confère un pathétique qui se reporte sur chaque instant de la vie de Marie. Les rencontres avec la jeune fille deviennent de brèves rencontres, celle que nous savons maintenant promise à une fin soudaine nous apparaît nimbée d'une grâce éphémère, d'une beauté aussi fragile que celle de la rose à laquelle, si souvent, elle se voit comparée. Sur cette Marie qui ne sera jamais 'bien vieille' souffle un air printanier baignant jusqu'à sa mort, cette mort légère et dite en images sereines. Après la mélodie animée, souvent tourmentée des 'Amours de Marie', la section terminale clôt le recueil sur un calme point d'orgue.

En dépit du modèle pétrarquien ou platonicien, Ronsard vit

une expérience qui est bien sienne; loin d'entraîner l'amant survivant dans la contemplation d'une âme qui se dévêt de son corps comme d'un voile pour mieux l'attirer dans son sillage, Marie nous est obstinément montrée dans sa réduction en *cendre*, *terre* et *corps*, cachée sous le sol, enfermée dans sa bière: 'La mort a son beau corps d'un cercueil revêtu', 'Vous n'êtes plus qu'un peu de cendre . . .', 'et cendre tu reposes'. Quand il arrive au poète de la placer dans le ciel, parmi les anges ou les astres, ce n'est pas pour susciter une union hors des sens, dans l'au-delà, mais pour mieux affirmer au contraire la séparation, l'opposition sans espoir des morts et des vivants, des *cieux* et de la *terre*, de *là-haut* et d'*icy*:

> . . . *tu possèdes les cieux,*
> *Et je n'ay, mal-heureux, pour ma part que la terre* . . . (Sonnet CXI)

Dans le sonnet de la rose 'Comme on voit sur la branche . . .', s'il y a métamorphose et transfiguration, c'est celle de la cendre en fleur, en beauté terrestre:

> *Afin que vif, et mort, ton corps ne soit que roses.*

Vif et mort: dans la mort comme dans la vie, ce corps toujours floral reste semblable à ce qu'il fut, pour une mémoire qui n'imagine la morte que sous les traits de la vivante.

On le sait par ailleurs (*Hymnes, Discours de l'altération et change des choses humaines*), la mort ronsardienne est une opération de vie, l'une des formes alternées de l'existence universelle. Aussi de la première à la seconde partie du recueil la coupure n'est-elle pas profonde, et l'amant ne subit nulle conversion; toujours amoureux du monde sensible, il aime ou rêve d'aimer Marie disparue comme il a aimé Marie présente; le pétrarquisme de la composition bipartite est ici plus apparent que réel. Ce qui n'a rien de surprenant de la part d'un poète foncièrement inapte à saisir l'esprit distinct du corps,

> *Car l'esprit ne sent rien que par l'ayde du corps.*[1]

---

[1] *Sonnets pour Hélène*, no. XXVIII.

Malgré sa vénération pour le 'docte Peletier' et quelques emprunts à la poétique de Ficin, Ronsard est bien éloigné de toute vision platonicienne, il souhaite trop d'avoir 'mille mains' pour 'toucher' la beauté qu'il aime.

La question de l'ordonnance doit être posée maintenant à la première partie du recueil considérée en elle-même, à l'ensemble de 103 pièces constituant la Vie de Marie. L'évolution du recueil, sa naissance en 1555, sa constitution en 1560 par regroupements, adjonctions, suppressions ont été excellemment décrites et commentées par M. Dassonville.[1] Je me limiterai, comme je l'ai fait jusqu'à présent, à l'état de 1578. Problème très ouvert, auquel je n'apporterai qu'une réponse partielle.

Un premier fait saute aux yeux : Ronsard répartit ses poèmes en deux grandes masses égales, encadrées par trois longues pièces à rimes plates, deux *Elégies* au début et à la fin, le *Voyage de Tours* au centre. Cette observation ne mène pas très loin, tout au plus prouve-t-elle une première volonté d'organisation. On notera du moins que l'Elégie initiale *A son Livre* justifie l'inconstance, l'abandon de Cassandre pour Marie, tandis que l'Elégie finale *A Marie* est une apologie de la constance couronnée dans le temple de 'fidèle amitié' :

> . . . *et ce temple aurait nom*
> *Le temple de Ronsard et de sa Marion.*

S'opposant aux canzonières pétrarquistes qui postulent d'emblée la constance inconditionnelle, celui de Ronsard semble aller de l'inconstance à la constance, au fil d'un amour qui hésite, se cherche, s'éprouve et finalement se fixe.[2]

Si l'on regarde plus attentivement à l'intérieur de cet ample cadre, on relève d'abord une disposition formelle qui n'existe ni dans l'*Olive*, ni dans l'*Amour des Amours* (mais que connaissaient les

---

[1] M. Dassonville, 'Pour une interprétation nouvelle des *Amours* de Ronsard', *Biblioth. d'Hum. et Ren.*, vol. XXVIII (1966), pp. 241–70.
[2] Ce qui confirmerait cette impression, c'est la suppression dans la seconde moitié, mais non dans la première, de quelques pièces qui faisaient l'éloge de l'inconstance.

Italiens, à commencer par Pétrarque) : la chaîne des sonnets, au lieu d'être continue, s'interrompt, à intervalles à peu près réguliers, pour faire place à des 'chansons' qui rompent le rythme et scandent la progression (1 ou 2 chansons tous les 6 à 10 sonnets). Aux sonnets, rigides et tendus, s'opposent les chansons, libres, mobiles, menues, figures formelles de la détente ; détente aussi dans l'esprit, car la chanson est souvent familière et badine, elle se laisse aller sans arrière-pensée au plaisir, à la tendresse légère. Fine agrafe entre deux groupes de sonnets, elle desserre l'étau des plaintes et des contraintes.

La chanson a encore une autre fonction, elle sert de charnière entre deux séries homogènes. Ces séries, dont M. Dassonville constate l'existence dès les premières éditions, le texte de 1578 les organise solidement ; elles rassemblent des pièces de sens voisin et de tonalité analogue en sections alternantes ; celles-ci progressent comme une grande phrase dont les unités lexicales seraient des sonnets ou des groupes de sonnets. A une série exprimant le servage douloureux, la tension ou la révolte de l'amant (sonnets XVIII à XXIV) en succède une disant l'abandon, l'acceptation ou le simple plaisir d'aimer (XXVII à XXXIII) ; vient ensuite une brève reprise des thèmes de l'amertume et de la femme inflexible (XXXVI à XXXVIII) puis du badinage (XLI à XLIII) ; la série suivante (XLV à LII) marque un progrès dans le cheminement en combinant les thèmes auparavant dissociés et successifs tout en maintenant les oppositions ; c'est que la passion est intime contradiction, mélange permanent de joie et de souffrance ; le bonheur se goûte dans les fers, le plaisir dans la tristesse ; aussi les vers multiplient-ils les oxymores : *plaisants tourments*, *soupirs agréables*, *déplaisir* et *liesse*,

> *Plus je suis en l'obscur, plus j'espère de jour* (LI).
> *Que l'amoureuse vie est un plaisant cercueil* (LII).

Sans pousser plus loin l'analyse de détail, on voit se dessiner un rythme et un approfondissement de la passion, qui attaque l'être avec soudaineté, l'assiège sauvagement, semble refluer devant ses rébellions, l'investit par vagues alternées de douleur et de plaisir, de présence et d'absence, le pénètre progressivement, se fait finalement accepter et souhaiter comme un tourment désirable, comme une loi de la vie commune à la Nature tout entière. Enfin, au bout de cette route qui consacre, en dépit des contestations et des tentatives d'évasion, un acquiescement à la gravité de l'amour, Ronsard a placé l'expérience de la mort, la fuite de l'être aimé, cette fois définitivement inaccessible.

Sponde

Il serait tentant d'explorer également quelques-uns des recueils qui abondent dans le dernier tiers du XVIe siècle. Un titre tel que *Hécatombe à Diane* y inviterait instamment : 'cent amoureux son-nets' qui sont autant d'offrandes sanglantes de l'amant sacrifié à la déesse irritée. Le chiffre *cent* a pour fin de renforcer l'idée centrale de sacrifice, d'effusion de sang métaphorique. Mais je m'en tiendrai pour terminer à un exemple plus tardif et bien différent, les *Sonnets de la Mort* de ce Sponde qui doit tant à Alan Boase.

Ce petit canzonière, non plus d'amour mais de mort, n'a pas été publié pour la première fois en édition posthume, comme on a pu le croire, mais du vivant de l'auteur. C'est ce que nous savons depuis la découverte par Alan Boase, en 1950, d'un exemplaire des *Méditations*; à leur suite figuraient les 'poèmes chrestiens'. Il n'est plus possible dès lors de suspecter l'ordre dans lequel ces sonnets nous sont parvenus. Acceptons-le tel qu'il est. On ne peut s'empêcher cependant, quand on suit attentivement ce développement si rigoureux, de s'étonner parfois de la disposi-tion reçue. On se prend à rêver : pourquoi ne pas brasser quelque peu les cartes et en retoucher l'ordonnance, ainsi que l'a fait pour les *Amours* le regretté Glauco Natoli ?[1]

En ce qui concerne les *Sonnets de la Mort*, ce jeu serait gratuit. Si je m'accorde témérairement la permission de m'y livrer un instant, ce n'est évidemment pas pour proposer à de futurs éditeurs la moindre modification, qui serait de toute façon irrece-

---

[1] *Problemi e Figure di Letteratura francese*, Florence (1956).

vable. Je ne donne ce petit exercice que comme un moyen commode et provisoire de réfléchir plus librement sur l'ordre d'un discours en en sondant les résistances, ainsi qu'aimait à le faire Valéry quand il soumettait à cette épreuve une suite de vers.

Il faut le reconnaître, Sponde résiste bien. Si bien qu'on a le sentiment, que ne donnaient pas les précédents recueils, d'avoir à faire à des pièces composées les unes par rapport aux autres en vue d'un groupement préalablement conçu. Cela est vrai surtout des premières, qui manifestent une logique, une sévérité dans l'enchaînement tout à fait exceptionnelles. C'est un caractère distinctif de ces poèmes de proposer une lecture rigoureusement continue, comme s'ils formaient un poème unique en plusieurs sonnets : I, les hommes mortels, entourés d'images funèbres, demeurent aveugles à leur condition mortelle ; II, 'Mais si faut-il mourir', l'attaque adversative désigne une affirmation antérieure qu'un mouvement propre à la pensée spondienne se hâte de renverser. Sur quoi le III reprend : 'Ha ! que j'en voy bien peu songer à ceste mort', ces 'vaissaux de verre' se croient des 'rochers', ces 'vermisseaux' se prennent pour des 'géants' capables de fonder les plus hautes entreprises ; mais, poursuit le IV dans un nouveau renversement, 'Pour qui tant de travaux ?' alors que la vie n'est que fuite et 'course à la mort' ; c'est la reprise du Ier sonnet que va confirmer le V :

> *Hélas! contez vos jours: les jours qui sont passez*
> *Sont desjà morts pour vous, ceux qui viennent encore*
> *Mourront tous sur le point de leur naissante Aurore,*
> *Et moytié de la vie est moytié du décez.*

Or c'est précisément la rigueur de ces enchaînements qui rend le lecteur exigeant et l'alerte sur d'apparentes ruptures. Pourquoi faut-il aller chercher au No VII la suite naturelle du V ? Et que vient faire, à la place qui nous est proposée, le sonnet VI ? Sa belle conclusion :

> . . . *Il faut que je revole à ces plus beaux séjours,*
> *Où séjourne des Temps l'entresuitte infinie.*
> *Beaux séjours, loin de l'œil, prez de l'entendement* . . .

213

semble sans relation directe avec ce qui précède, elle intervient trop tôt dans l'évolution du recueil, alors qu'elle en ferait si bien le dénouement. Où verrait-on mieux qu'au finale l'âme s'envoler et atteindre son haut *désir*, enfin délivrée de l'ombre, du mouvement, du temps qui ont fait le sujet dominant du canzonière?

Supposons un instant qu'il en soit ainsi et transposons le VI en XII. Que faire alors du No XII de nos éditions, le somptueux et complexe sonnet rapporté 'Tout s'enfle contre moy, tout m'assaut, tout me tente', dont les enchevêtrements et les contrastes formels disent les tensions internes de l'esprit et sa lutte contre le triple ennemi? Comment comprendre ces verbes au futur, dès le second quatrain, qui visent un avenir, dans l'espérance assurée de voir un jour la triple action divine vaincre

> *Et le Monde, et la Chair, et l'Ange révolté . . .* ?

On voudrait déplacer au début du recueil cette pièce inaugurale qui poserait d'emblée, au seuil de l'épopée spirituelle qu'elle annoncerait, le dur combat spirituel qui fait la condition de l'homme. Ainsi reconstitué, le petit canzonière de la mort dessinerait, dans un espace contracté à l'extrême, un trajet cohérent qui conduirait dramatiquement l'être en travail du labyrinthe à la délivrance, de l'*ombrage* de ce *temps* au grand jour de l'éternité.

Cette reconstruction n'étant pas licite, quel sera le profit de ce qui n'a été qu'une fantaisie? J'ai imposé une cohérence de lecteur moderne à celle de Sponde, qui seule importe; celle-ci devrait apparaître maintenant avec plus de netteté, l'attention étant alertée sur les divergences qui séparent les deux itinéraires. Si Sponde place, non pas en conclusion, mais au centre de son recueil l'appel aux "beaux séjours" de l'intemporel, c'est que cet appel n'est qu'un élan sans réalité ('je n'entends point quelqu'un de vous qui die . . .'), un élan sans lendemain, le désir d'un moment que suivra la rechute. La destinée de l'homme ici-bas est de poursuivre son cheminement par 'ces facheux détours'. Son désir de lumière ne peut s'exprimer qu'au sein d'un 'ombrage sombre' qui l'enveloppe de tous côtés. Il est donc dans la logique de cette pensée de placer le sonnet 'Tout s'enfle contre moy . . .' au dénouement, non à l'origine, de son trajet, parce que son trajet n'a pas de dénouement visible ; il n'est pas donné à l'homme spondien de sortir du labyrinthe ; la tentative du monde l'investira jusqu'au dernier jour, la délivrance sera sans cesse reportée à l'horizon.

D'autant plus forte sera la foi, la confiance en l'issue, d'autant plus 'invincible' la main de Dieu que la démarche humaine aura été incertaine et obscure.

Quelques années après ces *Sonnets de la Mort* paraissait à Lyon, en 1594, un petit ouvrage contenant une traduction des Psaumes pénitentiaux suivie de 12 sonnets – encore 12 ! – *sur le sacré mystère de nostre Redemption*. Une préface les présente comme des échantillons 'd'un plus grand œuvre'. L'auteur se nomme Jean de La Ceppède, le 'grand œuvre' annoncé, ce seront les *Théorèmes*.

Les douze sonnets de 1594 mettent déjà au cœur de la méditation la Passion du Christ. Des sonnets chrétiens de Sponde le Médiateur était absent ; le dernier vers du sonnet XI semble même rêver d'un salut sans le Christ, d'un saut immédiat dans la vie éternelle :

> *Mais quoy? nous n'avons plus ny d'Henoc, ny d'Elie.*

Avec La Ceppède, la conversion du canzonière profane de la Pléiade, amorcée auparavant par divers recueils de sonnets spirituels, est désormais accomplie. Le récit des Evangiles en fera toute la matière et le Christ en sera l'unique centre. L'ordonnance va s'en trouver totalement renouvelée.

Jean Rousset

'. . . ma douce fleur nouvelle'

(Ronsard, *Chanson*)

-》》-》》-》》-》》-》》-》》-》》-》》-》》-》》-》》-《《-《《-《《-《《-《《-《《-《《-《《-《《-《《-《《-《《

MY DEAR ALAN,

When reading your *Poetry of France*, vol. 1, 1400–1600, I could
not help remembering *le temps de notre jeunesse* when I was allowed
to teach linguistics beside you in Glasgow. It seemed to me then –
and I know you shared my opinion – that a linguistic criticism
could usefully supplement the literary criticism of which you are
a master. It seemed tempting to go back for a moment to our discussions of the 'thirties and try and make some remarks which
might help your less initiated readers to understand more correctly
the texts you published in your anthology. When I began the task
I quickly became aware of the truth proclaimed by Vossler: 'Der
Kunstwert liegt in der Einheit, nicht in den Einzelheiten der
Dichtung' (LGRPh, 1919, 246). As a linguist I had to deal with
Einzelheiten, whereas for you the *Einheiten*, i.e. the individual
works of art are of vastly greater importance. I became no less
discouraged at the thought of some kind of linguistically oriented
explication de texte of your poems; is not all *explication de texte* a
little 'stuffy' as you say in your foreword (p. xvi)? – After some
hesitation I finally decided to comment after all on a small,
seemingly insignificant, detail, a mere phrase in a *Chanson* by
Ronsard. I soon became engrossed in my subject and, having
nothing better to offer you, I put together what I have found so
far in the hope that you will not fail to see, in spite of my handicap,
the bridge that connects your interests with mine.

217

1 *French and Latin epithets*

In the first stanza of his *Chanson* (p. 95 of your anthology) Ronsard offers us an exuberant cascade of epithets of the beloved girl. Its music, its rhythmical qualities do not require to be commented upon, they are apparent to any reader. On the other hand, there may be those who feel a little intrigued by the vocabulary displayed here. In this respect a word of explanation may not be amiss. – *Ma chère amie, ma belle* are very ordinary; *ma douce rebelle* belongs to the tradition of the 'dame sans merci'. It stands beside *ma cruelle, mon inhumaine, l'ingrate, l'infidelle* in Deimier's later catalogue, which also mentions *ennemie, rigoureuse, guerriere, homicide* and *inconstante*.[1] Charmingly French and significantly paired are also *mon doux printemps, ma douce fleur nouvelle*. For *mon amour* one would likewise wish to invoke a French tradition (cf. *ma belle amour gracieuse* in Christine de Pisan's *Le Dit de la Pastoure* 2146)[2] and not go back to the Latin *amores* used in a plural.

All the other epithets are Neo-Classic or Latin. Marullus, whom you quote (p. 223) has the Latin originals for *mon coeur* (*meum cor*), *ma mignardise* (*mea suavitas*), *mes délices* (*mei lepores*), *mon passereau* (*mi passercule*), *ma gente tourtourelle* (*mi albe turturille*, where the choice of the masculine gender is somewhat surprising).[3] The *meos lepores* and the feminine *albam turturillam* are also found in Johannes Secundus' *Basia* VIII; he also has *meam columbam* exactly as Ronsard has *ma douce colombelle*; he has furthermore *meam vitam* (Ronsard: *ma douce vie*).[4] Of Latin models Plautus' *meus pullus passer, mea columba, mi lepus* (*Casin.* 1, 50) comes easily to mind. We may also quote from him *bene vale, ocule mi* (*Curc.* 1, 3, 47) which has found an echo in Ronsard's *mon œuil*. And

---

[1] Cf. F. Brunot, *La Doctrine de Malherbe d'après son Commentaire sur Desportes*, Paris (1891), p. 350.

[2] K. Glaser, *Altfranzösisches Lesebuch des späteren Mittelalters*, Halle a. S. (1926), p. 14.

[3] Cf. below, p. 220.

[4] F. A. Wright, *The Love Poems of Joannes Secundus*, New York (1930), p. 62, where *neaeque* (line 9) has to be read *meaeque*. Ronsard has imitated the Second Kiss in 1560; cf. p. 247.

Catullus' *lepores* are quoted in Leumann – Hofmann – Szantyr's Latin handbook.[1]

It is thus possible to divide up all the epithets into two groups according to whether they follow a French or a Latin tradition. In the eyes of learned poets such as Ronsard the loan-translations doubtless enhanced the poetic idiom; these foreign immigrants were supposed to be one day assimilated into French. Alas, the very fact that they require learned notes today shows up their later destiny. It is precisely because these borrowings have kept their foreign status that they are only of marginal interest to the French philologist who is rather drawn to the home-grown epithets. Of these the expression *ma douce fleur nouvelle* seems to me particularly intriguing, and my subsequent commentary will attempt to explain why this should be so.

2 *Flos – fleur*

The 'girl-flower' conceit may well be as old as lyrical poetry itself and lately Mr Peter Dronke has given us fascinating insights into its history.[2] He is obviously much more concerned with 'ideas' than with 'words', with 'conceits' more than with their linguistic formulations. Our interests here are quite different. We must ask whether or not the Latin word *flos* was identified with a girl, when *flos* in this sense appears combined with the attribute *novus* and in which sense *novus* is used. If we ask these questions it becomes immediately clear that in classical Latin not *flos* but *rosa* was the word used in erotic language. The rose was as much the flower of Venus as the dove was her bird. *Rosa* is the word all classical dictionaries list as being used as a term of endearment for the beloved girl from Plautus onwards. No corresponding entry is found s.v. *flos*. Nor does a consultation of the Thesaurus bring to light any significant material.[3] It thus appears that the literary

[1] *Handbuch der Altertumswissenschaft* II, 2, 2, München (1965), p. 18.

[2] P. Dronke, *Medieval Latin and the Rise of European Love-lyric*, I, Oxford (1965), pp. 181–92.

[3] The Thesaurus lists only one elaborate comparison found in Catullus (62, 39); *ut flos in saeptis secretus nascitur hortis, ignotus pecori, nullo convulsus aratro, quem mulcent*

fortunes of *flos* in our sense have been grafted on to those of *rosa*, and I shall endeavour to show that a grammatical accident was largely responsible for this.

First a word of introduction:

In the early Middle Ages the cultivation of the noble rose was apparently left to monks and clerics (FEW s.v. *rosa*). Thus it came to pass that such a popular symbol appears in a learned garb – the Latin vowel remained unchanged – and thus joins other learned words in the language of love such as the French-Provençal *amour* or the Spanish verb *amar* (against popular *querer*); even in Italy *ti amo* is slightly highbrow compared to *ti voglio bene d'anima*. *Fleur*, on the other hand, is popular in origin and penetrated into the sphere of noble sentimental conventions with the help of *rosa* as we have already said. In this it was doubtless helped by two linguistic properties. (*a*) *Flore* became of feminine gender and (*b*) its position was strengthened by the abstract collective sense which it possessed beside the individual, concrete, denotation. Both points require a brief commentary.

2a *Gender*

It is by no means a necessity that an epithet of the beloved girl has to be of feminine gender, otherwise how could Plautus use his *meus pullus passer* or Marullus address his girl as *mi albe turturille* (see above, p. 218)? And yet we know the use medieval poets made of the feminine *amour* subtly identifying and confusing Love and Lady. One example we quote from Christine de Pisan: *Et qu'avez vous,/ma belle amour gracïeuse?/N'estes vous pas bien joyeuse/du retour de vostre ami?* (see above p. 218); we can read another example in Chrétien de Troyes *Chanson* (2nd stanza), published by Bartsch-Wiese.[1]

We also know that *amour* became masculine (in the singular only!) in order to create a concordance between grammatical

---

aurae, firmat sol, educat imber . . . sic virgo (*Thes.* s.v. *flos*, 929, 54). Catullus's poem is reproduced in H. Weber, *Création poétique au 16e siècle en France*, Paris (1956), p. 337.

[1] *Chrestomathie de l'ancien français*, 11e éd., Leipzig (1913), p. 111.

gender and the masculinity of Cupid. True, grammatical concordance of a given word with the sex of the person denoted by
it, may even be avoided in certain well-known circumstances:
mon chéri used by a husband addressing his wife, *ma vieille* used as
a term of endearment between students. All the same, the expressive advantage of the concordance between gender and sex
can be a real one, and I should like to suggest that a feminine
flore was a better rival-companion of the feminine *rosa* than the
masculine *flos*.

The FEW does not proffer any explanation as to how the change
of gender of *flore* was accomplished. I should be inclined to see in
this the influence of *folia*, an old feminine collective of *folium*.
The Thesaurus notes an occasional neuter gender of *flos* in inscrip-
tions, and the collective, abstract meaning of our word, i.e.
'bloom', 'blossoming', could well have been a contributing factor
(cf. *la chaleur*, etc.). This would mean that *flore* became feminine
at a time when *folia* ceased to be felt as a plural. A grammatical
accident of this type may well have been responsible for the subsequent fashioning of a literary symbol that could play the role of
rosa, being partly confused with it, but sometimes being preferred
because of its lofty character: *flore* was less tied than *rosa* to a
hierarchy of flowers, to certain manifestations of colour, etc.

2b *Collective-abstract function*

The collective-abstract meaning of *flos*, i.e. 'blossom', 'flowering'
is old. From it stems the use of *flos* as an *elativus* 'the best kind of
something', which survives in the prosaic *fleur de la farine* and,
hence, in English *flour*. A girl could be referred to as *flos puellarum*
or, later, as *flors de domnas* (*Flors de domnas cui aclin e grazis, es
aicela que tan gen m'a conquis*. Giraut de Borneilh).[1] This does not
necessarily signify an identification between girl and flower, any
more than Deschamps wanted to identify a great warrior with a
flower by calling Bertram du Guesclin *la fleur des preux*.[2] Here we

[1] M. de Riquer, *La Lirica de los Trovadores* I, Barcelona (1945), p. 327.
[2] K. Glaser, loc. cit., p. 5.

must also mention the elliptic *flos* meaning *flos aetatis* which is important for the interpretation of a passage from Ausonius we shall have to discuss later.[1]

Besides *flos* other words can be used to denote an *elativus*. We find *sol* and *fons* in this quotation from Paulinus of Nola where Christ is called *Sol aequitatis, fons bonorum, flos Dei*.[2] In the 'Love Council' appears the *cardinalis domina* whose description culminates in the words *Ipsa virgo regia, mundi flos et gloria*.[3] This formula reminds us of Cervantes' *flor y nata de la andante caballería* where the abstract formal function of the *elativus* is much more strongly in evidence than any possible concrete metaphorical identification.

Besides the *elativus* we must take into account an *intensivus* of the form *flos florum*. In principle only words denoting an extreme degree in a scale of qualitative or quantitative values can be used in this way, which restricts somewhat the semantic range of this construction. Generally the *intensivus* is not used metaphorically: *the king of kings* is a king; *the song of songs* is a song (cf. also *summa summarum, saecula saeculorum* etc.). However, in particular circumstances metaphorical usage also occurs; *flos florum* may refer, not to a flower, but to a girl; *la crème de la crème* has a general metaphorical value.

A poet could be tempted to play with the various semantic values of *flos*:

> *Illius captus sum amore,*
> *cuius flos* [= 'flos aetatis'] *est in flore* [= 'bloom']
> *dulcis fit labor in hoc labore,*
> *osculum si sumat os ab ore.*
> *non tactu sanabor labiorum*
> *nisi cor unum fiat duorum*
> *et idem velle. Vale flos florum!* [= metaphorical *intensivus*][4]

[1] On pp. 223–4.

[2] P. Dronke, loc. cit., p. 184. *Flos Dei* might possibly be interpreted after the pattern of *crimen hominis*.

[3] Ed. G. Waits in *Zeitschrift für deutsches Altertum*, vol. VII (1849), p. 161.

[4] *Carmina Burana*, no. 78 in the edition prepared by A. Hilka and O. Schumann, vol. II, Heidelberg (1941).

The linguistic versatility of *flos-fleur* as exemplified in the usages as *elativus* and *intensivus* was no doubt a contributing factor in strengthening its position in the language as a generally hyperbolic term. It thus added, albeit indirectly, to the literary vigour of the *fleur–bien-aimée* symbol. What is more, it seems that *flos* was soon strong enough to influence the destiny of *rosa* and thus to establish itself as the leading symbol. The words of praise in *Carmina Burana* no. 77: *ave, decus virginum, virgo gloriosa, ave lumen luminum, ave mundi rosa* are doubtless a variation of those previously quoted from the 'Love Council': *Ipsa virgo regia, mundi flos et gloria.*[1] In a similar way the *rosa rosarum* of the *Carmina Burana* (no. 179): *Flos est puellarum/quam diligo/et rosa rosarum/quam sepe video* echoes the *intensivus flos florum.* In both cases *rosa* follows the path traced by *flos*.

3 La fleur nouvelle

Two early passages seem significant for the *fleur nouvelle* formula. One, dated 890, is very clear; *flos novus* is indeed the young flower:

> *Dulcis et preciosa puella!*
> *Relatu angelico habens*
> *Ultra omnes homines dona decoris!*
> *Vincens rosas rubore, lilia candore!*
> *Flos novus ex terra, quam polus colit arce!*

This prose adaptation of (pseudo-) Fortunatus by Gondacrus of Reims echoes the appearance of the divine rose Maria of the *Hymnos Akathistos* (τὸ ῥόδον τὸ θεῖον πεφανέρωται, καὶ κατευωδία ἐπλήρωσε σήμερον τὰ πέρατα).[2] The interpretation of the other quotation, from the fourth century Ausonius, is perhaps not quite as clear

> Collige virgo, rosas, dum flos novus et nova pubes et memor esto aevum sic properare tuum.

At least Helen Waddell's necessarily free translation suggests that

---

[1] The two passages have been compared from the literary point of view by H. Brinkmann in his *Entstehungsgeschichte des Minnesangs*, Halle a.S. (1926), p. 4.
[2] P. Dronke, loc. cit., p. 185.

flos represents as much as *rosa* ('while youth is with the rose').[1] However, *flos novus* must surely be considered as a synonym of *aevum* and equal a *flos aetatis* as in this passage from Terence (*Eun.* 319): (*virginis*) *anni?* – *Sedecim* – *flos ipse* 'c'est justement la fleur de la jeunesse.[2] We thus find in Ausonius' text a word *flos* used as an *elativus*, which does not imply an identification of a flower with a girl, in contrast to the later text of 890, where the identification is unambiguously clear. *Novus* in Ausonius' text shows semantic affinities with *primum* as in *primum ver* 'the beginning of spring'. It is interesting to note that this dynamic meaning of 'beginning' characterizes *novus* even when combined with *flos* taken in its concrete sense. The *fleur nouvelle* is not so much a 'young' flower in contrast to other, 'old', flowers, but it represents a stage in the life of the flower in contrast to later stages; *nouvelle* thus alludes to a brief dramatic life-span.

3a Naître *as an attribute to* fleur

It is perhaps not without interest to recall in this connection that in the old languages one does not say of a flower *elle pousse* but rather *elle naît* as if it were a human being or an animal. This poetic verb is already so used in Latin;[3] we remember Catullus writing *ut flos in saeptis secretus nascitur hortis* . . .[4] Littré (s.v. *naître*) quotes from the Châtelain de Couci: *Au temps que nest la rose et le lis, Et la rousée ou vert pré* (Couci XII). – Jean de Condé sings:

> En la douce saison jolie,
> que toute creature est lie,
> et que naist la flours en la pree,
> kantent oysiel main et viespree
> et mainent vie glorieuse.[5]

[1] *Mediaeval Latin Lyrics*. A Translation by Helen Waddell. The Penguin Classics (1952), p. 39.
[2] *Théâtre complet des latins* publ. par M. Nisard, *Térence*, Didot Frères, Paris (1856), p. 37.
[3] It still survives in Spanish and Italian.
[4] Cf. above, p. 219, n. 3.
[5] Bartsch-Wiese, loc. cit., 81, 4.

Of the examples I have collected from Old Provençal I shall merely quote two, where the flower is actually identified with the young girl.

> *Plus blanca es que Elena*
> *belazors que flors que nais*
> *e de cortezia plena* (Arnaut de Maroilh).[1]

> *Tan es sos cors gais et isneus*
> *e complitz de belas colors*
> *c'anc de rozeus no nasquet flors*
> *plus frecha ni d'altres brondeus* (Giraut de Borneilh).[2]

In my last quotation *naître* and *nouveau* are closely associated:

> *Trastot m'es belh ont ilh es e·m resplan,*
> *bos m'en son prat e vergier e roselh*
> *e m'agensa a chascun jorn de l'an*
> *cum la rosa quand ilh nais de novelh* (Guillen de Saint Leidier).[3]

The evocation of the birth of young life has its poignancy, for its very existence is threatened by death. Only one flower has conquered this menace; Maria.

> *flors de vida ses mort, maire de Dieu* (Guilhen d'Autpol).[4]

Surely a poet could elevate the flower to a symbol of young life with or without the linguistic association with *naître*. On the other hand, we must not underestimate the power of subconscious linguistic patterns.

3b *Flower and thorns*

The rose symbol is a natural paradox because it unites in one representation the symbol of desirability (corresponding to the blossom or flower) and that of repellence (the thorns). The proverbial 'no rose without thorns' has always alluded to the

[1] K. Bartsch, *Chrestomathie provençale*[6], Marburg (1904), 101, 20.
[2] M. de Riquer, loc. cit., p. 334.
[3] ibid., p. 383.
[4] C. Appel, *Provenzalische Chrestomathie*, Leipzig (1902), 58, 8.

condition of human enterprise: *inter vepres rosae nascuntur* writes Ammianus Marcellinus (16, 7, 4).[1] In erotic conventions the thorns symbolize the obstacles in the lover's path. In Goethe's *Heidenröslein* they become the weapon with which the young girl-flower defends her purity.[2] When Ronsard and his contemporaries thought of 'roses' and 'thorns' as literary symbols they could not help but remember Guillaume de Lorris as he developed the theme of the *bouton* in his celebrated work. Guillaume had given to the thorns an existence independent of the rose who is described as being surrounded by thistles and nettles:

> *Mais chardon agu e poignant*
> *M'en aloient mout esloignant*
> *Espines tranchanz e agües,*
> *Orties e ronches crochues*
> *Ne me laissent avant traire*
> *Car je me cremoie mal faire.*[3]

He has thus created a counter-symbol to the *fleur nouvelle*, independent of her, which explains the following usage:

> *C'est pour montrer que l'Amour est trompeur*
> *Amer, cruel, plein de crainte et de peur*
> *Comme celui qui porte en ses mains closes*
> *Plus de chardons que de lis et de roses.*[4]

We also know that the queen of flowers, the rose, is not the only one with which *la fleur nouvelle* may be identified, the lily is her closest rival. The lily, too, is found in a garden where she attracts the lover;

> *Can estav' en aquels bels jardis*
> *lai m'apares la bela flor de lis*
> *e pres mos olhs e sazic mo coratge* (Giraut de Bornelh).[5]

---

[1] K. E. Georges, *Ausf. Lat.-Deutsch. Handwb.*[9] (1951), s.v. *rosa*.
[2] Cf. also H. Weber, loc. cit., p. 336.
[3] vv. 1675 ss. in E. Langlois's edition.
[4] Ronsard, *A la Reine d'Ecosse*, Anthology, p. 104.
[5] R. de Riquer, loc. cit., p. 326.

She may also be surrounded by thorns, now transformed into
the image of relative ugliness;

> Si cum li liz est entre les espines,
> ensi est m'amie entres les filhes (Job, p. 441).[1]

The lily symbol is not without expressive advantages. Closely
associated with the Virgin it stood for 'purity'; but this was a
doubtful gain in view of its loss of sensuality compared with
Venus' flower. It also pictured the white colour of the beloved's
complexion. I shall refrain from quoting literary examples of this
widespread and well-known cliché and I shall also suppress
allusions to the eternal mixture of lilies and roses in praise of the
girl's delicate colouring.[2] All these stand for *attributes* of the
beloved; the *rose* or *fleur* alone seems to represent her *essence*.

We have repeatedly pointed out that the symbol of the *fleur
nouvelle* carries with it a strange poignant flavour of fleeting time,
of youth threatened by decay and death.[3] Under these circumstances it would seem almost unavoidable on the part of poets to
exploit the symbolism of the thorns to depict the sombre side
of existence. Yet, in the frequent poetic rendering of the *carpe
diem* theme[4] the thorns are gaily forgotten, in spite of the fact
that it was evoked in order to give expression to life's revolt
against decay. More astonishingly, they play no significant role
either in Ariosto's or Baïf's imitations of Catullus, where the
young rose dies because she is separated *de sa branche maternelle*.[5]
Other forms of the theme *la rose et la mort* as well ignore the
thorns.[6] All the more remarkable is their reappearance in a
Christian context, where the poet understands that life on this
earth may be nothing but a form of dying, that suffering is an

---

[1] Cf. Littré *s.v. lis.*

[2] We quoted one example above, p. 223.

[3] Above, pp. 224 and 225.

[4] Or the erotic *carpere rosas* for that matter. Cf. *Carmina Burana*, no. 140: *dulcius est
carpere iam lilium cum rosa, dulcissimum est ludere cum virgine formosa.*

[5] H. Weber, loc. cit., p. 339.

[6] ibid., p. 350.

essential attribute of our existence: flower and thorns, symbol and antisymbol are but one:

> *La vie est une fleur espineuse et poignante,*
> *Belle au lever du jour, seiche en son occident.*[1]

3c *Flora poetica*

Roses and *lilies*, though the most frequently used flower symbols, are by no means the only ones to celebrate feminine charm and beauty. The violet has been evoked in the later portion of the *Roman de la Rose* (vv. 8936 ss.): *Car les beautez des beles choses, Soient violettes ou roses, Sont en eux et non pas es dames* – not without irony, though. You are better acquainted than I am with R. Burns' mountain daisy or Shakespeare's *pale primrose* (*Cymbeline* IV, II, 220). Surely, some day somebody will write a *Flora poetica*, which no doubt would make curious reading, but it can hardly be our task here to pursue this matter further.

3d *Literary conceit and linguistic formula*

The 'girl-flower' conceit has survived all changes of poetic conventions. *My love is like a red, red rose* (R. Burns), *Sah ein Knab' ein Röslein steh'n* (Goethe), *Du bist wie eine Blume* (Heine), *La Rose de l'Infante* (Hugo), are some well-known landmarks; but the formula *la fleur nouvelle* is practically dead and easier to document from medieval texts such as Phyllis and Flora (*Sic emergunt lilia, sic rosae novellae*),[2] Giraut de Borneilh (*No posc sofrir qu'a la dolor/De la den la lenga no vir/E l cor ab la novela flor,/Lancan vei los ramels florir*),[3] Bernart Matí (*Lancan lo douz temps s'esclaire/e la novella flors s'espan*)[4] Marie de France (*E vit le lit a la pucele, Que resemblot rose nuvele, Eluduc,* 1011)[5] than from modern authors. It is true

---

[1] I owe the knowledge of this beautiful passage from Desportes's *Œuvres chrestiennes*, sonnet 12, to Littré who lists it s.v. *vie*.
[2] Ed. A. Bömer in *Zeitschrift für deutsches Altertum* LVI (1918–19), p. 235.
[3] *Romanistisches Jahrbuch* II (1949), p. 181.
[4] M. De Riquer, loc. cit., p. 117.
[5] Ed. A. Ewert, Marie de France, *Lais*, Oxford (1944).

Paulo used to sing in the *Lapin Agile* Bruant's ballad *Rose blanche* where the line occurs *Elle sentait bon la fleur nouvelle, Rue Saint Vincent.* Yet this is probably no more than an archaic survival, 'gesunkenes Kulturgut'. Such survivals exist elsewhere. Children sing *Noël nouvelet, Noël chantons ici* without understanding the meaning of *noël nouvelet.* Ostermann in his translation of Isaias XI, 1 (*Et egredictur virgo de radice Jesse et flos de radice ascendet*) writes *Mais il sortira un rejeton du tronc d'Isai et un surgeon* naîtra *de ces racines;* this does not prove, however, that *les fleurs naissent* is contemporary French.

If our contention is true that the formula *la fleur nouvelle* is archaic, a voice from the past, it would prove a curious phenomenon, namely that in our instance the linguistic formula is more sensitive to cultural change than its ideological content; the concetto certainly survives, but not in our formulation. To substantiate this thesis we have to go more deeply into the cultural background of *nouveau* than has been hitherto possible.

4 *Nouveau*

Nouvelle as an attribute to *fleur* seems to denote that brief span of time in the life of the flower when we have the illusion of life defeating death. The adjective denotes the crisis of youth, the moment before the dramatic opening up of *bouton* as Guillaume de Lorris describes it. Similarly the spring crisis of the year is called *l'an nouveau.* When Charles d'Orléans sings:

> *yver a sa peine perdue*
> *car l'an nouvel l'a fait bannir*
> *a vostre joyeuse venue*[1]

he does not refer to a 'new year' in contrast to older 'past years'; he rather alludes to the year 'as long as it is young'. Grammatically and symbolically the *fleur nouvelle* is inseparable from *l'an nouvel, le temps nouvel, le printemps, le renouveau;* it was this medieval tradition that lived on in Ronsard's *mon doux printemps, ma douce fleur nouvelle.* Equally important was the association of spring and

---

[1] K. Glaser, loc. cit., p. 23.

youth with the spiritual *renouveau* of man, so movingly celebrated in the spring rites of Easter. – We moderns have lost the feeling for the drama of youth in times where the average life expectancy did not significantly surpass thirty years, nor do we feel the drama of spring in central and northern Europe which in former times ended a long, cold, cruel, very dark, winter. Most of us have certainly lost a feeling for the unity of physical and spiritual experience that characterized the Middle Ages.

Mrs Eberwein-Dabkovich has had the merit of reminding us of the vital connotations of *novus* with spring, spiritual *renouveau* and youth in provençal and its echoes in Dante's *Vita Nova*;[1] but I think one will have to supplement somewhat her findings. Although she is aware of the importance of bringing *amor* some-how into the picture she has no example of *amor novus*. The existence of this expression is indirectly attested in Charles d'Orléans's *Jeunes amoureux nouveaux,/En la nouvelle saison,/Par les ruës sans raison,/Chevauchent, faisant les sauts* (Anthology, p. 14). It is directly evoked in the *Carmina Burana* (no. 179): *O! O! totus floreo! Iam amore virginali totus ardeo; novus, novus amor est, quo pereo!*[2] Indeed, the Latin text shows us how to interpret Charles d'Orléans's text correctly. In his *jeunes amoureux nouveaux* the word *nouveau* is not a quasi-synonym for 'young'; the *amoureux nouveaux* are rather a grammatical 'transposition' of *amor novus* in a similar fashion as we discover for instance *la petite bourgeoisie* in Zola's *petites bourgeoises*.[3] In other words: not the young people are 'new', but their love is.

Supplementing Mrs Eberwein-Dabkovich further I should like to insist more strongly than she has done on the unity of physical and spiritual experience expressed in the word *renouveau*, signify-ing 'spring', 'rebirth of nature' and also the spiritual rebirth of

[1] E. Eberwein-Dabkovich, 'Das Wort *novus* in der altprovenzalischen Dichtung und in Dantes *Vita Nova*', *Romanistisches Jahrbuch* II (1949), pp. 171–95.

[2] Cf. also: *Che fu en may . . ., Que damoisel, que damoisiellez Se pourchacent d'amours nouviellez . . . Richars li Biaus*, 916, Tobler-Lommatzsch, *Altfranzösisches Wörterbuch* s.v. *flor*.

[3] *Au Bonheur des Dames* II, Bibliothèque Charpentier (Paris), p. 51. Cf. also Engl. *the criminal lawyer*, meaning a specialist in *criminal law*.

man. Spring and Easter are wedded together. *Novus* has a distinctly dynamic sense, though lacking the prefix *re-*. The *homo novus* of the Apostle is 'man born again'. This idea, little known in Antiquity, is at the core of the message we call *Novum Testamentum*. Few things are more instructive than to compare the lexicological definition of *homo novus* in a dictionary of classical Latin with the Christian sense of these same words. As the *fleur nouvelle* becomes a symbol of life, so Christ appears under the symbolism of the death-conquering flower (*Es ist ein Ros' entsprungen* . . .), of the spring eternal.[1] When Christ was born there was indeed an occasion to celebrate the *noël nouvelet*, the birth that helps man to be reborn. – Certainly the medieval sense of *novus* finds an echo in Dante's *Vita Nova*, but the text we have to quote here was not written in Provençal as Mrs Eberwein-Dabkovich would like us to believe but in Italian:

FRATE GUITTONE[2]

> *Diletto caro, oi mio novo valore,*
> *che novo e bono amore*
> *à novamente in voi, odo, criata;*[3]
> *novella e dolcie aducie in me dolzore,*
> *che novel dàmi core*
> *nel qual novo cantar criar m'agrata,*
> *a memora del novo vostro vigore;*
> *e renovando ardore*
> *è tanto nova disianza orata,*
> *novo porgiendo sempre in voi onore,*
> *che novella dolzore*
> *ve renovi la mente onunque fiata.*
> *Renovi in voi, renovi uso e talento,*
> *e co novo stormento*
> *novo canto cantare i novo amore,*
> *di novello bono sengnore,*
> *onde be novo e velglio à nascimento,*

[1] Cf. P. Dronke, op. cit., pp. 186–7.
[2] E. Monaci, *Crestomazia italiana dei primi secoli*, Città di Castello (1912), p. 186.
[3] In this sentence *amore* is the subject and *diletto* the object.

231

> *e novo e vellio lui siate tut'ore,*
> *novello bono servitore,*
> *perchè* la nova *sua* vita,[1] *ove sento*
> *novo e piem piacimento,*
> *v'enduca en novo de santo omo lausore*

You may feel that we travelled far away from Ronsard. Certainly to the author of the *Vita Nova* this melting of worldly and spiritual symbolism and the medieval identification between the young *donna* and Maria was perhaps more familiar than to Ronsard. We label the great Florentine a medieval and Ronsard a Renaissance artist. But we also know that historical periods are not separated by fences. It is in any case important for the reader of Renaissance poetry to be aware of the medieval background of some of its symbolism. For only then will he see and experience what is new and original in the use a Renaissance poet makes of some of the old symbols.

In our particular instance the striking thing doubtless is that Ronsard and others are wont to place traditional French symbolism into contexts borrowed from Antiquity. It is this we have found, comparing Deimier's list of the beloved girl's epithets with Ronsard's Latin reminiscences.[2] The love of Antiquity is largely a symptom of the increasing secularization or worldliness of the sixteenth century. In this atmosphere the old medieval symbolism had to undergo an often subconscious re-evaluation, which in certain cases could mean a devaluation, a debasement of linguistic currency. It would be wrong to see in Ronsard's *mon doux printemps, ma douce fleur nouvelle* anything else but a wordly expression just because it is in tune with the loan translations from Latin. Purely worldly connotations were, of course, also possible in medieval contexts. Nevertheless we feel that in Ronsard's text the *fleur nouvelle* has been transplanted into foreign soil, it is in danger of no longer being felt in depth, of losing one once very important dimension. It is a usage symptomatic for a devaluation

---

[1] Stressed by us.
[2] *V. supra*, p. 218.

of a medieval symbol which was to become 'two-dimensional' and soon must have looked 'gothic'.

Epilogue

Another word was profoundly affected by changes in sentimental conventions; it is the word *doux*. Its vogue in Renaissance literature could be proved by statistics. It is probably the most frequently used epithet in the poems you collected for your anthology. It appears seven times in Ronsard's *Chanson*. It is the keyword in Baïf's poem:

> O doux plaisir plein de doux pensement
> Quand la douceur de la douce mêlée,
> Entretient et joint l'âme à l'âme mêlée,
> Le corps au corps accouplé doucement.

> O douce vie, o doux trépassement
> Mon âme alors de grand' joïe troublée
> De moi dans toi s'écoulant à l'emblée,
> Puis haut, puis bas quiert son ravissement.[1]

Its meaning often defies definition, but its courtly tone can be felt. It is very apparent in Desportes' lines

> Si tu es juste, amour, tu me dois delier
> Ou par un doux effort cette dure plier.[2]

Baïf's *doux pensement* makes us think of Guillaume de Lorris' *Doux Penser* and the others, *Doux Parler* and *Doux Regard*. *Doux* like *bel* in *Bel Accueil* used to be a conventional *mot de politesse*: *Bele douce fille, prenez/Cest cheval* we read in *Erec* (451). We still feel somehow the courtly charm in Ronsard's *ma douce fleur nouvelle*. This patina, too, has worn off. Or how would you look at me if I took leave with the words *Au revoir, biaus douz amis*?

Manfred Sandmann

---

[1] *Anthology*, p. 134.
[2] Malherbe objected to the epithet *dure*; cf. F. Brunot, loc. cit.

La Fontaine, Fables, Book X

[1]

IRIS, *I'd easily laud you in my rhymes,*
But praise you have dispraised so many times,
Unlike the rest of women, who, I'd say,
Seek nothing but fresh tributes every day.
Not one who nods when others puff her name:
And yet I'd rather suffer that, than blame
A foible Beauties share with Gods and Kings.
This potion which the tribe of poets sings,
This Nectar which for Jove alone should flow
And turns the heads of earthly gods below,
Is our applause, IRIS. *You disapprove,*
Being of those whom other topics move,
   Those gay exchanges, wit to wit,
   Which from theme to theme may flit,
   So that, when we converse with you,
Trifles may have their share. Who'll think this true?
   Whatever others think of this,
   Problems of Science, trivialities,
   Fantasies, baubles, all's in order:
I think good talk needs every kind of fodder;
It's like a plot where Flora spreads her blessings,
Where on a myriad flowers bees rest their wings
   And make sweet honeys of all things.
All this allowed, I trust you'll not condemn

234

La Fontaine: Discours à Madame de la Sablière

(FABLES, IX)

Iris, je vous louerois: il n'est que trop aisé;
Mais vous avez cent fois notre encens refusé,
En cela peu semblable au reste des mortelles,
Qui veulent tous les jours des louanges nouvelles.
Pas une ne s'endort à ce bruit si flatteur,
Je ne les blâme point; je souffre cette humeur:
Elle est commune aux Dieux, aux monarques, aux belles.
Ce breuvage vanté par le peuple rimeur,
Le nectar que l'on sert au maître du tonnerre,
Et dont nous enivrons tous les dieux de la terre,
C'est la louange, Iris. Vous ne la goûtez point;
D'autres propos chez vous récompensent ce point:
Propos, agréables commerces,
Où le hasard fournit cent matières diverses,
Jusque-là qu'en votre entretien
La bagatelle a part: le monde n'en croit rien.
Laissons le monde et sa croyance.
La bagatelle, la science,
Les chimères, le rien, tout est bon; je soutiens
Qu'il faut de tout aux entretiens:
C'est un parterre où Flore épand ses biens;
Sur différentes fleurs l'abeille s'y repose,
Et fait du miel de toute chose.
Ce fondement posé, ne trouvez pas mauvais

My Fables, if I sometimes add to them
Elements of the New Philosophy,
Subtle, engaging, even bold, maybe.
They call it New. Has it yet come your way?
  Now these modern thinkers say
  The animal is a Machine,
Behaving, not by choice, but driven by springs,
Without feeling or soul, but a material thing
Just like a Clock, whose movement is seen
To work, blind, purposeless, with even stride.
  Open a Clock, and look inside:
A mechanism of wheels replaces Mind;
One moves, compels a second wheel behind,
And that a third, and then a bell will ring.
These people say, a beast is such a thing.
Some object strikes it in a certain place
  Which sends the message on apace:
The neighbouring region registers the news
And then the Sense records the stimulus.
The Impression's made: but if we want a notion
Of how it's done, it's by Necessity, they say,
Neither through Will, nor any Passion's sway:
  The animal is set in motion
  By what the simple would maintain
Is sorrow, joy, love, pleasure, poignant pain,
  Or some other such emotion.
  Nonsense, they say: just think again.
What then? Clockwork. We men? Quite different.
That's how DESCARTES *conducts his argument,*
DESCARTES, *that mortal who might once have been*
Some pagan god, but stands halfway between
Man and the Angels, as between Oyster and Man
  We may distinguish Caliban.
But, to pursue the reasoning of this author,
He says, 'Of all the works of our Creator,
I have the gift of thought, and know I'm thinking.'

Qu'en ces fables aussi j'entremêle des traits
    De certaine philosophie,
    Subtile, engageante, et hardie.
On l'appelle nouvelle: en avez-vous ou non
    Ouï parler? Ils disent donc
    Que la bête est une machine;
Qu'en elle tout se fait sans choix et par ressorts:
Nul sentiment, point d'âme; en elle tout est corps.
    Telle est la montre qui chemine
A pas toujours égaux, aveugle et sans dessein.
    Ouvrez-la, lisez dans son sein:
Mainte roue y tient lieu de tout l'esprit du monde;
    La première y meut la seconde;
Une troisième suit: elle sonne à la fin.
Au dire de ces gens, la bête est toute telle:
    'L'objet la frappe en un endroit;
    Ce lieu frappé s'en va tout droit,
Selon nous, au voisin en porter la nouvelle.
Le sens de proche en proche aussitôt la reçoit.
L'impression se fait.' Mais comment se fait-elle?
    Selon eux, par nécessité,
    Sans passion, sans volonté:
    L'animal se sent agité
   De mouvements que le vulgaire appelle
Tristesse, joie, amour, plaisir, douleur cruelle,
    Ou quelque autre de ces états.
Mais ce n'est point cela: ne vous y trompez pas. —
Qu'est-ce donc? — Une montre. — Et nous? — C'est autre chose.
Voici de la façon que Descartes l'expose,
Descartes, ce mortel dont on eût fait un dieu
    Chez les païens, et qui tient le milieu
Entre l'homme et l'esprit, comme entre l'huître et l'homme
Le tient tel de nos gens, franche bête de somme:
Voici, dis-je, comment raisonne cet auteur:
''Sur tous les animaux, enfants du Créateur,
J'ai le don de penser; et je sais que je pense;

IRIS, *you know as well as anything*
    That if a brute could cogitate,
    Even then it could not speculate
About the Object, much less its own thought.
    DESCARTES *goes further, and maintains*
    There's no thought-process in such brains.
    For you and me there's surely naught
Incredible in this,

[II]

        although when, in the wood,
The horn, the hallooing huntsmen in pursuit
Afford no respite to the fleeing prey,
And every baffle of the beast at bay
Has failed to throw the scent and halt the pack,
The veteran ten-branched Stag doubles his track
And starts a younger beast, forcing the Hind
    To flee, and draw the hounds behind.
How could he reason more to save his hide,
With tricks and turns and twisting side to side,
With subterfuges, strategies and shifts
Generals could learn from, worth a better fate?
    But he'll be butchered, soon or late,
    Man's final tribute to his gifts.

[III]

When Mother Partridge sees her brood in fear
Of danger, featherless, with tender down
Which, even from Death, can't lift them through the air,
She feigns a hit, drags her wings on the ground
To draw the dog and huntsman after her,
Throws a false trail, and saves her little covey;
Then, when the hunter thinks his dog's retrieved,
She cries goodbye, flies off in mockery,
While he stares after her, vexed and deceived.

Or vous savez, Iris, de certaine science,
    Que, quand la bête penseroit,
    La bête ne réfléchiroit
    Sur l'objet ni sur sa pensée.
Descartes va plus loin, et soutient nettement
    Qu'elle ne pense nullement.
    Vous n'êtes point embarrassée
De le croire; ni moi.

      Cependant, quand aux bois
    Le bruit des cors, celui des voix,
N'a donné nul relâche à la fuyante proie,
    Qu'en vain elle a mis ses efforts
    A confondre et brouiller la voie,
L'animal chargé d'ans, vieux cerf, et de dix cors,
En suppose un plus jeune, et l'oblige par force
A présenter aux chiens une nouvelle amorce.
Que de raisonnements pour conserver ses jours!
Le retour sur ses pas, les malices, les tours,
    Et le change, et cent stratagèmes
Dignes des plus grands chefs, dignes d'un meilleur sort!
    On le déchire après sa mort:
    Ce sont tous ses honneurs suprêmes.

    Quand le Perdrix
    Voit ses petits
En danger, et n'ayant qu'une plume nouvelle
Qui ne peut fuir encor par les airs le trépas,
Elle fait la blessée, et va, traînant de l'aile,
Attirant le Chasseur et le Chien sur ses pas,
Détourne le danger, sauve ainsi sa famille;
Et puis, quand le Chasseur croit que son Chien la pille,
Elle lui dit adieu, prend sa volée, et rit
De l'Homme qui, confus, des yeux en vain la suit.

[IV]

Far in the North, beneath the icy Pole,
There lies a country whose inhabitants
Live like the savages of days of old,
Lost in their dark abysmal ignorance.
I mean, the men alone: the beasts are skilled,
   And many a stubborn wall they build
   Against the havoc of the swollen tide,
Raising a bridge to pass from side to side.
Their bulwark holds against the rushing water,
Made of a bed of wood, crusted with mortar.
Each Beaver toils in this communal work;
The fathers won't allow the sons to shirk,
And many a foreman irks them with his stick.
   Even Plato's Republicans
   Could learn from these amphibians,
   Who, through the winter, build wigwams
   And cross the Lakes on home-made dams,
   Solid constructions, laid with art;
Whereas our savage cousins cannot learn,
   And do no better, for their part,
   Than swimming naked through the burn.

[V]

No one will ever bring me to believe
Those Beavers are just Matter without Mind.
I'll not stop there: I heard this narrative
Told by a King revered among mankind.
The Saviour of the North will back my word,
A Prince whom Victory never left behind;
   His name's a bastion from the Turkish horde:
The Polish monarch. Kings can hardly lie.
He tells that on his frontier, there's a feud
Between two beasts who've always been at strife.
From sire to son, so long as there is life

Non loin du Nord il est un monde
Où l'on sait que les habitants
Vivent, ainsi qu'aux premiers temps,
Dans une ignorance profonde:
Je parle des humains; car, quant aux animaux,
Ils y construisent des travaux
Qui des torrents grossis arrêtent le ravage
Et font communiquer l'un et l'autre rivage.
L'édifice résiste, et dure en son entier:
Après un lit de bois est un lit de mortier.
Chaque castor agit: commune en est la tâche;
Le vieux y fait marcher le jeune sans relâche;
Maint maître d'oeuvre y court, et tient haut le bâton.
    La république de Platon
    Ne seroit rien que l'apprentie
    De cette famille amphibie.
Ils savent en hiver élever leurs maisons,
    Passent les étangs sur des ponts,
    Fruit de leur art, savant ouvrage;
    Et nos pareils ont beau le voir,
    Jusqu'à présent tout leur savoir
    Est de passer l'onde à la nage.

Que ces castors ne soient qu'un corps vuide d'esprit,
Jamais on ne pourra m'obliger à le croire;
Mais voici beaucoup plus; écoutez ce récit,
    Que je tiens d'un roi plein de gloire.
Le défenseur du Nord vous sera mon garant:
Je vais citer un prince aimé de la Victoire;
Son nom seul est un mur à l'empire ottoman:
C'est le roi polonois. Jamais un roi ne ment.
    Il dit donc que, sur sa frontière,
Des animaux entre eux ont guerre de tout temps:
Le sang qui se transmet des pères aux enfants

241

This enmity will be renewed.
These beasts are foxlike, of two strains,
But never were there such campaigns
With such great art and science waged,
Not even in great LOUIS' age.
They have their sentries, scouts, and spies,
Ambushes, and guerillas: no device
Escapes them, of this diabolic science,
Mother of heroes, daughter of the Styx,
And War, with all its cruel tricks
Perfects their wits and their experience.
To sing their battles, then must Lethe's shore
Release a Homer. If it could restore
Our anti-Epicurus, French DESCARTES,
What would he say of such a creature's art?
Just what I said: that Nature can impart
Such powers to beasts; but powers mechanical;
And that their Memory is all physical;
And that, if we examine each example
Which, in my lines, has served as demonstration,
These beasts require no nobler animation.
The Object, seen anew, probes Memory's store,
And following the previous path once more,
Repeats the pattern it had made before,
Which then returns by the same path again.
Thus there is no thought-process in the brain:
The Object merely caused the same reflex.
But Man, he says, is more complex:
We are determined only by our Will,
Not object, or instinct. Speak, walk, stand still,
I'm conscious only of my consciousness,
And all my organism, more or less
Can but obey my Reason's principle.
Distinct from Matter, it is better known
Even than the body, though it be our own,
And over all our actions, Mind presides.

En renouvelle la matière.
Ces animaux, dit-il, sont germains du renard.
    Jamais la guerre avec tant d'art
    Ne s'est faite parmi les hommes,
    Non pas même au siècle où nous sommes.
Corps de garde avancé, vedettes, espions,
Embuscades, partis, et mille inventions
D'une pernicieuse et maudite science,
    Fille du Styx, et mère des héros,
      Exercent de ces animaux
    Le bon sens et l'expérience.
Pour chanter leurs combats, l'Achéron nous devroit
    Rendre Homère. Ah! s'il le rendoit,
Et qu'il rendît aussi le rival d'Epicure,
Que diroit ce dernier sur ces exemples-ci?
Ce que j'ai déjà dit: qu'aux bêtes la nature
Peut par les seuls ressorts opérer tout ceci;
    Que la mémoire est corporelle;
Et que, pour en venir aux exemples divers
    Que j'ai mis en jour dans ces vers,
    L'animal n'a besoin que d'elle.
L'objet, lorsqu'il revient, va dans son magasin
    Chercher, par le même chemin,
    L'image auparavant tracée,
Qui sur les mêmes pas revient pareillement,
    Sans le secours de la pensée,
    Causer un même événement.
    Nous agissons tout autrement:
    La volonté nous détermine,
Non l'objet, ni l'instinct. Je parle, je chemine:
    Je sens en moi certain agent;
    Tout obéit dans ma machine
    A ce principe intelligent.
Il est distinct du corps, se conçoit nettement,
    Se conçoit mieux que le corps même:
De tous nos mouvements c'est l'arbitre suprême.

But how can Matter know what Reason says?
Here is the point. I see the tool obeys
The hand's dictates; but as for hand, who guides?
Who steers the stars on their unerring ways?
Do such vast comets fly on angels' wings?
Some Spirit works in us, and moves our springs.
The Impression's made — but how, I can't descry:
None but the Deity knows How and Why,
And, be it said in all sincerity,
To learn this truth, even DESCARTES had to die.
We are no different, he and we, in this.
　　I know that in these beasts, IRIS,
　　　Whose actions served me for example,
That Spirit does not move. Man's its sole temple.
　　　Yet we must grant to animals
A gift denied to plant-life, after all,
　　　Even though Plants may breathe, as well.
How will they answer what I have to tell?

[VI]

Two Rats came on an Egg, while foraging,
A hearty dinner for such tiny mites,
Who wouldha ve found an Ox embarrassing.
Full of good spirits and good appetites,
One was to eat the yolk, and one the white,
　　When Master Reynard came in sight —
Such an untimely call as he would make.
How could they save their egg? Just wrap it neat
　　　And carry it with their fore-feet?
　　　Roll it? Or drag it in their wake?
Out of the question, for the Egg would break.
Necessity, the Mother of Invention,
　　　Brought this device to their attention:
　　　As they were nearer to their nest
　　　Than to their uninvited guest,

244

Mais comment le corps l'entend-il?
C'est là le point. Je vois l'outil
Obéir à la main; mais la main, qui la guide?
Eh! qui guide les cieux et leur course rapide?
Quelque ange est attaché peut-être à ces grands corps.
Un esprit vit en nous, et meut tous nos ressorts;
L'impression se fait: le moyen, je l'ignore:
On ne l'apprend qu'au sein de la Divinité;
Et, s'il faut en parler avec sincérité,
    Descartes l'ignoroit encore.
Nous et lui là-dessus nous sommes tous égaux:
Ce que je sais, Iris, c'est qu'en ces animaux
    Dont je viens de citer l'exemple,
Cet esprit n'agit pas: l'homme seul est son temple.
Aussi faut-il donner à l'animal un point,
    Que la plante, après tout, n'a point:
    Cependant la plante respire.
Mais que répondra-t-on à ce que je vais dire?

LES DEUX RATS, LE RENARD, ET L'OEUF

Deux Rats cherchoient leur vie; ils trouvèrent un oeuf.
Le dîné suffisoit à gens de cette espèce:
Il n'étoit pas besoin qu'ils trouvassent un boeuf.
    Pleins d'appétit et d'allégresse,
Ils alloient de leur oeuf manger chacun sa part,
Quand un quidam parut: c'étoit maître Renard.
    Rencontre incommode et fâcheuse:
Car comment sauver l'oeuf? Le bien empaqueter,
Puis des pieds de devant ensemble le porter,
    Ou le rouler, ou le traîner:
C'étoit chose impossible autant que hasardeuse.
    Nécessité l'ingénieuse
    Leur fournit une invention.
Comme ils pouvoient gagner leur habitation,
L'écornifleur étant à demi-quart de lieue,

One seized the egg, and turned upon his back,
Then by the tail, along the bumpy track,
  His comrade dragged him like a sack.
  After this feat, may none maintain
  An animal can't use its brain.

[VII]

But, as for me, my simple explanation
Would be, were I the master of Creation:
Animals reason much as children do.
A child has simple thoughts, however few.
Creatures may think, then, without self-cognition.
  By this analogy, at least
  I would attribute to the beast
A power of reasoning different from ours,
  Yet more than blind machinery.
I'd postulate, Matter with higher powers,
  Hard to conceive though that may be;
A quintessential Atom, tempered Light
  Even more mobile and more bright
  Than fire itself. If wood gives flame,
Then flame refined may give us some insight
Of the Soul's nature; for gold all the same
Comes of brute ore. This Work I would endow
With feeling, judgement, and I would allow
Degrees of imperfection in its judgement,
Nor ask an Ape to lead an argument.
But as for Man, then I would favour him
With gifts superior to any beast's.
We'd have a double heritage, at least:
That common soul, in everything the same,
The wise, the mad, the child, the idiot, all,
  And shared with all that's Animal;
And then, a second Soul, which we may boast
To share with Angels to some sure degree.

L'un se mit sur le dos, prit l'oeuf entre ses bras,
Puis, malgré quelques heurts et quelques mauvais pas,
  L'autre le traîna par la queue.
Qu'on m'aille soutenir, après un tel récit,
  Que les bêtes n'ont point d'esprit!

  Pour moi, si j'en étois le maître,
Je leur en donnerois aussi bien qu'aux enfants.
Ceux-ci pensent-ils pas dès leurs plus jeunes ans?
Quelqu'un peut donc penser ne se pouvant connoître.
  Par un exemple tout égal,
  J'attribuerois à l'animal,
Non point une raison selon notre manière,
Mais beaucoup plus aussi qu'un aveugle ressort:
Je subtiliserois un morceau de matière,
Que l'on ne pourroit plus concevoir sans effort,
Quintessence d'atome, extrait de la lumière,
Je ne sais quoi plus vif et plus mobile encor
Que le feu; car enfin, si le bois fait la flamme,
La flamme, en s'épurant, peut-elle pas de l'âme
Nous donner quelque idée? et sort-il pas de l'or
Des entrailles du plomb? Je rendrois mon ouvrage
Capable de sentir, juger, rien davantage,
  Et juger imparfaitement,
Sans qu'un singe jamais fît le moindre argument.
  A l'egard de nous autres hommes,
Je ferois notre lot infiniment plus fort;
  Nous aurions un double trésor:
L'un, cette âme pareille en tous tant que nous sommes,
  Sages, fous, enfants, idiots,
Hôtes de l'univers, sous le nom d'animaux;
L'autre, encore une autre âme, entre nous et les anges
  Commune en un certain degré;
  Et ce trésor à part créé

This gift, created separately,
May neighbour in the skies the Heavenly Host,
Concentrate to the infinitely small,
  Infinity infinitesimal,
With a Beginning, but no end at all.
    These things are real, though strange to most.
    I'd say that in our tender years
    This heavenly Light in us appears
No more than a most frail and feeble gleam;
Yet, with the body's growth, Reason would pierce
The darkness of the flesh, however dim,
    Which, while it lived, would still contain
That baser soul, common to Mice and Men.

Francis Scarfe

Suivroit parmi les airs les célestes phalanges,
Entreroit dans un point sans en être pressé,
Ne finiroit jamais, quoique ayant commencé:
   Choses réelles, quoique étranges.
   Tant que l'enfance dureroit,
Cette fille du Ciel en nous ne paroîtroit
   Qu'une tendre et foible lumière:
L'organe étant plus fort, la raison perceroit
   Les ténèbres de la matière,
   Qui toujours envelopperoit
   L'autre âme imparfaite et grossière.

O si chère de loin et proche . . .

❧❧❧❧❧❧❧❧❧❧❧❧❧❧❧❧❧❧❧❧❧❧❧❧

UNIVERSITAIRE, ON SE défend mal d'une grande sympathie avec Jacques Peletier du Mans. *Moins et meilleur:* y a-t-il conseil plus salutaire à se proposer, ou à recommander à nos étudiants, que cette devise qui fut la sienne? Il était d'ailleurs des nôtres: principal, à différents moments de sa carrière, de trois collèges, il a enseigné aussi à l'université de Poitiers et vraisemblablement ailleurs. Il avait au plus haut point ce culte ardent et désintéressé du savoir que nous professons tous, et son œuvre entière est marquée au sceau d'un didactisme de bon aloi:

> *Enseigner la jeunesse est un bien grand mérite,*
> *Vu que par là science, un si grand bien, s'hérite.*[1]

Tenons-le-nous pour dit, encore qu'on eût pu le dire moins platement. Tel, d'ailleurs, n'avait pas toujours été le sentiment de Peletier. Parlant de ses débuts au collège de Bayeux, 'je me proposais, dit-il, l'opinion commune que ce n'est le moyen de garder sa dignité que d'enseigner';[2] il s'en dédommagea, dit son biographe le plus récent, 'par les publications qu'il fit'.[3] Le pauvre Peletier n'eut pas de chance au collège de Guyenne non plus: après avoir soutenu de vains combats contre l'insuffisance des crédits et l'hostilité de collègues difficiles – *praeceptores con-*

---

[1] *Les Louanges*, Paris (1581), fo. 48 verso. Cité par F. Letessier: 'Un humaniste manceau: Jacques Peletier' in *Bulletin de l'Association Guillaume Budé*: Lettres d'humanité, IX, Paris (1950), p. 258.
[2] *Dialogue de l'orthographe*, Poitiers (1550). Cité par Letessier, op. cit., p. 219.
[3] Letessier, loc. cit.

251

tumaces ac refractarios domi habui[1] – il ne tarda pas à se voir remercier. Quelques années plus tard, dans sa leçon inaugurale à Poitiers, il expliqua les déboires subis à Bordeaux dans des termes que nous comprenons sans peine : *vel propter juventutis illius gubernandae molestiam, vel ob negotiosam oeconomiam* . . . *Ea re,* continue-t-il, *quum primum potui, me ab ea sollicitudine redemi, ut ad mea studia me referrem.*[1] Que l'éminent collègue à qui ces pages sont dédiées et qui, lui, s'est si brillamment acquitté de ses fonctions de professeur, veuille bien faire abstraction de tout ce qui, dans ce rapprochement, est sans application dans son cas, pour n'y voir que le désir de lui souhaiter de longues et fructueuses années d'études personnelles : *sua studia.*

Comment ne pas éprouver une vive curiosité à l'égard d'un homme qui avait tant d'amis parmi les meilleurs esprits de son temps : Ronsard, Du Bellay, Maurice Scève, Pontus de Tyard, Montaigne, Cardan, et d'autres encore? Les travaux biographiques n'ont depuis quelque temps rien produit de nouveau sur lui, et il semble peu probable qu'il reste de grandes découvertes à faire dans ce domaine.[2] Mais, si tout a été dit, peut-être, sur ses relations de fait avec la Pléiade, on peut enregistrer une évolution très sensible dans l'appréciation de l'œuvre poétique de Peletier.

Ronsard, on le sait, disait de lui que c'était 'l'un des plus excellents poètes de (son) âge'[3] – remarque dont il serait difficile de déterminer l'exacte portée critique, et qui, d'ailleurs, précède la publication des ouvrages les plus intéressants de Peletier. Bornons-nous plutôt à des jugements plus récents. Ce ne fut qu'à la belle époque de l'histoire littéraire que se produisit un renouveau d'intérêt pour l'œuvre de notre poète. La thèse de l'abbé Jugé, divers travaux de Laumonier, l'édition de *l'Art poétique* procuré

---

[1] *Oratio Pictavii habita in praelectiones mathematicas,* Poitiers (1579). Publié par Laumonier in *Revue de la Renaissance* V (1904); et cité par Chamard, *Histoire de la Pléiade* III, p. 325.

[2] On consultera la synthèse claire et judicieuse de F. Letessier; voir ci-dessus.

[3] Préface *Au lecteur* des *Odes* de 1550.

par A. Boulanger, plusieurs chapitres de l'*Histoire de la Pléiade* d'Henri Chamard : autant d'hommages rendus par l'érudition à la mémoire de Peletier – et je n'en cite que les principaux. Malheureusement, le goût qui était, d'une manière générale, celui de la critique universitaire dans la première partie de notre siècle, goût formé par une certaine tradition romantique, était de nature à empêcher une appréciation suffisamment nuancée de la poésie du Manceau, ou même de sa pensée. Aussi bien s'intéressait-on surtout, à cette époque, à ses doctrines littéraires : parmi ses poésies on ne trouvait guère à louer que les odes rustiques de 1547. Peletier aura connu, en somme, un sort analogue à celui de ses amis et maîtres lyonnais : Scève et Pontus de Tyard.

Le renouvellement de la critique, une connaissance plus approfondie de l'univers intellectuel du seizième siècle ont permis depuis lors de voir Peletier sous un autre jour. L'esprit si ouvert et si rigoureux à la fois du regretté A-M. Schmidt, toujours à l'affût de l'insolite, était bien fait pour aborder l'œuvre du Manceau. Dans le long chapitre qu'il y consacre dans sa thèse sur *la Poésie scientifique en France au seizième siècle*,[1] il fait enfin bénéficier Peletier d'une certaine sympathie critique. Sans s'aveugler sur les déficiences poétiques de l'oeuvre, il en dégage avec netteté quelques aspects positifs : 'pour la première fois au seizième siècle, (Peletier) réussit à définir par des traits encore originaux cette atmosphère initiatique, où passent des divinités, des hiérophantes, des mystes, cette atmosphère de secret et d'amour où sous le signe de l'éternelle Uranie la plupart des poètes scientifiques tenteront de se plonger sans toujours y parvenir'.[2] Secret et amour : traits qui indiquent aussi un aspect personnel masqué par l'abstraction du style ; car, dit Schmidt, 'au seizième siècle, Peletier est sans doute l'un des maîtres de l'introspection pathétique'.[3]

Il est piquant et instructif de comparer les remarques de Schmidt avec celles de Chamard sur l'endroit où, dans *la Savoie*, Peletier parle du lac du Bourget. 'Ainsi, dit Chamard, devant ce

[1] Paris (1939).
[2] op. cit., p. 33.
[3] ibid., p. 68.

253

lac aux eaux mystérieuses, devant ce paysage aux horizons chargés de poésie, Peletier n'a pas vu d'autre chose à noter que deux poissons et trois oiseaux! O Lamartine!' Il se fait ensuite, reconnaissons-le, une leçon de relativisme: 'le Romantisme nous a gâtés'.[1] Mieux aurait valu sans doute chercher à définir quelques valeurs positives. 'C'est d'abord, écrit de son côté A-M. Schmidt, en douze vers, un blason d'animaux des mieux venus:

> *Là, le héron vole haut et crie aigre,*
> *Là est l'arlette au corps plumeux et maigre . . .*

puis le placement d'un fond lugubre:

> *Dessus ce bord est la fameuse tombe*
> *Des Ducs défunts, déserte Hautecombe . . .* (etc.)[2]

Fermons cette parenthèse sur ces paroles de Dudley Wilson: 'although Lamartine's tears, dropping slow to the beat of the alexandrine, are certainly more *personally* shed than those of Peletier, perhaps they are none the better for that'.[3]

Personne d'ailleurs de mieux qualifié que Wilson pour nous parler de Peletier. Il a notamment consacré au Manceau un important article paru en 1954: *The Discovery of Nature in the Works of Jacques Peletier du Mans*,[4] repris en partie dans son livre récent.[5] Les travaux de Wilson nous font pénétrer plus avant dans le système d'idées qui était celui de Peletier, nous montrant chez lui le jeu subtil et changeant de notions contraires ou complémentaires. Unité et diversité du monde, ordre et profusion des phénomènes: ces dualismes d'ordre cosmologique en ont d'autres pour contre-partie qui portent sur les relations de l'homme et du monde, opposant à une pensée neo-platonicienne: intuition du Tout, harmonie avec la Nature, amour cosmique, une connaissance progressive, scientifique si l'on veut, qui a pour ressort la

---

[1] Chamard, op. cit., III, pp. 322–3.
[2] Schmidt, op. cit., p. 56.
[3] D. B. Wilson, *Descriptive Poetry in France from blason to baroque*, Manchester (1967), p. 128.
[4] *Bibliothèque d'Humanisme et Renaissance, vol. XVI* (1954), pp. 298 et seq.
[5] Voir ci-dessus, note 3.

'vertu' personnelle du chercheur – et qui pourra, êut dit Peletier, 's'hériter'. Malgré l'attrait de doctrines capiteuses, la grandeur de Peletier aura été de sauvegarder l'activité autonome et consciente de l'esprit. 'The whole pattern of Peletier's poetry in and after 1955 suggests a desire for present equilibrium and for continual renewal in a scheme of things which is – if we may use the image – polyphonic rather than harmonious. This is much more typical of the Renaissance than is the conventional neoplatonic philosophy which indeed represents only a phase and a fashion in the century and dies out as swiftly as it is born.'[1]

On sait ce qu'est *l'Amour des amours*, 'cet étrange recueil' comme l'appelle Schmidt, publié à Lyon en 1555. Il comporte d'abord un *canzoniere* composé de 96 sonnets et de 2 *chants*. Suit une pièce strophique où le poète, porté sur les ailes de l'amour, parcourt les airs à la suite de sa Dame. Dans une seconde ode les deux se rejoignent au sommet du Parnasse, où la Dame reproche au poète la bassesse de son amour. Le moment est venu de la révélation:

> *Amour t'a ici attiré,*
> *Afin qu'à toi tu apparaisses,*
> *Et qu'à cette fois tu connaisses*
> *Le bien où tu as aspiré.*[2]

Il apprend, en somme, que l'amour est un premier pas vers la science. Aussi bien est-ce le chant encyclopédique – et polyphonique! – des Muses qu'il entend:

> *Durant ce céleste record*
> *Que me devise ma Princesse,*
> *Le doux chant des Muses ne cesse,*
> *Qui compose à el' son accord.*

---

[1] Wilson, art. cit., p. 310.

[2] *L'Amour des amours*, Lyon, 1555, pp. 68–69. Cité d'après l'édition en fac-simile publiée par A. van Bever, Paris, 1926. La graphie curieuse inventée par Peletier étant ce que l'on sait, j'ai cru devoir moderniser partout l'orthographe et la ponctuation. Cet ouvrage sera désigné ci-dessous par le sigle A.

> *Il me fait une telle oreille,*
> *Qu'un seul de choix je peux ouïr,*
> *Et de tous ensemble jouir*
> *D'une intelligence pareille.*

> *Lettres, parler ingénieux,*
> *Mesure, histoire, tragédie,*
> *Harpe, flûtes, cieux, comédie,*
> *Bruient un tout harmonieux,*
> *Qui de suavité ressemble*
> *A celle-là que vous départ*
> *La cueillette des fleurs à part,*
> *Et puis les fleurs toutes ensemble.*[1]

Se prévalant alors de cette possibilité de choisir, et suivant les conseils de sa Dame, le poète se met à transcrire les chants qu'Uranie lui fait entendre sur l'Air et sur différents phénomènes météorologiques. Une série de poèmes sur les planètes offre ensuite cette particularité de n'en comporter que cinq, là où l'on s'attendrait à en voir sept. A ce recueil déjà suffisamment disparate, Peletier juge utile d'ajouter des *Vers lyriques à Madame Marguerite*, où il explique pourquoi il a abandonné la poésie amoureuse vulgaire; un *Rossignol*, puis les quatre *Saisons*, retouchées, des *Œuvres poétiques* de 1547 viennent enfin clore le volume. N'oublions pas toutefois de signaler que le livre porte en guise d'épigraphe un sonnet *à la Fame*.

Cet ensemble a été abondamment commenté, à l'exception pourtant du *canzoniere*. Sur le peu d'intérêt de celui-ci l'accord paraît unanime: par une aberration surprenante chez un poète qui avait si bien compris, apparemment, les initiatives de ses amis de la Pléiade, Peletier a choisi de se mettre tout bêtement à l'école des Lyonnais et singulièrement de Pontus de Tyard. Son *canzoniere* n'est, dit Schmidt, 'qu'un simple décalque des *Erreurs amoureuses*'; Peletier n'a fait que 'varier les tropes d'un pétrarquisme toujours affecté, parfois languissant, souvent intolérable'.[2]

[1] A, pp. 71–72.
[2] Schmidt, op. cit., p. 25.

On fait valoir le témoignage du poète lui-même concernant le caractère composite du recueil : 'Je me suis mis à revisiter quelques miens écrits, que je gardais d'assez long temps par devers moi, lesquels j'avais tirés sur le sujet tant populaire de l'amour. Et les reconnaissant, me prit premièrement envie de les poursuivre ; si bien que je me trouvai tout ébahi que d'un passe-temps, et comme d'une dépendance d'étude, j'eus de quoi faire un sérieux jeu. Car, entrant en besogne, de dessein en dessein, me survint un certain avis, que l'amour était un sujet plus capable que ne l'avais pourjeté au commencement. Et de fait, suivant cette conception, me suis aventuré, d'un amour nu et simple, en faire un général et universel ; tellement que par ma déduction je démenasse un ébat amoureux qui comprît en soi profit et importance, faisant mon profit d'y pouvoir appliquer choses naturelles, cosmographie, astrologie, et autres choses dignes des plus nettes et plus graves oreilles : entreprise certes ardue et de longue exécution.'[1]

Ce qui ne ressort pas clairement de ces remarques, c'est le rapport qu'il convient de reconnaître entre le *canzoniere* et le reste du recueil. Peletier devait du moins croire suffisamment solide la logique générale de son projet. Dégager de l'amour une portée cosmique, l'entreprise assurément n'était guère nouvelle et avait de bons garants. Dans sa leçon de Poitiers, le poète en parle ainsi : *Amores scripsi, haud paulo diligentius elaboratos quam prima poemata : neque illos quidem amatoria levitate, sed, ut soleo dicere, Platonis imitatione scriptos.*[2] Ce dont on a cru pouvoir lui faire grief, c'est la maladresse avec laquelle il a cousu ensemble les différentes parties du recueil. Une transition violente, laisse-t-on entendre, nous arrache soudain du domaine de l'amour humain pour nous précipiter dans celui de l'amour cosmique. Cette transition s'effectue au moyen des deux derniers sonnets du *canzoniere* – où la Dame, c'est Schmidt qui le remarque, devient pour le poète à peu près ce que fut Béatrice pour Dante – puis des

[1] *L'Art poétique*, Lyon (1555). Cité d'après l'édition d'André Boulanger, Paris (1930), pp. 62–63.
[2] Cité par Chamard, op. cit., II, p. 131, n. 2.

deux *chants* intitulés *l'Amour volant* et *le Parnasse*. Une fois qu'Uranie a pris la parole, nous n'entendons d'ailleurs plus parler de la Dame du *canzoniere*, il n'est plus question que de 'météores'.

On ne saurait nier, certes, que l'effet produit par les sonnets XCV et XCVI ne soit assez inattendu et déconcertant. Sans doute faut-il convenir que le développement des thèmes du *canzoniere* n'est pas mené assez savamment, et que plus généralement la composition du recueil est fort défectueuse. Une lecture plus attentive m'induit pourtant à penser que la solution de continuité entre les deux parties du recueil n'est qu'apparente, que la transition, pour mal préparée qu'elle soit, est préparée quand même, que dans les *Vers lyriques à Madame Marguerite* le poète ne répudie pas le *canzoniere* tel que nous le connaissons, et que celui-ci, à supposer qu'il ait été à l'origine une simple série de poésies d'amour selon la convention pétrarquiste, a été profondément modifié dans le but, précisément, d'en faire une sorte d'allégorie philosophique. Ainsi s'expliqueraient, par exemple, non seulement les deux sonnets 'dantesques' de la fin, et le fait que les premières pièces sont adressées non à la Dame mais à l'Amour, mais aussi le poème *à la Fame*, et l'importance attachée partout à l'idée de *connaissance*. Il s'ensuivrait que c'est à la lumière des travaux de Schmidt et de Wilson qu'on doit essayer d'interpréter le *canzoniere*. Nombreux sont les rapprochements qu'on pourrait faire, si l'on en avait le loisir, entre les sonnets et *la Savoie* ou *la Louange de la Science*. Que, d'autre part, on retrouve dans le *canzoniere* la manière lyonnaise, c'est indiscutable. Mais Peletier n'y aurait-il rien mis de lui-même? De sa part, ce serait bien étonnant. Comme d'autres poètes au seizième siècle feront servir les conventions pétrarquistes à des fins dévotes, Peletier ne chercherait-il pas à exprimer, à travers les soupirs de l'amant, les ardeurs et les inquiétudes d'un esprit brûlé par la *libido sciendi* et amoureux – ou qui se croit amoureux – de la Nature?

On pourrait remarquer tout d'abord l'absence quasi totale, chez lui, de l'anecdote, du détail pittoresque. Aucune allusion, comme on en trouve dans les *Erreurs amoureuses*, à l'anneau de la belle, à son gant, ni au bal où elle danse à ravir, ni

> *Au mani'ment de ses deux mains marbrines*
> *Dessus le luth ou dessus l'épinette.*[1]

Malgré l'aspect cosmique du recueil de Pontus, sur lequel J. C. Lapp attire notre attention,[2] la part de la sensualité y est nettement plus importante que chez le Manceau. 'Rien n'est moins naturel, dit Schmidt, que l'abstraite passion qui transporte Peletier.'[3] Quelle qu'ait pu être Pasithée, en lisant Peletier on ne se soucie guère de savoir si la Dame anonyme qu'il chante était fictive ou réelle. Si, comme on l'a avancé, c'était Louise Labé, avouons que le poète méritait d'être éconduit. A cette abstraction accrue correspond d'ailleurs une plus grande austérité stylistique : les traits maniéristes – ornements mythologiques, métaphores filées, etc. – sont peu nombreux.

Il ne saurait être question de tenter ici un relevé systematique des thèmes du *canzoniere* de Peletier. Je ne voudrais pas non plus donner à entendre que l'ouvrage est parfaitement cohérent : rien ne me semble moins sûr, et l'on aurait certes fort à faire si l'on voulait y démêler, par exemple, les rôles respectifs de l'Amour, de la Dame, de la Beauté, de la Fame, de la Nature, de Dieu. On souscrit volontiers à la remarque de Wilson : 'at times, indeed, the reader must despair of such a poet'.[4] Puissent pourtant les quelques indications qui suivent servir à susciter des études plus poussées et plus précises.

Inutile d'insister sur l'idée même de l'amour cosmique, thème traditionnel :

> *Dirai-je pas bien sans erreur*
> *Que par l'amoureuse entreprise*
> *De ce Chaos la vague horreur*
> *Sa belle corporance a prise? . . .*

---

[1] *Erreurs amoureuses* I, xlii, Lyon (1549).
[2] Voir son édition des *Œuvres poétiques complètes*, Paris, STFM (1966), p. xxv.
[3] Schmidt, op. cit., p. 42.
[4] Wilson, op. cit., p. 130.

> *O pouvoir d'Amour assuré,*
> *D'avoir fait un Corps d'une Ombre!*
> *Cet Abîme avoir mesuré,*
> *Le Nul avoir réduit au Nombre!*[1]

On pourrait, il est vrai, signaler le parti que le poète a tiré de son 'application' des mathématiques. Il ne s'attarde pas, pourtant, à broder sur le mythe de l'amour cosmique en tant que tel, ni à jongler avec des concepts ou des catégories. Tâchons plutôt de distinguer quelques aspects de l'aventure intellectuelle vécue par le poète – nous rappelant que, quand il s'agit d'un homme de la Renaissance, qui dit aventure intellectuelle dit aventure spirituelle.

Il est remarquable, par exemple, que Peletier insiste tant sur l'éveil de l'esprit :

> *Mon songe obscur d'un beau réveil vaincu*
> *Me fait juger que ce que j'ai vécu*
> *Était la nuit du jour qui devait luire;*[2]

Nuit où, dit-il :

> *J'étais content, mais pour rien ne vouloir;*
> *J'étais joyeux de point ne me douloir;*
> *Mon heur passait sans que je l'aperçusse,*
> *Je jouissais en ombre de mon bien,*
> *Sans m'en sentir, sans entendre combien,*
> *Et sans avoir à qui le gré j'en susse.*[3]

Cette expérience est ressentie comme une libération, une exaltation, une expansion de l'être ; mais aussi comme une dépendance totale ou même une captivité. Dans le premier sonnet adressé à la Dame nous lisons :

> *Somme, je n'ai pour mon contentement*
> *Nul penser propre à mon commandement*
> *Qu'un souvenir de libre avoir été*[4]

[1] *A*, p. 10.
[2] *A*, p. 7.
[3] *A*, p. 5.
[4] *A*, p. 16.

Mais, dans le sonnet qui ouvre le recueil :

> *Je suis à toi, Dieu d'Amours, tu m'as pris,*
> *. . . tu m'as fait renaître:*
> *Par sa grandeur* (sc. de sa Dame) *je tiens vie de toi,*
> *Par ton pouvoir d'elle je tiens mon être.*[1]

Et plus loin :

> *Tout seul j'étais muni de mon effort,*
> *Dedans moi seul trouvais mon réconfort,*
> *A moi tout seul de moi je rendais compte;*
> *Mais or mon bien départi plus en croît,*
> *M'être amoindri m'est renfort et surcroît,*
> *Voire, et ma part plus que mon entier monte . . .*
>
> *Ailleurs qu'en moi, et en plus de cent lieux*
> *J'ai repris vie . . .*[2]

Joie d'amour, mais joie tout intellectuelle, joie de l'esprit attendant d'être admis aux arcanes, et s'ouvrant déjà

> *A la splendeur que me doit être infuse.*[3]

> *Bénis destins, qui par leurs cours secrets*
> *Ont ordonné de mes ans les degrés,*
> *Me réservant à si grand' connaissance!*[4]

Joie du poète aussi, qui compte bien

> *Faire servir le dire au concevoir*[5]

et conquérir ainsi 'la Fame', apothéose promise aux parfaits :

> *Quand seras-tu, o mon âme, accomplie*
> *En tes désirs comme en amour tu es?*
> *Au Ciel à coup volerais anoblie,*

[1] *A*, p. 3.
[2] *A*, pp. 5–6.
[3] *A*, p.39.
[4] *A*, p. 6: Connaissance non seulement du Monde, mais aussi de soi-même. Cf. *A*, p. 59 : Loyaux Amants, c'est miracle extrême,/Dont la raison assez je n'aperçois,/Qu'il est besoin être hors de soi-même,/Pour contempler ce qu'on a dedans soi.
[5] *A*, p. 59.

> *Ciel gardien des noms perpétués,*
> *Qui se saisit, comme signeur [sic] et maître*
> *De ce qui est le plus grand qu'il peut être.*[1]

Devant l'immensité de l'entreprise et de la grâce promise, l'humilité du poète et sa crainte sont aussi faciles à comprendre que l'ardeur de son aspiration :

> *Dois-je avancer ou retirer le pas*
> *D'amour si haut? qu'y pourrai-je acquérir?*[2]

La disproportion du sujet et de l'objet, du fini et de l'infini, ne serait-elle pas trop grande? Toute l'incertitude de l'amant pétrarquiste, l'alternance de la confiance et de l'abattement, sont transposées ici sur le plan de l' 'ardente quête'[3] du savant :

> *Or cesse donc, mon cœur, de désirer:*
> *Impossible est à ton indignité*
> *De joindre à toi si grand' divinité;*
> *Contente-toi, sans plus, de l'admirer.*
> *– Non, j'ai mal dit; aime, prie et persiste:*
> *En ces points-là ton heur gît et consiste,*
> *Si l'admirer si fort te doit repaître;*
> *Car par amour l'affection s'éveille,*
> *L'affection connaissance fait naître,*
> *La connaissance accroîtra la merveille.*[4]

Mais ce n'est pas par simple timidité que le poète se méfie; et c'est peut-être ici qu'une lecture du *canzoniere* montre le plus clairement la justesse de certaines remarques fort intéressantes de Wilson. Peletier ne veut pas s'abandonner à la transe mystique. D'une part l'ardeur de la quête, le feu de l'enthousiasme s'affirment avec confiance :

> *Cette beauté d'éternité vêtue,*
> *Portant d'honneur les immortels présents,*
> *Rend à mon cœur les longs siècles présents,*
> *Et en rondeur mes désirs perpétue;*

---

[1] *A*, p. 36.
[2] *A*, p. 15.
[3] *A*, p. 42.
[4] *A*, p. 27.

> *Elle m'enflamme, monte et évertue*
> *Le sens, le cœur, les esprits et les ans*
> *A ces labeurs péniblement plaisants*
> *Dessous le joug qui à mon gré me tue.*
> *Mon feu prend force, et croît infiniment,*
> *Ayant trouvé son semblable aliment;*
> *Toujours en soi s'entretient la matière,*
> *Mon feu sans cesse a de quoi s'allumer;*
> *Car elle étant si durable et entière,*
> *Il s'y nourrit, sans rien en consumer.*[1]

D'autre part, cependant, l'idée de la jouissance fait peur au poète :

> *O beau Soleil, cachez votre splendeur*
> *Si vous pouvez, de peur que j'en jouisse;*
> *Ou permettez qu'elle par sa grandeur*
> *Avec mes yeux la vie m'éblouisse;*
> *Car par ses rais votre face aimer j'ose,*
> *Par votre face, encore plus grand' chose.*[2]

Ecartelé ainsi entre le désir et la peur de se perdre, il est bien tenté de s'en tenir à l'espérance, et, précise-t-il, s'adressant a l'Amour :

> *S'il doit sortir effet, dépars-le-moi,*
> *Pour ne point voir à coup mon tout en main;*
> *Ou le détrempe au moins de quelque émoi,*
> *Pour donner mode à ce que j'ai d'humain.*[3]

Le débat entamé dans ce sonnet XXV se poursuit dans les deux sonnets suivants et n'aboutit à aucune conclusion. Le poète le reprend vers la fin de son *canzoniere* :

> *Plus mon désir d'emprises me prépare,*
> *Plus d'entre-deux s'offrent pour m'en refreindre;*
> *Tant plus je cuide aux mérites atteindre,*
> *Plus au milieu des grâces je m'égare.*
> *Trop de splendeur la vue me sépare,*

[1] *A*, p. 58.
[2] *A*, p. 35.
[3] *A*, p. 25.

263

> *Trop grand' ardeur ma flamme vient éteindre;*
> *Trop grand accueil d'approcher me fait craindre,*
> *Ce m'est rigueur d'une douceur si rare.*
>   *Je suis l'oiseau qui dans sa longue cage*
> *A désappris la vie du bocage;*
> *Le près me plaît quand d'elle je m'étrange,*
>   *Le loin je quiers lorsque près je me range;*
> *Tous les endroits où elle n'est, me nuisent,*
> *Tous les endroits où elle est, me détruisent.*[1]

Dans un autre sonnet, il se rappelle avec quelle ardeur il s'élançait d'abord à la poursuite de son 'ennemie';

> *Mais maintenant qu'en pieds elle s'arrête,*
> *Mon cœur à coup demeure sans conduite,*
> *Et mon emprise à son néant réduite,*
> *Moi dépourvu en mon heure plus prête.*[2]

Ce qu'on pourrait appeler la mise au point: l'exacte relation à établir entre le sujet et l'objet, semble donc constituer pour Peletier une grande difficulté. La connaissance qu'il cherche, c'est, comme l'a bien vu Wilson, une connaissance d'ordre 'scientifique' qui pourtant ne se laisse pas ramener à un simple empirisme. Entraîné vers l'extase, vers l'union mystique, le moi doit se ressaisir. Au lieu d'un abandon et d'une absorption, il faut qu'il y ait échange et réciprocité:

> *Oh! je crains d'être trop ardent,*
> *Amour, et que je me transporte*
> *En lieu où je m'aille perdant:*
> *Rends-moi à moi, et me rapporte.*[3]

Il est vrai que la strophe suivante semble aller à l'encontre de notre thèse:

> *Ainçois rends-moi à celle-là*
> *A qui être tu me commandes;*
> *Rends-moi à elle, car elle a*
> *Tout ce que de moi tu demandes.*

[1] *A*, p. 54.
[2] *A*, p. 41.
[3] *A*, p. 11.

Mais on pourrait tout aussi bien interpréter ces vers comme exprimant le désir du poète de reprendre ses recherches scientifiques.

Bien loin de se perdre, l'esprit doit jouer, vis-à-vis de son objet, un rôle analogue à celui d'Aristée luttant avec Protée :

> *Tant que voudrez, par rigueur et licence,*
> *Vous pouvez faire envers moi ce Protée,*
> *Comme faisiez, éprouvant la portée*
> *De mon amour lors en adolescence;*
>   *Car moi, de qui en présence, en absence,*
> *L'affection ne s'est pas désistée*
> *Serai toujours l'obstiné Aristée*
> *Pour vous choisir en votre vraie essence.*
>   *Mon cœur pièça je vous fis apparaître,*
> *Ne vous aimant sinon pour vous connaître;*
> *Devrai-je donc être dit importun,*
>   *Pour vouloir voir d'œil ferme votre face,*
> *De telle ardeur, qu'endroit moi c'est tout un*
> *Vous contempler et être en votre grâce?*[1]

Citons enfin un sonnet qui offre une sorte de schéma du grand problème que l'intelligence pénétrante quoique versatile de Peletier semble avoir si bien compris :

> *Celle pour qui mon heur tant se soucie*
> *M'est un portrait, et pour telle la prends-je,*
> *Qui a un point fini auquel se range*
> *Chacune ligne en vue raccourcie;*
>   *Si je la sens plus ou moins adoucie,*
> *Plus grande ou moins, ce n'est point chose étrange,*
> *Non plus qu'à l'œil, ainsi comme il se change,*
> *La chose vue ou moindrie ou grossie –*
>   *Qui toutefois une mesure garde,*
> *En quelque sorte, et sans qu'on la regarde.*
> *Oh qui sera la conduite certaine*
>   *Pour me garder que je ne me déçoive,*
> *Tant qu'en ma Dame ou voisine ou lointaine*
> *Cette Beauté en son point j'aperçoive?*[2]

[1] *A*, p. 37.   [2] *A*, p. 22.

Le chercheur de sources aura vite fait de montrer le point de départ de ce poème dans les vers bien connus de l'épitre *ad Pisones*:

> *ut pictura, poësis; erit, quae, si propius stes,*
> *te capiat magis, et quaedam, si longius abstes;*

et de nous rappeler qu'au seizième siècle la théorie de la perspective était connue de tous. J'aime mieux, pour ma part, mettre en regard de ce texte de Peletier le petit poème des *Pas*, où Valéry, autre esprit tourmenté par le jeu du Songe et du Savoir, cherche lui aussi un point d'équilibre, un état d'attente, d'espoir continué, de tension ardente et lucide, entre le sommeil et la jouissance; distanciation, mise au point effectuée par la modulation grammaticale des deux derniers vers, nullement mystérieuse:

> *Tes pas, enfants de mon silence,*
> *Saintement, lentement placés,*
> *Vers le lit de ma vigilance*
> *Procèdent muets et glacés.*
>
> *Personne pure, ombre divine,*
> *Qu'ils sont doux, tes pas retenus!*
> *Dieux! . . . tous les dons que je devine*
> *Viennent à moi sur ces pieds nus!*
>
> *Si, de tes lèvres avancées,*
> *Tu prépares pour l'apaiser,*
> *A l'habitant de mes pensées*
> *La nourriture d'un baiser,*
>
> *Ne hâte pas cet acte tendre,*
> *Douceur d'être et de n'être pas,*
> *Car j'ai vécu de vous attendre,*
> *Et mon cœur n'était que vos pas.*

Et sans doute aurions-nous mauvaise grâce de regretter que Peletier, s'il a chanté 'le bois épais d'horrible solitude',[1] ne se soit pas aventuré plus loin dans la 'forêt sensuelle'.

Alan Steele

---

[1] *A*, p. 44.

Proper Names in Renaissance Poetry

➤➤➤ ➤➤➤ ➤➤➤ ➤➤➤ ➤➤➤ ➤➤➤ ➤➤➤ ➤➤➤ ➤➤➤ ➤➤➤ ➤➤➤ ⬅⬅⬅ ⬅⬅⬅ ⬅⬅⬅ ⬅⬅⬅ ⬅⬅⬅ ⬅⬅⬅ ⬅⬅⬅ ⬅⬅⬅ ⬅⬅⬅ ⬅⬅⬅ ⬅⬅⬅

WHAT IS THE relation between, for example, the proposition 'I am forty years old' and me? By what right do I connect this 'I' with the living, breathing, moving concretion of sensa that constitutes my empirical specificity? For the first person singular of the pronoun in no sense belongs to me, nor can it refer directly and unambiguously to me; how can that belong specifically to me which has been used and is being used and will be used countless billions of times by all who are familiar with the English language? Indeed, it is this very familiarity, by which words are to us closer than breathing and nearer than hands or feet, which masks from us the fantastic nature of the link which binds sentience to symbol. Between my actual, existent, palpable, empirical self and the language I utter there is an ontological gulf which I cross every time I *do* utter a word; and the gulf must be crossed if I am to be a man, and not an animal on all fours like a cow or a cat. In the uttering of 'I am forty years old' I cross the gulf into another and fundamentally different ontological dimension; and in the crossing of the gulf I give up, I have to give up, my existential actual self; in the saying 'I am forty years old' I erase that self and create, as it were, a new self which is totally virtual and set for ever apart from my existent self which it annihilates. The link, that is to say, which binds my sentience to the words I utter is a link which is forged by first being snapped; it is a contact which is made by first being broken; a bridge which is thrown across by first being blown up; and a light which is switched on by a plunging into darkness. The proposition 'I am forty years old' does not and cannot *refer* to me; it *projects* a new 'me', a 'me' in virtuality which in a manner endlessly baffling and paradoxical wipes me out and in the wiping out creates me for ever, no longer in actual but in virtual specificity.

It is the mark of symbolic utterance that it is free-standing, detached from all existent, actual examples of the things which we say it 'refers' to, but which I think it does not and cannot refer to, but create and project. It is in essence totally non-discursive, non-referential; the prerogative – or curse; call it what you will – of man, who is at once its creator and its creature, its master and its slave; its master because it was forged in the incredible cortex of the mind; its slave because only the symbol can show sentience its own face, and only *homo fictus* can show *homo sapiens* what he is. It is my contention that the essentially non-referential nature of language is obscured for us by the fact that we must use language *as if* it referred to our actual empirical selves, in order to orient our activities and go about our daily business. That is, we use what is essentially *symbol* as if it were *signal*; we take with the symbol a liberty which is at once illicit and essential: illicit since the symbol is free-standing, non-referential and serving only for contemplation; it is held in the mind and is thrown out of gear with all practical activity; essential since to contemplate the symbol and to treat it non-referentially would make all practical life impossible. The proposition 'I must go to the bathroom' is like 'I am forty years old', in essence simply the projection or creation of my virtual self; it has nothing to do with *my* existent self, since at the very instant I am saying it thousands of other users of the English language are saying it; but if I treat it as pure symbol and simply contemplate the microcosm of virtual life which it projects, I shall never actually get near the bathroom and things will look exceedingly black for both my large and small intestine. Let now a kitchen-sink dramatist come along and put the above proposition in a play; instantly it is seen as part of the structure of the art-form which is the play and which uses language as symbol not signal from beginning to end.

The difficulty we have in seeing that the symbolism of language is precisely analogous to – not, of course, identical with – that of music, for example, stems entirely from the fact that language is the only symbolism which does double duty; it is the only symbolism which makes practical life possible; it would be extravagant to order a *tête de veau vinaigrette* by whistling the first bars of the 'Eroica' Symphony or by uttering a couple of quadratic equations, and then expect that hirsute concoction to be served up to us, so to speak, on a plate. But in essence the symbolisms of music, mathematics, painting are exactly analogous to that of language; their relation to human sentience is alike; between each and every one of them and existent, actual life there is the same gulf; the crossing of the same Rubicon and the throwing of the same irrevocable die – 'iacta alea est'; 'nescit vox missa reverti' – in each case actual, 'real' specificity is cancelled out, erased, displaced and annulled, and is replaced by a musical or pictorial or verbal projection in a mode totally virtual, impalpable, ideal, inorganic. All symbolic structures are in their essence completely non-referential whether they are employed in works of art or outside them, whether in *poesis* or in *praxis*; and I think that once one sees this a vast amount of mystery is removed from the criticism of works of verbal art. As soon as one sees that the ontological gulf is crossed by every man, woman and child who, instead of a growl, a snarl, an ululation, or a belly-noise, opens his mouth and utters the intrinsically absurd concatenations of letters that we call words, then it will be seen that from the least to the greatest and regardless of our power over language, we simply project ourselves, in our utterance, into a new dimension.

The difference between the poet and the ordinary man-in-the-street is that the poet knows, though he may never formulate or conceptualize this knowledge – since those who can, do, and those who can't, teach – that language is in essence projection, creation of virtual life, and has nothing whatsoever to do with his actual existent self. He is, as Keats says, the most *unpoetical* thing in nature, for he is continually filling and informing some other creature.

Nowhere do the divided and distinguished worlds of symbol and sentience come closer than in the proper name; nowhere does language appear to be so obviously and inescapably referential than in a proposition of the type 'John Smith is forty years old'. John Smith denotes unmistakably, so we suppose, and points unambiguously to, the actual person of flesh and blood who runs under that name. Yet a little reflection will disclose to us that this is not so; that the sentence 'John Smith is forty years old' is no more denotative or apodictic than the proposition 'I am forty years old'. Why is this? It is because all sentences have a monadic structure, i.e. they are totally autonomous and self-sufficient, impenetrable by other propositions. A sentence, like a single word, like a complete play or poem, is not an aggregate of discrete and independent parts, but an interpenetration of elements. All these linguistic forms present, in the world of symbol, the same symbiosis and welding together that we have in our physical corporeality. Just as an eye or a limb has no meaning except in the contextual relationship furnished by the entire organism which is the body, so no element in a sentence has any meaning detached from the totality to which it is wholly subservient. The meaning of a sentence is not acquired *paulatim vel seriatim*; the last element in the sentence must be uttered before the sense is complete; and when it is uttered, but not before, the whole meaning flashes forth together as a single intuition. The understanding of a sentence, that is to say, is always from the whole inwards, never from the elements outwards; the whole is prior to the part. Single word stands to sentence as single frame stands to the reel of film, as single dance-step to the whole dance, as single cipher to our friend of a couple of pages back, the quadratic equation, as single note to the melody, as single point of light to the whole complex of light which is the image on the television screen. To go up close to the TV image is to be lost in a *tintamarre* and *brouillamini* which is totally meaningless. Likewise to go up close to the single word is to plunge into meaninglessness, for it is essentially absurd and incomprehensible, therefore it must be made meaningful, and it *is* made meaningful by convention; it is accepted and intuited; it is not understood. Who can understand 'galimatias', 'loquimini', 'fero, ferre, tuli, latum', 'ferio, ferire, ici, ictum'? Anyone who claims to understand any or all of those monsters wants, as they say, his head examined. Nevertheless the single word is the frail and unspeakable plank, the all-powerful nullity, which yet, by convention, shelters man from the abyss. It is 'vox et praeterea nihil' and therefore 'vox et praeterea omnia'. In each case we have, as it were, to throw a mental lasso round them before we can capture them; and, very like the medieval definition of God, word, sentence, total poem, are each of them a circle whose centre is everywhere and circumference nowhere. It is with word as with sentence and poem; the form must be closed before it can be opened; we must have, in Eliot's phrase, 'the whole consort dancing together'.

In the domain of *praxis* the proper name is the great means of pinning word and person securely together: a pinning which is, as I have said, as essential to human activity as it is a fallacious use of the symbol. This is why this kind of denotative language is pre-eminently the sphere of all whose concern is with practical affairs; i.e. the world of contingence, the everyday world in which babies are born and old men die and couples get married and linen gets soiled and has to be sent to the laundry and houses are bought and sold and malefactors are arrested and flung into jail; and so on and so forth. This is why it is the language of the lawyer and the police dossier and the customs official and the estate-agent and the public registrar of births, marriages and death. 'Yesterday at Glasgow Magistrates' Court Jeannie Brown or Davidson or McTavish pleaded guilty to a breach of the peace and was fined £5 or 14 days in jail': the plurality of proper names tethers securely the miscreant to the misdemeanour wherewith she is charged. Now this kind of language, which purports to be entirely denotative not connotative, signal not symbol, referential not non-discursive, is at the very antipodes from the language of the poem. The specificity at which it aims is an actual, alive, 'real-life' specificity which is perpetually pointing beyond itself to, in this instance, the aforesaid hapless Jeannie Brown or Davidson or McTavish. It is, as Valéry has pointed out in his *Poésie et Pensée abstraite*, totally centrifugal, wholly means not end; and, given the essentially

271

detached, free-standing, non-referential nature of symbolic utterance, the pursuit of an ever-receding mirage and the great
delusion. The proper name used referentially never means or can
mean; it has no semantic content, it points; and, of course, it can
point only when there is something to point to; which is why it is
significant only in a context in which all are alive and kicking.

In poetry, however, the proper name never refers to a specific
creature of flesh and blood, it never alludes to any person in
contingent life, but invariably projects a virtual person (or persona) who has that name, whose significance it owes entirely to
the rest of the ordinary, common, vulgar words of the poem of
which it is a part. When Ronsard says

> *Je vouldroy bien richement jaunissant*
> *En pluye d'or goute à goute descendre*
> *Dans le beau sein de ma belle Cassandre,*
> *Lors qu'en ses yeulx le somme va glissant*[1]

the name 'Cassandre', like all the other elements in the sonnet, is
an intrinsic part of the poem and has meaning only within its
ambit. The poem is a structure of value defined by, consisting in,
and coterminous with, the large primary organizing devices of
rhythm, metre and rhyme, working together with the words and
syntax of the French language to project and create the illusion of
life. The name 'Cassandre' is a prisoner of the intuition which is
the poem and has no meaning or significance whatsoever outside
it. She is entirely a creation made up out of the whole cloth which
is the web and fabric of the language. It is therefore as senseless to
ask 'Who was the real Cassandre?' as it was senseless to ask 'How
many children had Lady Macbeth?' It is as pointless to detach the
name 'Cassandre' from the poem as it would be to detach a
theme from a sonata or a square inch of paint from a Van Gogh
canvas and then expect these mutilations somehow to be meaningful on their own. Cassandre therefore is a prisoner of the poem,
but because it *is* a poem and not a title-deed or a bill of lading,

[1] In the case both of Ronsard and d'Aubigné the text I am using is that of the S.T.F.M.
edition.

this prisoner finds perfect freedom in the service of the centrality which is the sonnet. Ronsard, as a man, knew in his 'real' life a girl called Cassandre, he could see with the eye of flesh that she was a good-looker; but being a man of common sense he knew it was impossible, in the days before Cook's Tours, to arrange visiting parties to come and see the lady in person; and, being a poet, he knows that if she is to be shown to others she must be conveyed entirely by the inert, inorganic, inanimate structure of rhythm and meaning which is the French language. Nor will it do to talk *about* Cassandre; she must be *shown* in full presentational immediacy. 'Don't tell me,' says Henry James, 'show me'; don't describe a happening; let it happen.

Proper names are, in themselves, totally opaque, inert and meaningless, which is why they never figure in a dictionary but only in a telephone directory, which is nothing but a series of pointers towards specific individuals. The problem facing Ronsard is somehow to disperse the opacity and activate the inertia of the proper name; to endow it with full connotative, qualitative value and thrust it upwards, so to speak, into the light of the universal, which is the light of the common noun, verb, adjective and pronoun. It is a commonplace of Ronsard criticism that he is a great master of rhythm; now, rhythm is, of all the elements in the poem, which is itself altogether non-discursive, perhaps the least amenable to critical analysis. It is resistant ultimately to analysis because, as Eliot says, it operates at levels far below the level of conscious cerebration; Valéry says that the very definition of the relation between sound and sense is that it is indefinable; rhythm in poetry has the same nature as time had for Saint Augustine: 'What is time? If you don't ask me, I know; if you do ask me, I don't know.' But precisely because rhythm *does* operate subliminally, *therefore* it must never be lost sight of for an instant. To remove it from the poem is, as Yvor Winters says, comparable to emptying the blood from the body; the result is a desiccated corpse. Of course, it is never the poem which thus becomes a corpse; what is impoverished is not it but we, if we wantonly treat as referential what is palpably given as non-referential. The damage is never done to the poem with which now there is no variableness neither shadow of turning, but to the reader whose co-operation is essential to that *I–Thou* reciprocal relationship which alone is really, fully and truly the poem. Rhythm is used by Ronsard therefore with the function of semantic; rhythm in Ronsard is the great in-former. These considerations apply throughout the entire canon: whether it is Cassandre, Marie, Hélène, Sinope, Genèvre, Astrée, or whoever, in every case the original 'real-life', 100 per cent girl of flesh and blood is erased and her virtual persona created in her place; or, if I may be permitted to put the matter in somewhat cruder terms, a lady in a bed and a lady in a book are two entirely different ladies; both highly desirable no doubt – who but a pathic would care to contest it? – but desirable, surely for totally different reasons. The 'real' Cassandre, Marie, Hélène, is always 'the girl he left behind him', just as he himself is, in his poem, a self-made man and his own creation.

The question whether Hélène was ugly or not is never to be answered by appeals to documents – (documents, like poems, are made with words, which can do nothing but project the illusion of life wherever they are employed, and in whatever language they are couched) – but only by inspection of the *Sonnets pour Hélène*. There are as many Hélènes as there are sentences to put them in, since every verbal Hélène wipes out all actual creatures of that name and makes up an enduring Hélène in virtuality. Claude Binet, the writer of the *Discours sur la Vie de Ronsard*, says Hélène de Surgères was beautiful; Cardinal Du Perron says, or rather implies, that she was ferociously ugly: when she asked him to preface one of the posthumous editions of Ronsard with an 'epistre' to show 'qu'il ne l'aymoit pas d'amour impudique', that surely not – too – 'révérend-père', worthy to be placed cheek-by-jowl with that other Cardinal, de Retz, 'l'âme peut-être la moins ecclésiastique qui fût dans l'univers', retorted 'Au lieu de cet epistre, il y fault seulement mettre vostre portraict'. Now we reject Binet's 'belle Hélène' and we cleave to Du Perron's 'thrawn Janet'. Why is this? Binet saw her, Du Perron saw her; the lady herself has been dead these 400 years, give or take a couple of score, and therefore – La Palice *dixit* – none of us have ever set eyes on her; yet Du Perron's girl makes more impact than Binet's. The reason is that Binet's *Discours* is not so much written, composed or constructed as flung together, 'bâti à la diable', and is the perfect simulacrum of a dog's breakfast; 'ces phrases embarrassées et d'une terrible lourdeur', says Henri Chamard; whereas Du Perron's anecdote fairly rings with inner authenticity. We accept it for dramatic and artistic reasons which have nothing to do with historical or biographical precision. 'Se non è vero, è molto ben trovato'; if she wasn't ugly *before* the anecdote, she must needs be ugly *after* it; the Cardinal's brilliant cameo has thrust ugliness upon her in perpetuity; and Du Perron can now add another to that list of definitive 'stet's in the last chapter of Revelation: 'and she that is ugly, let her be ugly still'. Now if this applies to Du Perron's Hélène, it applies *a fortiori* (not to say *a fortissima*) to Ronsard's:

> *A l'aller, au parler, au flamber de tes yeux,*
> *Je sens bien, je voy bien que tu es immortelle:*

this creature is numinously lovely because she stands forth in and by the power and beauty of Ronsard's incomparable alexandrines 'et vera incessu patuit dea'. Ronsard's Hélène would still be what she is, a symbol which is the focus of a great poet's vision of human life, even if tomorrow fifty thousand letters and portraits were to be unearthed showing her plainly to be as ugly as that pattern of Caledonian homeliness, Willie Wastle's wife, of whom it is recorded:

> *She has an ee, she has but ane*
> *The cat has twa' the very colour,*
> *Five rusty teeth, forbye a stump*
> *A clappen tongue wad deave a miller;*
> *A whiskin beard about her mou*
> *Her nose and chin they threaten ither*

> *Sic a wife as Willie had*
> *I wad na gie a button for her.*

275

She's bow hough'd, she's hein shinn'd,
Ae limpin' leg a hand-breed shorter;
She's twisted right, she's twisted left,
To balance fair in ilka quarter;
She has a hump upon her breast
The twin o' that upon her shouther

Sic a wife, etc. etc.

Roger Sorg was deemed to have deserved well of the republic of letters when, busily grinding the axe of a thesis whose absurdity is equalled only by its irrelevance, the thesis, namely, that Cassandre was the first and only real love of Ronsard's life, he 'proved' that the poems '*Sur la Mort de Marie*' were originally written to lament the death not of Marie de Bourgueil, as everyone, including Sainte-Beuve, Pierre de Nolhac, Blanchemain, Marty-Laveaux and Paul Laumonier – to name but a few – had ignorantly and erroneously supposed, but of Marie de Clèves, madly beloved of that sexual conundrum Henri III; and the beauty of the sonnet which everyone knows by heart:

Comme on voit sur la branche au mois de May la rose

is often explained by those who accept Sorg's 'proof' as being due to the recollection by Ronsard, when he was composing it, of his love for the peasant girl. But this is another example of the same fallacious jumbling together of symbol and signal, the same epistemological blunder and confusion of categories, the same false coupling in the mind, of word with real, actual, empirical thing instead of with virtual, unreal, immaterial thing. There is no way by which an existential awareness of any kind, envy, hate, love, volition, intention, passion, lust, can be poured directly into language in the way one would decant sherry into a copita or whisky into a plain straight-up-and-down tumbler. The emotion in the poem is not and can never be the personal, actual, empirical emotion of the poet; it is and can only be created by the poem and in the poem by the patterning and configuration of the elements which the poet puts together in a creative act which is neither

276

wholly active nor wholly passive, but is a reciprocal reaching out across the gulf which divides sentience from symbol: in the precise formula of Montaigne 'Je n'ay pas plustost faict mon livre que mon livre ne m'a faict; livre consubstantiel à son autheur'. The poet and his word are like the shades in Virgil's underworld: 'Tendebantque manus ripae ulterioris amore'; each says to the other: 'come over into Macedonia and help us'. The emotion is not put into the poem; it is discovered in the act of writing; the words mean what they say and they say what they mean, they do not mean what the poet says and they can never say what he means. The Marie therefore who is bewailed in these poems *Sur la Mort de Marie* is neither Marie de Clèves, nor Marie de Bourgueil, nor Mary Magdalen nor Marie Dressler nor Marie Curie nor Mary Queen of Scots nor any one of that unfortunate lady's 'fow'r Marys'; she is, in John Donne's famous retort to Ben Jonson apropos the Elizabeth Drury of the *Anniversaries*, Ronsard's 'Idea of a Woman, and not as she was'. His Marie suppresses them all and subsumes them all in a new creature, impalpable, inorganic, virtual, who endures as long as the French language, the 'damoiselle de bonne maison' in the great phrase which d'Aubigné gives to Ronsard in the preface to *Les Tragiques*, shows her bright face to men. Similarly, when Ronsard in the 1578 edition of the *Second Livre des Amours* transposes eleven poems originally written 'for Sinope' and alters that name to 'Marie', by the simple act of substituting the five letters of 'Marie' for the six of 'Sinope', he wipes out Sinope and creates Marie; there is no question of biographical sincerity or, in Desonay's phrase, of 'désinvolture inexpiable', but only of concern for the whole poem. The girl in the poems is now no longer Sinope but Marie because Ronsard says so; and their place now is with the other sonnets in the *Second Livre des Amours*, for just as all the elements in the single sonnet hang together or not at all, so the sonnets in the sequence as a whole form a total import which is greater than the sum of the individual poems which make it up.

The poem is a pattern of interrelatedness; to drop perpendiculars from names in it to their supposed prototypes or originals in 'real' life is to devise a nexus of relationships wholly inimical to the integrity of the poem and altogether destructive of the pleasure and value which the poem was written to promote. It is to make that confusion between poet and historian against which Ronsard himself, following Aristotle, is always telling us to be on our guard; for, of course, the perpendiculars are, and can only be, dropped into the darkness of our own minds.

These remarks apply with the same force to all the proper names in Du Bellay's *Regrets*. The names Gordes, Bailleul, Panjas and so on function exclusively in the poems to further the dramatic illusion of 'papiers journaux, ou bien de commentaires'. The names are not pointers but *dramatis personae*; and information 'about' the 'real' people to whom they 'refer' is not merely gratuitous but inimical to the apprehension of the poem and goes directly against its grain, since all such information is material not element, and has not been used by the poet. It is much more useful to remark that practically all Du Bellay's names are dissyllables, appropriately masculine, and that each in its 'sound-look' aspect shows us *in petto* that four-square, masculine Latin quality which is seen in the best of the tightly articulated sonnets of the *Regrets*. It is the careless user of language who 'alludes' or 'refers' to things; the artist must show, project, exhibit and thrust up into the light. *Poesis* is a 'making' from first syllable to last. Certainly the poet *uses* proper names, since poetry serves for the enhancement of the imaginative life of men and women; but he uses them never to point beyond the poem, but always in such a way as to stay within its frontiers.

The question of proper names is posed with the utmost urgency in d'Aubigné's *Tragiques*: here, surely, is a poem which inhabits firmly the matrix of contingent actuality and which is inseparable from that matrix. Yet a consideration of what makes *Les Tragiques* a poem and not a document will lead us to the same kind of conclusion as we reached in the case of Ronsard. There is no more sustained passage of poetry in French, whether of the sixteenth or any other century, than the image of Catherine de Médicis in the first book, *Misères*. Now, of course, as in the case of Hélène,

Marie and Sinope, d'Aubigné's Catherine is for ever cut off from
the real-life Catherine de Médicis, that unfortunate whipping-girl
of the Renaissance. His Catherine is made out of an enormous
tissue of imagery drawn from nature and the elements in their
most sinister and hostile manifestations; when, after several
hundred lines, d'Aubigné leaves her, she stands forth as the very
embodiment of the confusion and disorder which is tearing out
the vitals of France. M. Henri Weber suggests that the epic poet
needs a 'recul dans le temps' before his epic can be successful.
But it is not so much *temporal* distance which he needs as what E.
Bullough[1] in a famous article has called *psychical distance*: what he
needs is a large formal integument or organizing framework which
will withdraw his poem from traffic with actuality and permeate it
with the virtuality of the symbol. (This is true of all poets: thus
Ronsard, for example, finds artistic freedom in myth, in submission to the strict demands of sonnet structure, in his impeccable ear and sense of cadence and rhythm.) The success of the
passage from *Misères* which I am discussing is due, I think, to
certain large and simple formal devices. One of them is the way in
which the poet alternately uses the third and second person
singular of the pronoun, the switch from apparently impersonal
narrative to direct apostrophe producing a great sense of urgency,
crisis and personal involvement; for example, the switch at line
747:

> *Pleust à Dieu, Jesabel, que, comm'au temps passé*, etc.,

where the immensely long sentence, interrupted by a double
digression, and which continues for twenty lines, to 766, has the
structure of a delayed imprecation, beginning at line 747, then
held up for ten lines which, ostensibly explanatory, have as their
real function the building up of a head of dramatic pressure; then
the repetition of the optative at line 758

> *Pleust à Dieu, Jesabel, que tu euss' à Florence*

[1] E. Bullough, 'Psychical Distance as a Factor in Art and an Aesthetic Principle',
British Journal of Psychology, June 1912.

acts at one and the same time, paradoxically, as a release from the pressure of tension and also its augmentation. This interweaving of passages alternately in the third and second person contributes powerfully to the thickening, as it were, and the apparent solidification of the image; of course, the syntactical idea would be nothing were it not for the flashing lines of great power and for the vibrant energy of the language throughout: for example:

(763) *Cinq cens mille soldats n'eussent crevé, poudreux*

in which the adjective standing apart simply shows us the disintegrated soldiery; but this effect is not conveyed by the syntactical placing alone of the adjective, cunning though that is, but also by the co-operation of the strong verb *crevé*, the violent consonants of *poudreux*, the vicious and strong keenness of the vowel and sibilant in the subjunctive *n'eussent*, and the dramatic import of the imprecation as a whole which seals up all the elements and in the sealing-up endows them severally and collectively with vastly increased explosive power. Next, that line of quiet and sinister beauty

(785) *C'estoit un beau miroir de ton esprit mouvant*

whose semantic meaning is prosaic in the extreme: 'Anybody could have told, from your ploys and cantrips in the convent, just what a hell-cat you were going to be later on'; but, as the line *reads*, one sees a magic mirror in which is reflected not a face but a baneful restless dynamic spirit; and this is the first mention of that motif of sorcery, witchcraft, pestilence, poison and unnaturalness harnessed to immense power which keeps coming back every so often as the image unfolds. Perhaps the most spectacular of these passages comes at line 827:

> *Mais toy qui au matin de tes cheveux espars*
> *Fais voile à ton faux chef branslant de toutes parts,*
> *Et, desployant en l'air ta perruque grisonne,*
> *Les pais tous esmeus de pestes empoisonne,*
> *Tes crins esparpillez, par charmes herissez,*
> *Envoyent leurs esprits où ils sont adressez*

where Catherine *is* the Gorgon scattering destruction broadcast.
The fact that the bits and pieces of these images are culled from
Horace, Lucan, Juvenal, the Bible *et al.* is totally irrelevant to the
new thing that d'Aubigné is here making, since the semantic,
rhythmic, and syntactic structure of the French language is *sui
generis* and completely different from that of Latin or Greek or
Italian or Urdu or Ancient Hittite; 'chacune Langue', says du
Bellay, 'a je ne sçay quoy propre seulement à elle'; 'la disposition
des matières est nouvelle', says Pascal; and it is with the structure
of French and no other language that d'Aubigné is working. Now,
just as the recurring apostrophes create and maintain that sense of
crisis and involvement mentioned earlier, so the repeated passages
in which we are shown the baneful sorcery and unnaturalness of
Catherine, recurring, as they do, symphonically, supply the
image with a central whirling core of immense and flashing power,
and since the lines are deployed in a dimension of pure virtuality,
i.e. detached absolutely from the physical space-time continuum
in which bodies evolve, part adheres to part and fuses with it by
an impalpable osmosis whose effect – totally illusory – is of the
greatest possible concretion and 'thingness'; the first and greatest
of all Catherine-wheels. It is certainly possible to point to parts
which are weaker than others; but of the integrity and authenticity of the image there can be no doubt. The point I wish to
make is that this image is nothing but a huge extended metaphor
which simply absorbs and sucks up into itself all the particulars of
contingent circumstance, including, of course, the proper name
of Catherine herself. Geographical names, historical 'references',
the fear and hatred of the foreigner, the anti-feminism at the
beginning of the passage, are all taken up into the web of the
imagery and transformed into a vision of terror and beauty which
is the 'monde à l'envers'. As Walter de la Mare puts it:

> *It's a very odd thing*
> *As odd as can be*
> *That whatever Miss T. eats*
> *Turns into Miss T.*

Professor Boase is absolutely right in refuting the suggestion

281

that this poem is propaganda, and that, as has been said, d'Aubigné's pen is fighting the same battle as his sword; if so, so much the worse for the pen. In the first place, if the poem is propaganda, why was it published at the singularly inept date of 1616, a score of years after all the soldiers had gone back home and when some of them were no doubt already in receipt of the Louis Treize equivalent of the old-age pension? In the second place, if I had been sitting with d'Aubigné in the trenches at Castel-Jaloux at the first reading of it in 1577, I would certainly have had this question to put to him: 'Let's get one thing clear, Agrippa *mon ami*: this dame now, is she on *our* side, or on theirs?'; and on receiving the answer 'on theirs, *mon vieux*', I would have let the blunderbuss fall from my nerveless fingers and been off like the hammers of hell and like Cicero's Catiline: 'abiit, excessit, evasit, erupit'. If this is propaganda, it is propaganda for the other side and d'Aubigné is the original Quisling. The propagandist invites to action; the poem serves uniquely for contemplation. The use of the art-symbol, as Allen Tate has said, lies in its perfect inutility; it is for the enhancement of the life of the imagination and works immanently; it is a potentiality, a world to look at not to live in. The image of disorder which is Catherine holds us to it, we cannot choose but look at her; and in the looking at this 'appareil sanglant de la Destruction' we are at one and the same time terrified and comforted. Because she is total symbol, wholly out of gear with actualities and practicalities, she possesses what the psychoanalysts call pluri-signation or polyvalence; that is to say she bodies forth not merely upheaval and disintegration in the political state but upheaval, separation from grace, and the terror of death, wherever they are found. So far from conveying merely the struggle of a historical, local and particular Protestantism set over against a local, historical and particular Catholicism, she is like a great spinning orb, full of inner fire, which throbs and vibrates with energy and throws light into every corner of the little room of man.

Wherever d'Aubigné is working within the web of this kind of imagery, the imagery of natural forces and of the elements, the imagery of the outcast, of man abandoned to the mercy of a hostile universe that threatens destruction, he speaks with the voice of a great, original, true poet. Thus, in the passage at the beginning of *Vengeances*, drawing on the episode of Jonah in the Old Testament, he projects himself to us in an extraordinary image of being cast adrift on the oceans of the world:

> *Je m'enfuyois de Dieu, mais il enfla la mer,*
> *M'abysma plusieurs fois sans du tout m'abysmer.*
> *J'ay veu des creux enfers la caverne profonde;*
> *J'ay este balancé des orages du monde;* (lines 115–18)

or in the equally powerful figure of Cain in the same book, which is simply a transposition into *Les Tragiques* of the tempestuous self-created outcast who rushes headlong through the first *Stances* of *Le Printemps*; or again, in the unforgettable passage in *Jugement* which begins at line 770

> *Pourquoy, dira le feu, avez-vous de mes feux*
> *Qui n'estoyent ordonnez qu'à l'usage de vie,*
> *Fait des bourreaux, valets de vostre tyrannie?*

in which the ordinary interrogative *Pourquoy*, by simple repetition ('what I tell you three times is true') and by cunning variation in spacing within the alexandrines, does not function merely semantically but becomes itself a metaphor, takes on flesh and is the stabbing finger of God himself.

There are, of course, hundreds and hundreds of bad lines in *Les Tragiques*, and I think the worst book of the seven is *Les Feux*; it is bad because fundamentally it presents us with a fight to the death between language used as symbol and language used as signal. D'Aubigné is, in this book, on his own admission 'tout entier au sentiment de (sa) religion'; and there's the rub, 'hinc illae lacrimae'. It is clear from the passage I have discussed from *Les Misères* that for this subject he needs a lot of elbow-room and space in which to deploy his resources. Since, as Wordsworth says, the poet must create the taste by which he is to be judged, we must, if we are to apprehend his power, submit ourselves to his tempo and run in the rhythm of his alexandrines, thus supplying ourselves with an aesthetic thermostat which is the only means by which we can enter into possession of the poem and the one infallible defence against anachronism. Catherine grows and increases rather like Virgil's *Fama*: 'vires adquirit eundo', by a kind of creative anfractuosity and in a sinuous widdershins movement, caught by Montaigne in a phrase which he applies to his own *Essais*, but which I think tells us something essential about *Les Tragiques* and indeed about a great many artistic structures: 'Mes fantasies se suyvent, mais par fois c'est de loing, et se regardent, mais d'une veuë oblique.' But in *Les Feux* the movement is choked and impeded by an excess of proper names, names of martyrs to whom he wishes to do justice; but if he has done historical justice to them by mentioning them in his verse, he denies to all of them the poetic justice which he grants so overwhelmingly to the enemy. The fact that, at one point in the book, he pays a compliment to the 'valeureux Escossois' should not, I think, induce a denizen of *Ultima Thule* to accept with any better grace this wretched dreary cortège of Protestant Oliver Twists each presenting to the poet his little bowl to receive his ration of rhythm and imagery; and the reaction of the bored reader is that of Nicole towards her master's phonetic lesson: 'De quoi est-ce que tout cela guérit?' The whole of the book is strictly *poésie de circonstance*, which is to say a formal contradiction in terms and that coupling of horse and donkey which notoriously produces nothing but a sterile mule. The verse of *Les Feux* like all verse is an amalgam of rhythm, metre and rhyme, it is language doubly objectified and made corporeal; it is ends and means in an indistinguishable totality. But the proliferation of proper names constantly solicits our attention beyond the objectified structure; it is as if the poem were trying to compete with the telephone directory or the *Daily Express*. It is the empirical, conative, volitional d'Aubigné trying to get into the poem; but the language forbids it absolutely. It is disobedience to Ronsard's impeccable principle, that poet and historian belong to different categories; and for that disobedience d'Aubigné has to pay. He has stopped looking at the virtual image

in the mirror and has turned aside to look at 'real' life; and therefore he suffers in his verse the fate of the Lady of Shalott:

> *She left the web, she left the loom,*
> *She made three paces thro' the room*
> *She saw the water-lily bloom,*
> *She saw the helmet and the plume,*
>   *She look'd down to Camelot.*
> *Out flew the web and floated wide;*
> *The mirror crack'd from side to side;*
> *'The curse is come upon me', cried*
>   *The Lady of Shalott.*

The verse is no longer saying 'Look at me', or, as the Roman priest
said at the high point of the ceremony, *Hoc age*. It says *'Don't* look
at me; look anywhere but at me'; it solicits a centrifugal not a
centripetal gaze; which is to say, it commits the unforgivable
artistic sin.

For what shall we see if we do look beyond? If we check up on
all the proper names, look up and verify all the 'references', and
fill our minds to overflowing with information? We are then but
piling up a mass and a slag-heap of unformed, inartistic, consti-
pated data which, being outside the poem, are brute materials.
We no doubt in the process become mines of information on the
historical 'background', and depositories of that polymathic lore
which Montaigne, with unerring disdain, dubs 'la science'; but
not one particle of this information is relevant to the illumination
of the poem. It is as pointless to try to illumine the poem by
supplementary information of this kind as it would be to fling a pot
of paint at a Rembrandt in hopes of seeing it better. To say that the
poem must be placed in its historical 'background' is to turn the
problem on its head and look through the wrong end of the telescope. It involves a double fallacy: a delusion as to the nature of the
tie that binds man's sentience to his symbol, an incomprehension
of the nature of the poem; a fallacy as much ontological as artistic.
For just as the word as primary imagination is the one thing which
can orient our life in *praxis*, so only the word as secondary imagination, which is to say, only non-discursive artistic projection, will

give us the illusion of what it must have been like to have lived in past time, as E. M. W. Tillyard says of the Epic. It is the heroic couplet of Pope that really gives us the measure of the Augustan age, and only the rhythms of Mozart can capture and present to us the fundamental rhythms of the eighteenth century; a film like John Ford's *The Informer* conveys the 'troubles' of Ireland incomparably better than any factual account could ever do. It is the difference between *la durée* and *le temps*.

Just as there is nothing behind the word, which is the great *Urphänomen*, so there is nothing behind the poem, which is made with words. 'Procedes huc, et non ibis amplius'; 'Thus far shalt thou go, and no further.' The poem is the 'jewel hung in ghastly night' that lightens the darkness of contingence, stamps a shape upon the void, and gives a meaning to the senselessness of flux. All words whatsoever proceed from dead men's mouths, for the link between symbol and sentience is established by being severed, and the contact is made in the breaking. We shall fully receive the poem when we accept fully the fact of our own mortality in the here-and-now.

> *For poetry makes nothing happen; it survives*
> *In the valley of its saying where executives*
> *Would never want to tamper.*[1]
>
> . . . .
>
> *O chestnut-tree, great-rooted blossomer,*
> *Are you the leaf, the blossom or the bole?*
> *O body swayed to music, O brightening glance,*
> *How can we know the dancer from the dance?*[2] [3]

G. M. Sutherland

[1] W. H. Auden, 'In Memory of W. B. Yeats'.

[2] W. B. Yeats, 'Among School Children'.

[3] I have attempted in this article to apply to one specific problem of French Renaissance poetry (a problem which turns out after all to be a pseudo-problem), some of the ontological and epistemological insights of Ernst Cassirer in his great work *The Philosophy of Symbolic Forms*, trans. R. Manheim, New Haven (1953–7) (3 vols). My debt is great also to Susanne K. Langer's *Feeling and Form*, London (1953), especially to her chapters on lyric poetry (pp. 208–79), whose pregnant generalizations are applicable to poetry in all languages.

Ballad for Tenor and Vehicle

A first step is to introduce two technical terms to
assist us in distinguishing from one another . . .
the two ideas that any metaphor . . . gives us. Let me
call them the tenor and the vehicle. . . . With
different metaphors the relative importance of the
contributions of vehicle and tenor . . . varies
immensely. At one extreme the vehicle may become
almost a mere decoration or colouring of the tenor,
at the other extreme, the tenor may become a
mere excuse for the introduction of the vehicle.
(I. A. RICHARDS)

The Bedouin, guiding the plough, will sing tunes to the
camel that he can only sing to the camel, because
in his mind the tune and the camel are the same thing.
(E. M. FORSTER)

I

TENOR:

Walking the thirsty road, I lead horse and caravan —
Jaunty, with loud shirt and braces,
And voice louder still: mellifluous scarcely,
But clear; you can hear every word.
Dazzled and deafened, the passer-by
Has barely a glance for the lagging, dispirited vehicle.

287

II

VEHICLE:

He has moved now (ignoring the Highway Code)
To the horse's far side ('off' side, you should call it);
Hugging the hedgerow, he falters from earshot and view.
Now I, in my unobscured gaudiness, take the eye stunningly:
Plume of smoke from my chimney, checked curtains,
Gay red-painted wheels — their bold creaking
Quite drowning his raucous roulades.
He may bawl as he may: all ears and all eyes are for me.

III

TENOR:

I have climbed to my perch; with reins gathered,
Trim I sit, your trim coachwork prefigured
In me as its figurehead: to a strumming of horses' hooves
My vibrant melisma weaves in with your wheels' clatter.
A fine pair we make: each enhancing the other.

VEHICLE:

You have climbed to your perch; with reins gathered,
Trim you sit, my trim coachwork prefigured
In you as its figurehead; to a strumming of horses' hooves
Your vibrant melisma weaves in with my wheels' clatter.
A fine pair we make: each enhancing the other.

IV

TENOR AND VEHICLE (in unison):

From within the caravan now are our reins guided;
Voice and wheels, as we bowl along smoothly, blend
In one journeying song; at the window
A single gay pattern dazzles: is it curtain or kerchief?
Who can say? Who has won?
It is we; we *have won – and are* one.

NOTE: For a prose typology corresponding to the four 'movements' of this Ballad, see my article, 'Intention in Metaphor', *Essays in Criticism*, vol. IV (1954), pp. 191–8.

F. W. Leakey

Questions

(for *Alan Boase*)

'*Where*' cried the *Ivory Gull*
'*where will they find it now*
une forme sienne une forme maîtresse'
skimming low over Fidra in April
('*maybe in the study at Culross*'
said the Long Ghost '*or maybe*
at St Andrews by that tower and window
or maybe on any island')

'*And where are the* beaulx livres
the beaulx livres de haulte graisse'
cried a fat rabelaisian Laughing Gull
dropping skite over Glasgow
('*maybe in the Gorbals*' said the Long Ghost
'*maybe in the Canongate*
maybe even, God knows, in Aberdeen
anywhere a soul has richly ripened')

291

'And where' cried the Rosy Gull
le cerveau ivre . . d'une gloire confuse
'where are the words of cunning beauty
saying actual relations to the universe'
(*'maybe where the tree stands on the moor'*
said the Long Ghost 'where the rock
has its hold in the sea, anywhere
that highest intellect meets wildest nature')

'Where' cried the gulls *'where'*
            'maybe' said the ghost

Kenneth White

List of Subscribers

List of Subscribers

Olivier Abrioux
Ian W. Alexander
R. Alexander
Elizabeth Armstrong
Lloyd J. Austin
Elizabeth A. Babister
Carl Paul Barbier
H. T. Barnwell
J. J. Beard
Alistair H. Blyth
Nicholas Boyle
Grahame Castor
T. C. Cave
H. P. Clive
Norman Cohn
Joan Crow
Beverley Evans
A. G. Falconer
Donald M. Frame
Austin Gill
C. A. Hackett
M. I. Henderson
F. M. Higman
Leighton Hodson
Margaret I. Holmes
S. J. Holyoake

A. Basil Jackson
C. R. Jessop
K. Lloyd Jones
Rhys S. Jones
James R. Knowlson
Harold W. Lawton
Katherine Lever
A. H. T. Levi
J. Lough
I. D. McFarlane
D. McMillan
Elizabeth Moles
Jennifer Ann Moss
Anne Prestwood
Sylvia D. Raphael
Elizabeth Ratcliff
Bodo L. O. Richter
R. A. Sayce
Christine M. Scollen
Robert Shackleton
Marjorie Shaw
J. P. Short
W. McC. Stewart
A. J. Steele
Elisabeth Stopp
Bernard C. Swift

Margaret G. Tillett
Kenneth Varty
I. H. Walker
M. G. Wallas
D. A. Warren

M. B. Winch
Mark S. Whitney
Barbara Wright
C. M. Zsuppán

Bangor, University College of North Wales Library
Basel University, Romanisches Seminar
Belfast, Queen's University Library
Brighton, University of Sussex Library
Cambridge University, New Hall Library
Genova University, Istituto de Lingue Estere
Leeds University, The Brotherton Library
London University, Birkbeck College Library
London University, University College London Library
London University Library
London University, Westfield College Library
Newcastle upon Tyne, University Library
Oxford University, Taylor Institution
Sheffield University Library
St Andrews University Library
Warwick University Library